™

Ummac Dan

YOUR GALACTIC NEIGHBORS

SHELDAN NIDLE

Illustrations by Miriam de Vera
Book Design by Miles Simons

Blue Lodge Press
Vancouver and Maui

Your Galactic Neighbors by Sheldan Nidle

Blue Lodge Press First Edition Printed in June 2005

ISBN: 978-0-9665791-8-5

Cover Art and Book Design: Miles Simons
Illustrations: Miriam de Vera
Typeset in Caslon Book BE and Frutiger

Blue Lodge Press
P.O. Box 880151
Pukalani, Maui, Hawai'i 96788, U.S.A.
Blue Lodge Press Website: http://www.paoweb.com

10 9 8 7 6 5 4 3 2 1

Printed in USA

Dedication

This book is lovingly dedicated
to my son, Narturi.
Know that your father loves you very, very much.

Table of Contents

LIST OF ILLUSTRATIONS

Acknowledgements

First, a warm 'Selamat Jarin!' (Sirian for 'Blessings') from my Galactic Federation book committee and from me. And a cordial 'Aloha', freely given, from the island of Maui to my readers. To these, I add a greatly appreciative 'Mahalo nui loa' to the wonderful Hawai'ian people and their marvelous and ancient culture. I also formally call upon the blessings of the Hawai'ian goddesses Pele (fire), Kapo (manifestation), La'Ieikana (rainbows) and Haumea (wisdom). May they bless this book and attract to its pages those readers for whom its information will smooth the way for first contact and the coming grand reunion with our many space families.

The physical preparation of this manuscript was made possible through the efforts of a great many dedicated people who willingly assisted in its birthing. My sincerest thanks go to Colleen Marshall, whose thoughtful suggestions made possible the writing of this book, and, especially, to Rhonda Wettlaufer for her painstaking ways with words. Special appreciation goes to my former wife and paoweb's content coordinator, Miriam de Vera, whose abundant illustrations enhance these pages, and whose attention to detail and gift for problem-solving have enabled the gracious resolution of occasional difficulties. I am deeply grateful to Miles Simons, my magnificent Webmaster, who created the cover graphics and, with the expert technical advice of Jaynne Wellygan, designed the formatting and styling of the book. Thanks, too, to Miriam de Vera and Miles Simons for the computer expertise that they so generously provided and to Eugenie Smallman for her attentive proof-reading. I am also indebted to Tazz Powers for her kind and practical advice and loving support.

I am grateful to my partner, Colleen Marshall, for the enduring love and unconditional support she gives to me and all of my work. Kudos, too, to my team of dedicated co-workers at the Planetary Activation Organization (PAO), whose encouragement and direction helped make this book's publication possible. Finally, eternal thanks, love and utmost regard to Mother/Father God, the Spiritual Hierarchy, the Ascended Masters of Sirius and Earth and, especially, to Washta, a Sirian Ascended Master and my major spiritual guide. Let it be known that Spirit's miraculous work has been completed!

Introduction by Susan Nidle

Those who choose to accept what society has taught us about the universe believe that the stars, in their private milieu, exist in a finite universe. What is real is limited to what the five senses reveal. For many of us, however, the real truth is much more complex.

When we were growing up in the 1950's, my brother and I spent a great deal of time with Beings that visited us to remind and educate us about life on other planets and dimensions. Their method of communication was telepathic and 'psychic', but also involved physical contact. These contacts did not evoke any fear or trepidation, only wonder, and grateful happiness. We accepted the information and responded as children would, who are given an endlessly rewarding learning experience by familiar, loving and unfathomable teachers.

We were duly receptive to their lessons; in fact, there were no distractions for me at all, even though I was a young child. I was severely ill with asthma and spent hours in a rigid sitting posture, motionless, struggling for breath. In the 1950's, there was very little treatment available for asthma, other than middle-of-the-night doctors' visits involving intramuscular epinephrine injections in my emaciated little butt. I remember my poor pediatrician appearing at the hysterical begging of my panicked mother, and I remember the sudden, fleeting relief, calling me back from the edge.

On normal nights, I would assume my usual posture and, gasping for air, subside into a state of trance-like receptivity. During my hours of forced meditation, I would be shown patterns and colors in a tonal mode. These patterns would be explained to me telepathically, as waves of energy influencing the evolution and growth of this planet. Many nights were spent with my two particular teachers, who also managed to help me maintain connection to my physical body, which was tenuous at best.

In the room across the hall, a synonymous ritual was enacted; my brother would be communicating with his teachers for similar purposes. They seemed to tailor their activities with us to show us shifting facets of the same truths; they designed our education according to our personality, karma, physical body and chosen task.

When I was a child, I often thought of my brother and myself as strangers stranded in a strange land. Suburban western New York was our habitat; it was our classroom and our prison. We were curious about this place we found ourselves stranded in; I loved to park myself in the backyard and watch the local ant colony. Everywhere in my early environment, I found endless examples of diversity and similarity. We lived near Niagara Falls; the complexity of surviving there was fascinating. Wherever I looked, the struggle to learn, grow and survive was manifested. We felt stuck here, yet strangely detached. Yes, we were interested in our surroundings, yet their inherent limited reality, at this point of time on the planet, was constantly brought home to us. Logic and knowledge continually confirmed to us the reality of unlimited life across the universe.

The three-dimensional limits of this planet, now, are still an astonishment to me when I remember the lessons of my childhood. Living in a multi-dimensional environment, as most Beings who live off-planet do, presents its own set of limitations and problems. But the difference between the reality of other Beings' existence on other levels and planets, and ours, is difficult to describe. The nearest analogy would be the notion of flatlanders.

OK, picture two-dimensional Beings without depth, possessing only width and height – Beings who are flat. Now, picture three-dimensional Beings who possess width, height and depth, and ponder the real differences and what they entail. This may give a little bit of a hint of the extent of the discrepancies between three-dimensional living and the next level 'up'. OK, then multiply by at least 10 (the distinction between layers of consciousness is not measurable to us, but expands exponentially), factor in the idea of time and consciousness, and think about those disparities.

Oh yes, keep in mind that I am discussing only the very next level surrounding us; the level that is directly less dense than ours. There really is no limit to the expansion of the levels of consciousness and existence.

If you follow my logic, you can imagine how silly it is to think that only three-dimensional Beings living on this planet exist in the universe. It reminds me of what I would call 'galactic fundamentalism,' for lack of a better English expression. It smacks of the notion that Earth-based human life is the highest extent of the imagination of the Creator of this vast universe.

We were astonished that the humans we knew had the audacity to deny the simple fact that an endless array of Beings actually live and move and have their essence in our galaxy, and that countless, inhabited stars and planets exist around us. To us, logic and knowledge continually affirmed the reality of unlimited life across the universe.

Now, as an adult, I live in the Pacific Northwest. The other day, a sea creature washed up on a Puget Sound beach. It looked like no normal creature known to us previously. Some bright, local scientist determined that this beast called the deepest part of the Pacific Ocean its home.

This Being's existence is a testament to survival and adaptation in what, to us, seem to be difficult circumstances. It sustained life under tremendous pressure and in an utterly 'alien' environment. Think about the amount of resourcefulness and evolution required by this guy to continue to exist in his native habitat. Sea Beings living in shallower waters do not need nearly the amount of diversity to endure.

We could not survive where this creature lived its daily life; its ancestors surely multiplied over millions of years under adverse circumstances. Alien to us, normal to its environment, this amazing creature survived, largely unchanged as a species, since the time of the dinosaurs.

Again, if our own mysterious world is teeming with endless types of Beings, it is patently absurd (I love that phrase) to assume that there is not an equally amazing array of life forms existing throughout the universe.

This is one of the tenets taught to me as a child. There is a simple law that, if certain forms of life are very successful, they are repeated as often as possible. "If it ain't broke, don't fix it."

Mother Nature, God the Creator and all Beings above and below have wonderful, rapturous, even 'silly' imaginations, appearing in varied forms in order to keep surviving, generation after generation. Try anything, and if it works, repeat it. All across the universe, sentient Beings strive to adapt in their quest to continue living; adaptation manifests in many forms.

The idea that our beautiful, blue planet is unique in the entire universe, in terms of life forms, is a sweet and naive notion. It rings about as true as the crooked notion that any one religion contains the only pathway to God the Eternal.

We are not an anomaly; we are a continuation of a pattern, repeating itself in slightly different designs, across the universe. We are unique yet the same throughout the 'known' universe, like cousins in a large extended family.

Twentieth century Earth scientists have 'discovered' (verified via their clunky instruments and rudimentary math) that many chemical substances are formed in the centers of stars. This is, supposedly, a cornerstone of modern astrophysics. I ask you, does this not indicate that familiar compounds exist throughout the universe, the very 'building blocks' of life on Earth? If this is true, and generally accepted on Earth, then can we not fantasize/hypothesize that, since these substances originated off-world, they 'may' have spawned the same type of genetic response 'there' as they have here, on our home planet?

Truly, the 'neighborhood' is really not so different. We can travel throughout our small planet and discover surprisingly similar environments, family situations, likes and dislikes. Across cultures and, I believe, across species, we are very alike. Just imagine that this is true of our 'kin' who exist on other worlds and dimensions. Things are stunningly different, yet strangely, and essentially, the same.

The other side of this coin also concerns building blocks of life. What if carbon-based life forms occur on planets with carbon bases only? Therefore, planets that are based on other substances evolve life forms according to their most frequently occurring elements. To us, that which is created from a different base compound may seem alien, but, to the local area, it is perfectly logical, or they could not survive. The advanced form of life created under those circumstances would, on the surface, seem strange indeed to us. Let me emphasize the idea that surface differences are arbitrary and superficial, on this planet and the next.

My advice about this book is to read a chapter or two slowly, in the evening, and then pause if you can. Gaze up at your local universe. When my brother and I were children, we observed the sky nightly, for hours, sometimes through a small hallway window. The pure act of looking fixedly upwards has always evoked awe and wonder within me; it seems to help activate our mystical heart and imagination.

This book is an activator. If you allow yourself to stay open to its concepts, as you gaze at the night sky, you will find yourself understanding more about our world. We really are just a tiny speck in the universe, yet we are also crucial to a greater plan.

We are in troubled waters now, reaching the moment of transition on a grand scale, and one of the keys involves holding perspective. Understanding our larger place in the scheme of things can only help us, as we attempt to hold the light and maintain the grid.

In this book, my brother speaks of many complex concepts and odd Beings in a matter-of-fact way. I would just like to attest that this material is consistent with concepts he has discussed throughout his life. I enjoyed reading it, as he discusses civilizations and their inhabitants in a clear, concise way, including many details I have not heard before. He describes strange ideas so simply that we can see the greater image if we open to it.

Let this book serve as another testament to the complexity, diversity and beautiful simplicity of the universe. May it help us to understand more of the mysterious information available to all, if we, as sentient beings, open our inner hearts to life off and on this blue world.

Susan Nidle

Introduction

How I Came to Write This Book

This book was conceived more than a year ago when, during one of my 'update' sessions, I was approached by a committee of 22 Beings from across this galaxy. They affirmed that the time had come for me to help the peoples of Earth overcome their strong aversion to the appearance of many of this galaxy's highly intelligent inhabitants. To enable me to do so, Washta, my Sirian guide, and a number of chosen others would act as my 'way-showers' in writing this book. Its purpose is to introduce you to a very narrow segment of the extraordinary array of cultures and species found throughout this star system. These Beings are your galactic neighbors and, even though their home worlds may be many thousands of Light Years from yours, they belong to the vast entity that is the Milky Way Galaxy.

Your galactic neighbors are humans from constellations such as Pegasus and Aries, and Reptilians and Dinosaurians from many former Anchara Alliance home worlds. These former Alliance members hail from star-nations as far apart as Draco, Orion or Reticulum. Despite fierce and prolonged wars, each of these former foes ceased their long-standing hostilities and willingly became part of the Galactic Federation of Light. As a result of their union, these star-nations are experiencing phenomenal growth and, through their solemn efforts, are carving out their own diverse galactic societies. Now, having observed your own progress, these fledgling galactic societies look to Mother Earth's experiment in consciousness for inspiration. Its successes can pave the way for your future role as wise teachers and unifiers of this galaxy. Ultimately, your nascent galactic society is destined to become a most welcome model for their continuing endeavors.

The Star-Nations Chosen

To serve as our examples, we have chosen twenty-two star-nations. Five of these are former members of the Anchara Alliance, while fourteen are long-time members of the Galactic Federation and three are former neutral star-nations. They were selected to serve as prime examples of the different types of diversity that exist in this galaxy. Many species, however, are not represented in this initial sample. They were omitted for a reason: their physical appearance is less than pleasing to limited conscious humans, particularly those who dwell on Mother Earth. Each star-nation represented here encompasses Beings that are now serving in some capacity with our first contact mission. For that reason, it seemed that a brief introduction was necessary.

As I have stated in my many messages, the first Galactic Federation of Light members that you will meet after first contact are galactic humans from constellations as diverse as Andromeda, Taurus, Aries and Pegasus. These delightful Beings have been part of my life since childhood. Their wisdom, knowledge and technology will provide most welcome support to this unfolding project - the turning of this chaotic world into our own unique galactic society. This unfurling planet will become a way-station for the Galactic Federation. Many special conferences, encompassing Beings and organizations that span the totality of physicality, will meet here. Thus, it is vital for us to move beyond our present xenophobia and begin to embrace sentiency in whatever physical form it may choose to take.

To Start: The Galactic Humans

To begin with, we will learn about galactic humans and about the many varied hybrid forms with which they are associated. From there, we can be more accepting of other Beings that resemble them. Next, we will move on to physical entities that are far different from us. This book will assist in preparing you for these extraordinary adventures. Accordingly, most of the Beings represented here are not human in form. Some of them, in fact, manifest bodies startlingly unlike what we are used to. Even their cultures and their disparate societal structures are dramatically dissimilar to our own. They are included in this book to illustrate the true diversity of this galaxy. Through them, you will also be made more aware of the obvious differences between the cultures of the former Anchara Alliance and those that originated with the Galactic Federation.

The Role of Former Anchara Alliance Star-Nations

Yet another important point to emerge from this work is the degree to which the former Anchara Alliance star-nations are engaged in modifying their cultural and societal structures. Like us, they are transforming from a realm ruled by the dark to one that is speeding toward the Light. In us, these Beings see fellow explorers. They fervently believe that their change can mirror our own, and they take great strength and encouragement in what we are achieving. The Anchara Alliance members are really most anxious to greet us and express their true appreciation for what we are doing. For that reason, they have undertaken much of the detail work in planning this coming first contact. Still, they realize that gradually, our society must be prepared for their formal arrival.

As you will see, each species described in this book is an example of the multiplicity of life forms found in our star-system. Some are among the most known, or have been the most dreaded, in the galaxy. Others, after long migrations, formed star-nations or were brought to sentiency by their Local Spiritual Hierarchy. In all cases, these star-nations are part of the divine plan and its sacred decrees, which have unfolded a most wondrous diversity of Life throughout this Milky Way Galaxy.

Part I

Humans

An Introduction from the Humans

Humans in this galaxy are descended from aquatic apes, who became fully sentient approximately eight million years ago. These apes lived near the edge of a large ocean on the third planet from their sun. Known to your astronomers as Alpha Lyra or Vega, this star is located in the constellation of Lyra. Vega is about 26 Light Years from Earth.

Approximately seven and one-half million years ago, the first human colonies in the Lyra constellation joined with other nearby sentient societies to form defense leagues against the constant incursions of various dark forces that threatened their freedom. Over the next several million years, as these defense alliances grew, humans gradually ventured out from their original 'homes' into other parts of this galaxy.

Human colonists chose worlds that resembled their own origins, that is, water worlds similar, in many respects, to Mother Earth. These worlds featured rolling oceans, continents abounding in lakes, streams and rivers, and an almost immeasurable diversity of animal and plant life forms. Seeing themselves as planetary and solar guardians, these humans quickly established rituals and other forms of energy work to maintain and sustain their beautiful water worlds.

As you read this section, you will notice clear similarities among the countless solar systems and home worlds it describes, which result from the human soul's intense and immutable attraction to such environments. Solar systems having as many as four water worlds were highly sought after by most human civilizations.

These solar systems consist of between six and twelve planets, with smaller worlds rotating closer to their sun and much larger ones revolving in wider, more distant orbits. Usually, these larger planets are gas giants, similar, in many respects, to your Jupiter, Saturn and Uranus. Many have multicolored rings, ranging in size from the narrow bands encircling Uranus to the magnificent ones displayed by Saturn.

Now, we ask you to consider your ancestors and kin. As you do so, view them as both examples and exemplary prototypes of the many forms of galactic society. Let this slim volume serve to help you as you make your own future choices, and prepare you for the coming of first contact.

1

The Andromedan Confederacy

Present Status and Location

Frequently, Washta would reveal to me the long history of the Andromedan Confederacy located in the constellation of Andromeda. Its many thousands of members are positioned between 150 and 4,000 Light Years from Mother Earth. This grand union of star-nations was first accepted into the Galactic Federation of Light some 3.5 million years ago, and forms one of the Federation's original 14 Regional Federation Councils.

My first meeting with a group from the Andromedan Confederacy occurred when I was about five. An Andromedan mothership had come to Earth to assess the current condition of the solar system. Washta, my Sirian guide, gave me frequent lessons, filled with examples of how knowledge garnered by the Andromedan Confederacy had saved the Galactic Federation of Light from ruin.

The Andromedans, known throughout the Galactic Federation of Light as great scientists and healers, had originally manifested many of the technologies that powered the Sirian mothership and effortlessly ran her computers. These wise and enlightened Beings were deeply dedicated to bringing peace to our galaxy. Washta's wonderful lectures and informative discussions on Andromeda gave me a profound appreciation of these galactic humans and their heartfelt civilizations. The key to Andromeda's galactic society is its members' loving acceptance of their immense divinity.

Andromedan Society

With the exception of the Lyrans, the Andromedans pride themselves on being perhaps the oldest and farthest-ranging members of the Galactic Federation of Light. Owing to their confederation's sheer size, the Andromedans decided that their primary headquarters should not be limited to just one solar system. Instead, they decided to pay homage both to their diversity and the large size of their Regional Council.

The Andromedans created a rotating system whereby each different segment of their council would have an opportunity to act as host to Regional Council meetings. Every few thousand years, the Andromedans switched the location of their Regional Council's headquarters.

According to this rationale, every Council member able to provide a potential meeting place was allowed to use that site to house the sessions of the entire Regional Council and its various staffs.

In this way, they nurtured deep loyalty, Love and inner joy that endure to this day. Andromedans are justifiably very proud of their achievements. They have used this profound satisfaction to make incredible scientific discoveries and are, actually, the leading human scientists in the Galactic Federation. Andromedans view such successes as proof of their potential, and are eager to bring that potential to every aspect of the Galactic Federation of Light.

Their co-operative efforts are famous all over the Galactic Federation for doing just that – showing how they work and function, demonstrating their joy and how they use it to transcend groups, showing how easily they can release and reveal their full creative abilities and, with no great difficulty, effect impressive changes.

They have also shown how these cultural differences, when worked at, can actually be used to strengthen any group that is culturally distinct. Andromedan liaison teams are celebrated throughout the Galactic Federation of Light for their wondrous ability to explain and express unity and creativity by diversity. For that reason, they are one of the major groups working on your first contact.

Andromedan Confederacy's Cultural Nuances

The types of clan structures found throughout the Andromedan Confederacy vary greatly from sector to sector. The most common prototypes are the Lyran/Sirian model, with six clans, and the Andromedan/Pleiadean with twelve. The Andromedan use of these two prototypes is unique, since most of their galactic societies contain subcultures that have continued to practice their own distinct language and traditions.

Crucial to this is their use of cultural liaisons and counselors. Places such as Pi Andromeda apply a Lyran/Sirian model. However, each of the three inhabited home worlds in this solar system enjoys a rich layer of unique subcultures.

Each world has cultural liaisons that serve as semi-official interpreters for its many cultures. In addition, a special inter-world liaison board provides creative solutions for whatever cultural problems may arise.

When tied into advanced translator technology and their natural telepathic abilities, this system allows each individual and group to communicate freely with each other. The result is a constant stream of data, which applies these differences and allows this remarkably diverse society to manifest frequent and countless new innovations.

Yet another way to accomplish this is found in the stars that make up Gamma Andromeda. Home worlds here use the Andromedan/Pleiadean model, which has 12 clans instead of the Lyran/Sirian six. In this model, three clans are especially devoted to counselors, liaisons and culture.

Such clans developed because it was found easier to maintain a separate system to train these important individuals. Each clan serves as a repository of specific wisdoms, which can be applied within the other nine clans. Further, any problems that cannot be resolved within the nine-clan framework may also be presented to one of the three clans most capable of solving it.

This 12-clan system permits the Star-Nations of Gamma Andromeda to be clearly viewed as autonomous star-nations, containing many of the most successful scientific research groups in the galaxy.

Their reputation is due mainly to how well their specially modified, 12-clan system formally addresses their broad diversity. This social system, carried throughout the Andromedan Confederacy, was the model used when many star-nations from Lyra and Andromeda first colonized the Pleiades some 400,000 of your years ago.

Andromedan Confederacy Solar System and Description of Some of their Home Worlds

Andromedan home worlds range from watery planets, resembling Mother Earth, to semi-arid realms. Those we intend to concentrate on are located in the multiple stars of Gamma Andromeda and Pi Andromeda, which are between 350 and 650 Light Years from Earth.

The Home Worlds of Pi Andromeda

Pi Andromeda, yet another important binary star system, is about 650 Light Years from Mother Earth. Her smaller star is a blue-white mass, similar in overall appearance to Sirius-B. A colony dedicated to advancing the principles of spiritual science was established here nearly 2.78 million years ago. Her colonists discovered a solar system that contained two large water worlds.

They located their headquarters inside the planet, closer to a sun resembling that of Sirius, where the climate was semi-tropical. Exotic ferny orange, blue and brown trees formed endless forests that reached down to the edges of green and black beaches. Red or blue mountains, occasionally streaked with purple and as tall as Earth's Himalayas, towered over most continents. Within these dazzling surroundings live strange mammalian and reptilian life forms.

The two founding scientist colonies quickly considered their new home worlds a great treasure abounding with extraordinary energies. In this habitat, they devised novel technologies for interstellar travel and uncovered the reasons for the Arcturians' powerful healing energies. Discoveries such as these soon confirmed the Andromedan Confederacy as a major center for scientific research and healing.

The larger star is known for being home to three immense water worlds, each more than three times the size of Mother Earth. The middle of these worlds bears a close resemblance to the main home world of 'Akonowai' (Sirius-B). Washta likes to see this as proof of how the sacred spiritual energies of the Great Blue Lodge have spread across the Milky Way Galaxy.

To the Andromedans, this world is extremely sacred. On her, they erected a great temple, similar in size and location to that found on Sirius-B. Regularly, the priest and priestesses from the Spiritual Warrior clan of Sirius-B arrive here to take part in divine ritual with their Andromedan counterparts. Here, also, the sacred blue dolphins of Sirius-B join in these same rituals. The rites celebrated on this Andromedan world are, in fact, deeply connected to those on Sirius-B. The Great Blue Lodge of Creation has often affirmed to the Sirians that this sacred place in Andromeda is their other galactic home.

The outer water world in this same solar system is regarded as the main repository for information on the histories and cultures of the Andromedan Confederacy. On this world filled with sunken, swampy plains and low-lying mountain ranges, there stands a distinguished university and research center.

This inner-world facility often sends renowned scholar/representatives to the main Galactic Federation of Light cultural center in the Vega system. These educators have studied virtually every form of galactic human culture. They have trained millions of associates from across this galaxy and are justly proud of Andromeda's rich cultural diversity.

We have examined only a few of the thousands of home worlds that make up the Andromedan Confederacy. Each one boasts a diverse cultural tradition and unique history. While those we have just described are the most celebrated, the rest are equally beautiful and, in their own way, even exotic. The inhabitants of these worlds take understandable pride in their environments. We have given you only a brief tour of these worlds: you are left to hear the rest from the galactic humans of the Andromedan Confederacy themselves when you meet them at first contact.

The Home Worlds of Gamma2 Andromeda

Let us continue our examination of the Andromedan Confederacy with the home worlds of the blue-green triple stars that your astronomers recognize as Gamma2 Andromeda. Initially colonized by humans nearly 3 million years ago, these stars contain the Confederacy's largest water world, which her inhabitants call Sirrai. Sirrai is the fourth planet in a cluster that includes two other stars in orbit around a central star. She is famous for her vast oceans, teeming with many species of life, and for her polar night skies, which boast rare pastel auroras, multicolored and resplendent.

Here, as well, are large, silver, spinner dolphins that guard the approach to immense underwater caves dotted throughout the largest continent's inland sea. These caves are celebrated for their ability to harmonize and balance both the physical body and the soul. Here, more than two million years ago, in an island cave connected to these underwater caves, a most renowned counselor, known as Toudok, articulated the concept of the 12-clan system.

This he did following a long, 28-hour meditation, in which he examined his society's future and identified the solution to a recurring problem: how to develop a new program to properly train and administer every liaison and counselor in his diversified society. His method was first to immerse individuals, such as new-borns, into clans that were specifically dedicated to these noble goals. Heart logic dictated that, for such clans to exist, souls would be urged to incarnate as counselors or liaisons and to seek out these new clans for embodiment.

He also reasoned that some new clans must be dedicated to the study and preservation of the world's rich history, while others would be exclusively focused on the multiple cultures of his home world. These concepts led him to formulate a new model for galactic society. Its concepts were quickly laid out

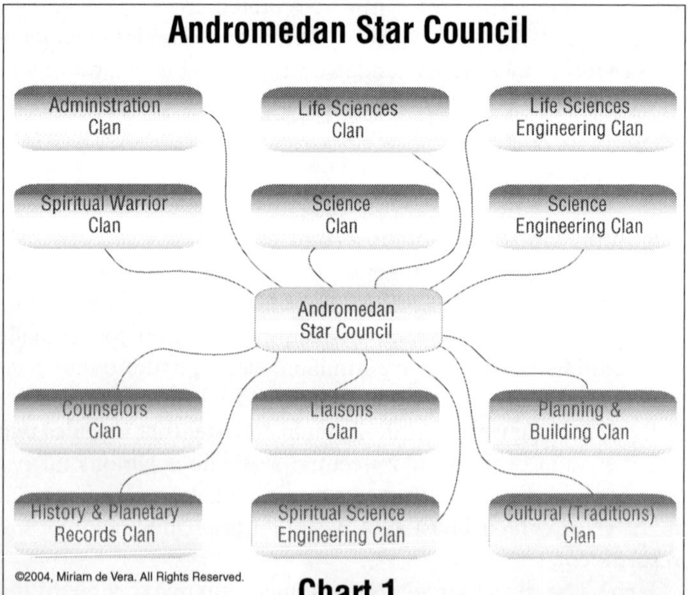

Chart 1

here on Gamma2 and used to resolve many complex societal problems. Soon, this model spread throughout Andromeda (see page 8, Chart 1: Andromedan Star Council).

While the central star of this cluster of three initiated the 12-clan system, the inner star orbiting this center also contains worlds renowned for their immense beauty. Within the two inner planets of this sun exist semi-arid, extremely volcanic regions with pools of multi-colored hot mud and pliable, constantly shifting rock formations. In this world, there were many small, scattered continents. When humans from Lyra colonized the third planet in this system, they discovered a world of reddish-blue seas, orange-blue skies and many small, scattered continents.

This world, known in Andromedan as 'Dosna Man', is significant because it further modified Toudok's 12-clan model. Here, among lands covered by 800-feet tall purple trees similar to redwoods and swarming with bear-like creatures hardly a foot long, an innovative new way to conduct a main star council was embarked upon.

Previously, main star councils such as these had simply accepted a particular clan council's advice on a specific issue and given it their uncritical approval. Now, a meeting of the clans became an open forum in which the decisions of each clan council were fiercely debated.

This procedure gave the other clans a chance to review what another clan had agreed upon and determine how it related to their own issues. Counselors and liaisons well versed in the decision-making process assisted this discussion. By adhering to this process, many precedents were set, and creative ways found to resolve questions to the satisfaction of all involved.

Descriptions of the Andromedan People

Andromedans resemble Earth humans in appearance and can walk among us almost unnoticed. Aboard ship, they most often wear the traditional, multi-colored Galactic Federation of Light jumpsuits. However, Andromedans also dress in traditional attire, which ranges from a type of ancient Greek gown to a combination of shirt and pants very similar to that worn by the ancient Vikings. Andromedans fall into either one of two basic Earth human types.

The first type is a Caucasian, whose features vary from the

so-called 'Nordic' (blonde hair, blue eyes, pale skin) to a 'Mediterranean' type (dark to light brown hair, gray to brown eyes, tanned-looking skin). The second is typically Asian, with dark hair, dark, almond-shaped eyes and brown skin that can vary in color from very pale to dark brown.

The eyes of all Andromedans are a little larger than those of Earth humans. The thin lips are very pale pink, while the ears are fitted slightly lower on the side of the head and are somewhat smaller in size. The hands and the feet are delicate in appearance, with long fingers and toes.

The men vary in height from 5 feet, 7 inches to almost 7 feet (1.7 to 2.12 meters). The women's height ranges from 5 feet, 4 inches to almost 6 feet, 4 inches (1.63 to 1.93 meters). Andromedan woman are noted for their alluring energies and their buxom figures. They need about 2 hours of sleep per day.

In the Galactic Federation of Light, Andromedans are noted for their mastery of all forms of scientific endeavor and usually form the core of most S&E fleet science liaison teams/boards. Andromedans are a key part of the many Galactic Federation of Light medical teams assigned to assist Earth humans in their transformation to fully conscious Beings of Light.

Andromedan languages range from a dialect that resembles Earth's romance languages, like Spanish or even Italian, to a variant found mostly in the Mu and Nu Andromeda star-nations, which is more guttural.

Andromeda's Role in Creating an Expanded Galactic Federation of Light

During the last few years, the Andromedans have applied their skills to all of the different reptilian, dinosaurian and even insectian groups who, though not fully understanding the exact nature of the Galactic Federation, have struggled to transform their societies from tyrannical to galactic. Although these former dark Beings aspire to be part of the Galactic Federation of Light's activities, they are very apprehensive. Their key issues are those of trust: they question whether a new, more open reality can indeed be constructed in their midst.

The Andromedans excel at exhibiting joy and openly expressing it. That, combined with their capacity for demonstrating the unity created within diversity, brought about the wondrous resolution of many potentially difficult situations within the former Anchara Alliance's far-flung Empires. This was one of the major factors that enabled the Galactic Federation to move dramatically forward in unifying the many disparate Anchara Alliance members who have joined the Galactic Federation in the last six to seven years.

Through these cultural exchanges and their great acceptance of the Andromedans, the former Ancharans have helped to largely overcome their deep suspicions. Liaisons and counselor teams from Andromeda have assisted in training many Anchara Alliance star empires in the best ways of dealing with the momentous changes that are necessary for their spiritual evolution. The study groups that these former galactic foes have sent to Andromeda have given them a better understanding of the steps that are needed to transform their societies. Their studies have focused on the importance of retaining certain cultural nuances in their society during the re-evaluation process.

Andromedan Ships

Andromedan ships piloted in the atmosphere of Mother Earth range from the traditional, sombrero-shaped scout ships of between 20 and 50 feet (6.1 and 15.3 meters) in diameter, to lens-shaped, small atmospheric command ships that measure up to one-half mile (805 meters) in length. The Andromedans used these older types of beamships to provide an observation fleet that was not too technologically advanced. They felt that, since Earth's society was still rather primitive, a display of the Galactic Federation's newest ships was unnecessary.

In space, the Andromedan Confederacy operates two types of motherships. The first is a series of large, oval vessels, up to five miles (8.1 kilometers) long, which are tied together by large tubular connectors. Formerly, these motherships comprised the core (command) ships for many S&E (Science & Exploration) fleets. They normally housed a fleet of about 400 auxiliary ships.

The second mothership, a flattened orb-shaped vessel that is often as large as your moon, is used to survey star systems from a distance. It maintains a fleet of between 4 and 6,000 support ships.

Andromedan Ships

Approx. 20 - 50 feet in diameter

Multi-Purpose Ships

Figure 1

2

The Star Dominion of Altair

Now, as we continue our journey through the roster of twenty-two of your galactic neighbors, we arrive on the Star Dominion of Altair (pronounced Al-tear). During this and other journeys, we will explore the birth of the many different galactic cultures and their progress down through the ages to our own time. We will also examine how the present wave of peace and co-operation, spawned by the last decade's Treaty of Anchara, has brought this galaxy together as never before. The Altairians are a case in point. Previously, by acting as either mediators in peacetime or unwilling go-betweens during hostilities, they had depended on the 'on and off' nature of the galactic wars to gain certain cultural, diplomatic and technological advantages.

I first came to meet them as a child of seven when Washta, my guide and mentor, took the time, first, to talk with and, later, to introduce me to an Altairian ambassador and his entourage of nine liaisons. These envoys were on a mission to this solar system that included a number of private 'informal discussions' with some of Earth's secret governments.

The Altairians have long seen themselves as the one group of galactic humans the many dark empires of the Anchara Alliance occasionally heeded. They secured this advantage millions of years ago, during the galactic wars, when they were able to negotiate a truce that lasted for nearly 300,000 years.

Present Status and Location

The Star Dominion of Altair was last accepted into the Galactic Federation of Light nearly nine years ago. Formerly, Altair was a neutral star-nation with a habit of resigning from the Galactic Federation of Light when it best suited them. They also had a long history of sporadic collaborations with the dark star empires of the Anchara Alliance. Because of its proximity to the headquarters sector of the Galactic Federation, Altair has long been a major participant in the current diplomatic and cultural exchanges between the former dark empires of the Anchara Alliance and the Galactic Federation of Light.

Now, owing to her long, collaborative history with the Anchara Alliance, Altair once more has become a natural conduit between these formerly dark empires and many of the Galactic Federation cultural and diplomatic teams. This role has enabled them to assume a degree of authority, which they otherwise would have been unable to garner, in its Regional Galactic Federation Council.

Altair, Arabic for 'Flying One' (Alpha Aquila), is a large, white star located approximately 16.8 Light Years from Mother Earth. She is the brightest star in the constellation of Aquila (Latin: 'Eagle'). Together with Deneb (Arabic: 'Tail of the Hen') – Alpha Cygnus – and Vega (Arabic: 'Stooping Eagle') – Alpha Lyra – Altair forms a glittering triangle in the summer skies. The twelfth brightest star in this galaxy, Altair is noted by your astronomers for her rapid spin. The Altairian solar system consists of six large planets. The third, a water world, is the Altairians' main home world.

Description of Altairian Solar System

Like most solar systems, Altair has six worlds, the smallest closest to her sun and the largest farthest away. The Altair home world has two moons; the rest of her solar system lays claim to another twelve. The innermost planet in this system is about the size of your Earth. Because constant discharges from Altair, her sun, electrify this planet's atmosphere and cause continual electrical storms, her atmosphere has transmuted to a mixture of methane and hydrogen. The sole remaining primary life forms in this acrid air are a series of complex bacteria and algae. Frequent clouds of sulfuric plasma drift through the planet's lower atmosphere.

The next planet, more than twice the size of Earth and with an atmosphere similar to your own, is more supportive of life. She is semi-arid, with large deserts covering most of her one continent. Two large, mainly shallow seas surround it. A soaring mountain range bisects the landmass, and chains of other high, saw-toothed mountains line its coasts. Although wildlife here is diverse, reptilians predominate on the arid lands while amphibians, strange mammalian and other bird-like creatures rule the coastal regions. Primitive, armored fish, bizarre sand worms, arthropods, deep ocean worms and jellyfish, together with assorted crab-like creatures, command the seas. Altairians research this planet and value her for her immense biological diversity. Flora and fauna found nowhere else in their solar system exist here in abundance.

The remaining outer planets in the Altair solar system are so-called 'gas giants', similar, in many ways, to the large planets in your Sun's outer solar system. For most, the difference lies in their rate of rotation, which is faster than that of your Jupiter, Saturn, Uranus or Neptune: in one case, its rotation is oddly slower than that of most of this galaxy's gas giants. Thus, their atmospheres exhibit other anomalies, such as the giant red spot visible on Jupiter, or the strange blots that connect to form mystifying geometrical patterns. The two outer planets are surrounded by a ring system that is the equivalent of Saturn. They were formed when a number of large space objects (comets, asteroids and small planetoids with erratic solar orbits) passed too near the planets, colliding with their small, outer moons and exploding into a series of beautiful, multi-colored rings.

Description of Altairian Home World

The third planet in the Altairian solar system is a large water world close to three times the size of Mother Earth (nearly 23,000 miles or 37,000 kilometers in diameter). On her surface are three large continents surrounded by an interconnected ocean. This water world's highly oxygenated atmosphere has a distinctive orange tinge. Her skies are alive with billions of large birds and with enormous bat-like mammals. Two of her continents are known for vast blue and purple grasslands. On the third continent, which vaguely resembles a large human hand, is an inland sea connected to the ocean by a narrow strait located near the base of the 'thumb'. A three-tiered firmament keeps the planet ice-free and the climate semi-tropical.

Like most galactic humans, Altairians prefer to live inside their world. There, huge crystal cities support a population of close to 1.3 billion souls. Due to their constant negotiations with both the former Anchara Alliance and the Galactic Federation, Altair has acquired technology that is equal to that of any in the galaxy. This technology powers their cities and is used to create homes, clothing and food for all her citizens.

Altairian Society

The Altairians' culture is highly unusual. It is noted for a multi-level ruling class that grew to dominate the twelve clans that formed its galactic society. That society is undergoing a transition to a more traditional form of galactic society. The core of Altairian society is a ruling council, consisting of reigning classes from each of the twelve clans. It is in charge of the day-to-day activities of the Altairian Dominion. The governing council elects a chief ruler, a King or Queen, who serves in that capacity for ten years.

Beneath this ruling council is a group similar to your planet's nobility (princes, dukes, counts, etc.). This body oversees the day-to-day administration of each of the ten major political regions on their world. By using their great influence as regional heads to direct critical socio-political activities, such as negotiating important economic contracts and monitoring every detail of their region's economy, they rose to elevated positions of power.

Below them were twelve clans, subdivided into groups that supplied workers, administrators, technicians and researchers in charge of manufacturing technologies, building trades and enterprises that maintained Altairian society. Rules dictated by the governing council compelled these clan members to swear loyalty to the intermediary nobility (see page 17, Chart 2: The Altairian Galactic Society Prototype).

From this middle group of regional governors, which had the status of royalty, was chosen the ruling council's 'chief ruler'. Seeing that it was prudent, now, to rejoin the Galactic Federation of Light, these groups quickly began to open up Altairian society and set in motion a complex process that, by ending the 'royal order', in time can restore a more traditional, clan-based system of governance.

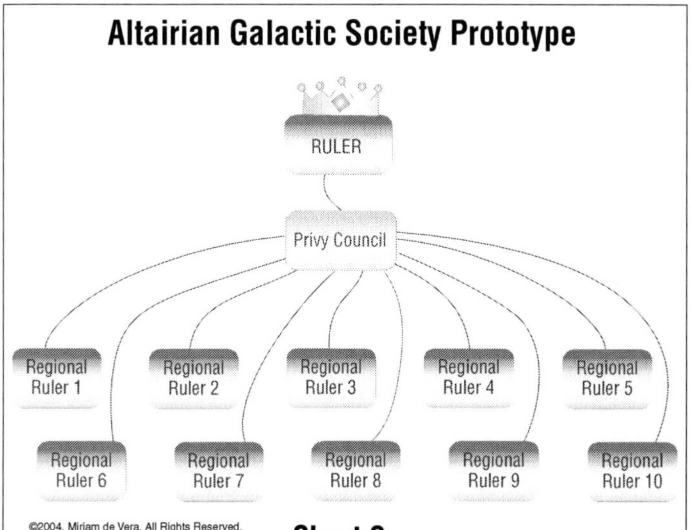

Chart 2

To do so, each regional assembly began to appoint true representatives of their society's clan system to the main ruling council, replacing former members drawn from the intermediary nobility. These regional rulers also initiated reforms that transformed each clan from a worker group into a truer example of a galactic human clan with all of its many and varied sub-divisions.

Over the past nine years, Altairian 'nobility' has radically opened up their society, which they have used as a prototype for others. This prototype, a modified version of the Andromedan/Pleiadean galactic society model, can be used by many other former members of the Anchara Alliance to transform their societies. These one-time Ancharan societies existed according to the concept of simple, unjustifiable loyalty to their dark lord, Anchara, and to the rulers and their appointed representatives who manipulated them to create vast galactic empires in the name of Anchara.

Altair's Former Role in the Anchara Alliance

As noted, the Altairians were trusted negotiators between some empires of the Anchara Alliance and other neutral star-nations. They occasionally even served as overseer for the Alliance on important secret projects. A case in point is their dealings with Earth's 'secret governments' and the former overlords of your world – the Anunnaki. This task quickly gained in importance as many of the dinosaurian and reptilian dark empires felt that the overt efforts of your 'secret governments' to counter their agendas were exceedingly foolish. Thus, from the 1950s to the 1990s, the Altairians acted as mediators between these various groups. The result was a series of clandestine treaties designed to resolve difficulties and ensure that each party's interests were served. The undertaking occurred once again when, in the mid-1990s, the Anchara Alliance asked the Galactic Federation of Light for membership.

Since the dark empires of Anchara did not trust the emissaries of the Galactic Federation, they approached the Altairians to barter this deal. In 1995, the Altairian ambassadors were able to quickly piece together an acceptable agreement, the Treaty of Anchara. It remains the basis upon which the former empires of the Anchara Alliance were accepted as members of the Galactic Federation of Light. However, the Altairian role did not stop there. For nearly a decade, they have worked hard with a number of other star-nations to help the formerly dark sectors of this galaxy make their peace with the Light.

Changing Altair's Society

The Altairians are starting to democratize their society by restoring the ultimate basis of the 12 clans and adopting the Four Laws as their other guiding principle. The model for their society is the Andromedan/Pleiadean prototype. As the Altairians continue in their societal transformation, they are using their increased understanding to assist former members of the Anchara Alliance in transforming their own tyrannical societies.

To do so, the Altairians assembled a working group that consisted of the reptilian and human societies from Aldebaran (Alpha Taurus). The Aldebaran reptilians, which have belonged to the Galactic Federation of Light for more than 800,000 years, have developed their own remarkable and singular prototype of galactic society.

The Aldebaran model is being shown to former Anchara Alliance members. The Altairians' liaison and negotiating skills have proved invaluable to this process. At the same time, the

Altairians have observed many nuances in the Four Laws that they, in turn, are applying to their own societal changes.

This process of change applies, also, to the actions of the reformed Anunnaki (now called the Annanuki), who look to the galactic society model and the Altairian guidelines for assistance in their own societal transformation. Clearly, the recent drastic changes in our own galaxy have caused a great many far-reaching consequences, affecting not only the Altairians, but also tens of thousands of former members of the Anchara Alliance. They understand the need for change and desire to know how it can be implemented so that their societies can become welcome additions to the Galactic Federation of Light.

Description of the Altairians

The Altairians are, primarily, a humanoid species with a few Reptilian and Dinosaurian hybrids living among them. Let us describe the physical appearance of each of these Beings.

The Altairians tend to resemble us in many ways, despite some major differences. First, they are tall in stature. Regardless of gender, the average Altairian stands over seven feet (2.13 meters) tall. Their skin is naturally very smooth and hairless. It is also noted for its white tones, which range from extremely pale to those of the average white European.

Their eyes, unlike ours, are large and recognizable for their round or almond shape; most often, they are sapphire blue, but occasionally green or yellow. The nose is either large and aquiline or small and slightly bulbous. Altairian lips are extremely thin, and their canine teeth are large. Their ears are delicate and somewhat larger than ours. Hair is thick and blond, red or brown-black.

The Altairian head is in proportion to the rest of the body, and the neck is long and graceful. Body, arms and legs are very muscular. Each limb has five or six extremely long, thin digits.

Males are slightly taller than females, and stand between 7 and 8.5 feet (2.13 and 2.59 meters) in height. Females range from 7.5 to 8 feet (2.29 to 2.44 meters) tall. Altairians are celebrated for their flair in dress, which varies from silver or gray jumpsuits to spectacular, iridescent robes intertwined with multicolored, flowing gowns. Altairians need only 2 to 4 hours of sleep per day. Altairians are renowned for their great psychological proficiency, and for their skills in the many ways of manipulating the mind and manifesting the desires. Their vast body of knowledge is gleaned from close interaction with star-empires formerly allied with the Anchara Alliance, and their capacious scientific libraries date back more than 25 million years.

While the language of Altair is very melodic, its speech can also be guttural.

Altairian Ships

Altairian scout ships are disc-shaped, with large, flat, rounded objects protruding from the disc's upper edge. The scouts vary in diameter from 50 to 150 feet (15.2 to 46 meters).

Altairian motherships are extremely large, extending from 100 to 10,000 miles (160 to 16,000 kilometers) across. Smaller ones resemble tadpoles, while larger ones look like rounded, stacked loaves of bread. Larger motherships are extremely self-sufficient and usually keep only to deep space.

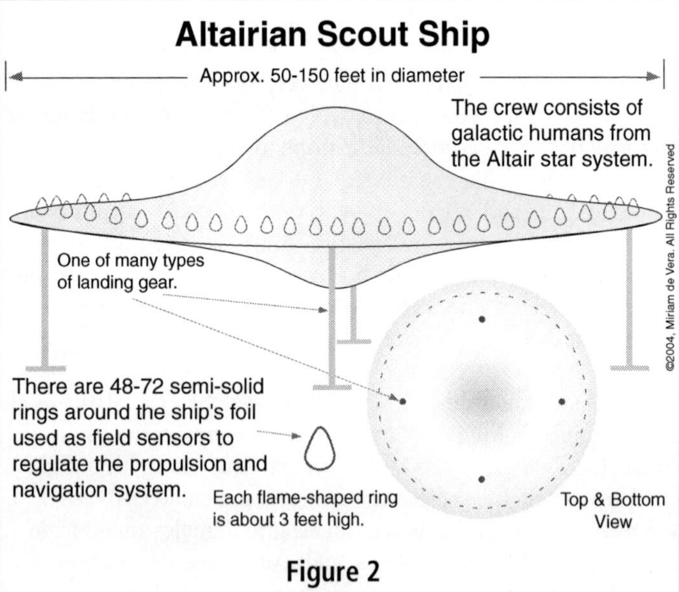

Figure 2

3

The Star-Nation of Epsilon Eridani

Time and again, Washta, my main Galactic Federation of Light guide and mentor, would delight in describing to me the importance of 'heart logic'. He would explain that it is through this higher reasoning that our heavenly guides and our True Self communicate with us. In this way, it is possible for us to imaginatively solve any possible problem and, by using our true abilities, to manifest new ideas, create beautiful art and pioneer clever inventions. One star-nation that had honed this logic to its highest point was Epsilon Eridani.

During one of his teaching sessions with me, Washta introduced me to Bilok, a liaison team member on his Sirian mothership. Bilok, who originated on Epsilon Eridani, told me that 'heart logic' was taught to the children of his home world (in their language, 'Erza' or 'Heart Being').

Epsilon Eridani society centered on the discovery of methods that can enhance the use of 'heart logic' in a galactic society. Among such uses was the assisting of any galactic society in carrying out its responsibilities to each individual member, to its society as a whole, to your solar system and to the Milky Way Galaxy. Indeed, entire institutes were created to teach the various methods of achieving greater resonance with this sacred process. Such organizations were highly honored by the Galactic Federation of Light. That very recognition, in fact, led Bilok to travel to Sirius-B on a mission to instruct eminent counselors, such as Washta, in the latest 'heart logic' technologies.

Location and Status

The constellation of Eridanus (which in Greek means 'River'), is located between the constellations of Orion (Greek for 'Hunter') and Taurus (Greek: 'Bull'). Eridanus is best known for its second-brightest star (Beta Eridani), known as 'Cursa' (Arabic: 'Foot Stool'), which sits near the bright star Rigel (Arabic: 'Foot'), at the foot of Orion. This very bright star is about 89 Light Years away from Earth. Epsilon Eridani is positioned about 10.5 Light Years from Earth, near the middle of the constellation of Eridanus. Celebrated as one of the first solar systems ever discovered by Earth's astronomers, in the late 1990s, this star is very similar in size and composition to Earth's Sun.

Epsilon Eridani, known to her inhabitants as the star-nation of 'Jadok-san', was accepted into the Galactic Federation of Light nearly 3.7 million years ago. Like Sirius and the Star League of the Pleiades, Epsilon Eridani is one of the star-nations that together forms part of the Sirian Federation Regional Council. This is the same Galactic Federation Regional Council on which your solar system's star-nation will sit.

Epsilon Eridani Solar System and Description of Home Worlds

The solar system of Epsilon Eridani consists of six planets, and is similar in configuration to that of Sirius-B. Like Sirius-B, the Epsilon Eridani solar system encompasses two main home water worlds, the largest being her third planet, called Erza ('Heart Being'). This prime Epsilon Eridani home world much resembles Earth, except that she is one-quarter larger. Erza, with six main continents and five large, deep oceans, is nearly 70 percent water. Like Earth, she teems with life. By contrast, Bertak, Epsilon Eridani's fourth world, whose oceans contain the planet's supply of just less than 50 percent water, is known as a large, Saharan continent. On this planet stands a main temple of the Epsilon Eridani people that is dedicated to the study and dissemination of 'heart logic'.

The Epsilon Eridani people enjoy a galactic society very similar to that of Sirius-B. You should understand that every Lyran/Sirian type of galactic society is not exactly alike, and that each possesses many crucial differences. Here, to accommodate the broad study of 'heart logic' in Epsilon Eridani galactic society, the six-clan Lyran/Sirian social order has been modified to an eight-clan system.

Origins of Epsilon Eridani Society

Epsilon Eridani, as well as the next star-nations to be discussed, Eta Hercules and Alpha Aries (Hamal), was first colonized by expeditions from Sirius-B. Although each had initially embraced a galactic society very similar in concept to that of their former Sirian home worlds, Epsilon Eridani also maintained a large contingent of colonists from the more distant Andromedan star-nations.

The Lyran/Sirian model for galactic society is built on six clans. Each clan possesses its own council, which is overseen by a main governing council that acts as the Sirius-B government. In turn, this administrative body convenes with similar governing councils from Sirius-A and the other Sirian solar systems to create the Sirius Star System's Main Governing Council. This Main Council rules over a traditional community that is based upon the Four Laws of galactic society (see Addendum, p. 195).

If we examine the achievements of the people of Epsilon Eridani, we find that, while they are passionate about the role of individual inner logic in enunciating truths, they feel that they themselves are blessed with a highly intuitive heart-logic. They developed these talents at the time the colonists from Sirius-B united with those from Andromeda. The result was a new understanding of how spiritual science could be applied to solve a society's problems and advance its levels of technology.

By applying both, the Epsilon Eridani became distinguished scientists in much the same way as their Andromedan ancestors. Consequently, their many logic schools support the Andromedan concept of unity created through diversity. These same schools also embrace the great Sirian concepts of duty and spirit. The Epsilon Eridani combined these two components and created a society slightly different from either the Andromedan galactic societies, which possess twelve clan councils, or the Sirius-B model, which has six.

Epsilon Eridani Galactic Society

The Epsilon Eridani people created their own unique eight-clan galactic society. This modified model was based upon the retention of the original six clans, which are called the Spiritual Warrior, Administration, Science, Science Engineering, Life Sciences and Life Sciences Engineering clans. In a departure from the classic Lyran/Sirian example, the people of Jadok-san added two additional clans (see Chart 3 below). The first, known as

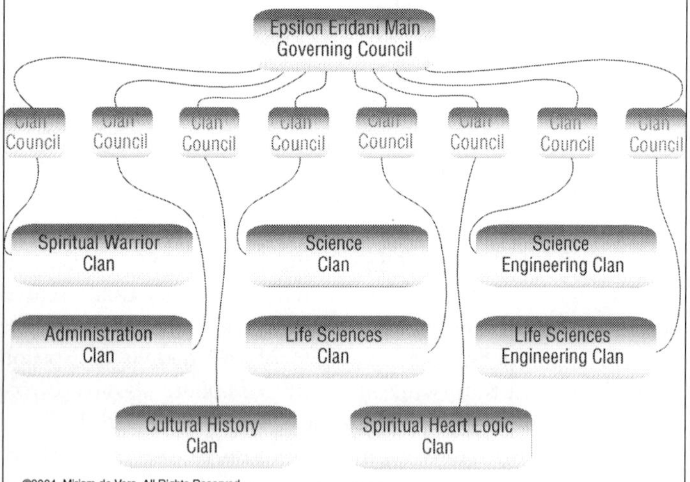

Chart 3

the Cultural History clan, deals with the concepts of creating cultural unity within an extremely diverse cultural society. It is a modification of the cultural tradition and history clans found in the 12-clan Andromeda model. The second, known as the Spiritual Heart Logic ('Baruk') clan, is unique to this Epsilon Eridani 8-clan prototype. This second clan develops techniques to make different tasks work holistically. That is, this clan has been given the crucial task of presiding over the development and use of 'the spiritual logic of the heart'.

Following the classic model, all of these clans establish their own main clan governing councils. The councils, in turn, send representatives to Epsilon Eridani's main governing council. At this point, we notice another difference. During sessions of this governing council, distinguished liaisons from the Spiritual Heart Logic clan serve as special presiding referees to assist members of the main governing council in solving whatever problems or difficulties may arise.

As you can see, the people of Epsilon Eridani found a way to combine components from the Lyran/Sirian and Andromedan models for galactic societies. This wondrous talent has made them celebrated throughout the Milky Way Galaxy. In effect, the Epsilon Eridani people have applied the Andromedan ability to create unity out of diversity. These they combined with two great traits of their Sirian ancestors: a wonderful spiritual aptitude, and a famous sense of shared and personal spiritual loyalty to the Great Blue Lodge of Creation.

For this and other reasons, the Epsilon Eridani people are renowned, galaxy-wide, for what they refer to as 'spiritual logic of the heart' – their applied, intuitive reasoning – and for using that reasoning to analyze and successfully resolve any given situation. The Epsilon Eridani people are highly regarded as truly gifted logicians – a trait this society deems its greatest characteristic. The logicians of Epsilon Eridani are often called upon to apply this 'spiritual logic of the heart' to other sectors of the Galactic Federation of Light. Galactic human societies throughout the galaxy acknowledge the great skills of the people of Jadok-san, and are quite happy to call upon them whenever they are needed.

Physical Description of the Peoples of Epsilon Eridani

The Epsilon Eridani human resembles the original Sirius B humanoid colonist. Men's bodies vary from perfectly formed, muscular physiques to child-like builds, and range from 6 feet, 6 inches to 7 feet, 4 inches (1.98 to 2.24 meters) in height. Hair is blonde to light brown and eyes are light blue to green. Women are extremely voluptuous and stand between 6 feet, 2 inches and 6 feet, 8 inches (1.88 meters and 2.03 meters) tall. Epsilon Eridani skin tones are extremely pale, light red or light blue. Like their Sirian relatives, they require only two hours of sleep per day.

The clothes of the Epsilon Eridani people are unique. Unlike their Sirian ancestors, the people of Jadok-san have shied away from the sheer, flowing, short or ankle-length Sirian gowns, adorned with ribbons and other signs of rank or high honor. The traditional Epsilon Eridani outfit consists of gauzy, billowing pants, topped by waist- or knee-length gossamer blouses. Like the Sirian original, these outfits take the colors of their respective clan. But, rather than special ribbons or epaulettes, various special geometrical designs in the outer blouse determine the individual's rank and the honors accorded them.

Aboard Galactic Federation spacecraft, the outfit changes to a one- or two-piece jumpsuit that adheres to the uniform requirements of Federation dress codes. Normally, the one-piece design is worn only when there is a mixed crew, consisting of members from several other Galactic Federation of Light star-nations. This often occurs on Science and Exploration (S&E) fleets assigned to a first contact mission.

The two-piece jumpsuit design more closely resembles the traditional Epsilon Eridani costume. The pants are baggy, like those worn on their home worlds. The jacket extends just below the waist, much like one of their more popular traditional styles. This jumpsuit also adheres to the clan color codes, with the special geometric designs that determine rank and conferred honors. The boots, an integral part of this costume, are designed to merge into the pants so that they appear as one undivided unit.

Epsilon Eridanians are recognized as avid explorers and consummate scientists. They have led some of the most successful Science and Exploration (S&E) expeditions into previously unexplored parts of this and other galaxies.

The Epsilon Eridani are also noted for their superior abilities as administrators and Galactic Federation of Light Liaison Counselors. They excel in organizing Science & Exploration fleet missions to the outer reaches of this galaxy and have led several first contact missions to other galaxies.

The syntax of the original Epsilon Eridani language very closely resembles that of Polynesia. Subsequent Andromedan colonists influenced the language, eventually producing speech patterns whose style and sound are very similar to Chinese. The outcome is a unique and graceful hybrid language, famed for its sweetness of sound. Chants intoned in this language are renowned for their powers to heal and soothe.

The Ships of Epsilon Eridani

Epsilon Eridani ships observed in Earth's skies are part of a large fleet of scout ships, designed to monitor Mother Earth. Frequently, they resemble ships from the Andromedan Confederacy or the Star League of Centaurus.

The all-purpose science ship, one of the most common, has a diameter of about 45 feet (14 meters) and a height of nearly 28 feet (8.5 meters). Its shape resembles that of a Mexican sombrero, and is similar to Andromedan scout ships, or even those from Centaurus. Unlike them, however, the Epsilon Eridani ship's main dome (housing the crew and command sections) and its disc ('wing') areas are much thicker. Therefore, these scout ships can carry more scientific instruments and remain in cloaked hover mode for much longer.

A second Epsilon Eridani craft is the atmospheric command ship. Shaped like a giant rod, it is approximately 4,000 feet (1.22 kilometers) long and usually carries a crew complement of 541. Together with a corresponding Pleiadean command ship, it coordinates the daily flights of scout ships in a given sector of your atmosphere.

Such command ships transport a crew of special liaisons who analyze preliminary data and ensure that each ship in its sector successfully carries out its mission and returns safely to base. These ships keep in touch with their assigned motherships and make certain that each oncoming wave of scout ships perfectly dovetails with the next. Out of this elegant, galactic ballet flows a constant stream of vital information about Mother Earth.

A third type is the special fleet mothership. It is shaped like a large, oblong lozenge, half-surrounded by a group of smaller 'lozenges' that are connected to one another by a series of large, round pylons. Its main hull is 4,000 miles (6,440 kilometers) long. Generally, it serves as the main command mothership on an assignment for the Science and Exploration (S&E) fleet. These motherships are only a fraction of the many thousands of ships selected for the science mission of your first contact.

4

The Star-Nation of Alpha Aries (Hamal)

Many times, Washta would describe to me the extent to which human galactic society can vary in character, conduct and creative focus. One of the prime examples most often mentioned by my wise counselor is the Star-Nation of Hamal (Alpha Aries). The people of that star-nation are celebrated throughout this galaxy for the wondrous beauty of their art. In fact, they are unofficially described as the 'art ambassadors' of the Galactic Federation of Light.

In the late 1980s, I was first 'reintroduced' to the almost overwhelming abundance of material I would have to learn in order to launch my first contact mission. The symbolic 'living' art of the peoples of Hamal was used to gently guide me through the many concepts I needed to know. Among them were the history of, and underlying reasons for, the creation of human galactic society; and the way the driving forces behind 'fluid dynamics' (the main management tool of the Galactic Federation) operate to offer creative solutions to specific problems. For all of this, I am deeply grateful to the 'living artisans' of the Star-Nation of Hamal.

Present Status and Location

The Star-Nation of Alpha Aries (Hamal) was first accepted into the Galactic Federation of Light nearly 2.13 million years ago. Originally, Hamal had been part of a series of strategically positioned defense colonies, settled 2.5 million years ago by Galactic Federation of Light human colonists from the Andromedan Confederacy and human star-nations located in the constellation of Lyra.

The star Hamal in Arabic means 'Head of the Sheep'. Her inhabitants call Hamal 'Japos Da'La' ('Being of Joyous Light'). She is the brightest star in Aries, and is approximately 66 Light Years from Earth.

The constellation of Aries (Greek for 'Ram') appears in your night sky as a far-flung region consisting mostly of larger-magnitude stars. She is positioned between the constellations of Andromeda (Greek: 'daughter of Cassiopeia') and Pisces (Latin: 'Fishes'), and just above that of Pegasus (Greek: 'Winged Horse'). The easiest way to find Hamal is to look for a triangle in the head of the ram that is located just below Andromeda. This triangle consists of Hamal and two other major stars, which form the ram's horns. These stars are Beta Aries or Sheratan (Arabic: 'signs'), and Gamma Aries or Mesarthim (Arabic: 'Fat Lamb').

Alpha Aries: Solar System and Description of Home Worlds

The solar system of Alpha Aries contains eight planets. The outer three are huge 'gas giants', similar in size and appearance to your planets Saturn, Uranus and Neptune. In the center of this solar system are two semi-arid worlds, each about one-quarter the size of Neptune and Uranus, and about 7,400 miles (11,900 kilometers) in diameter. Next closer to their sun is the planet that serves as home world for the Alpha Aries star-nation. Her natives know this planet as 'Joo'Doo', and she is the third planet from Japos Da'La.

At first glance from space, the planet of Joo'Doo appears very Earth-like. At 7,000 miles (11,270 kilometers), Joo'Doo is close to Earth in diameter. But, unlike Earth, she contains only three large continents surrounded by five deep oceans and a three-tiered firmament that supports an ecosystem famous, like that of Mother Earth, for her wide variety of life forms.

The climate of the Joo'Doo' home world is semi-tropical, and cooler only at each pole. Like all planets, Joo'Doo is hollow, enclosing an inner world populated by creatures that, even to this ecosystem, are highly unusual. Alpha Aries' inhabitants, who number 700 million, live in special crystal cities scattered across her inner realm.

The hybrid human (dinosaurian/human) species, in particular, prefers to be the primary guardian for Japos Da'La's two semi-arid planets. They feel more at home in these planets' extremely hot, dry environments. There, it is much easier for them to share their sacred planet-keeping rituals with their human counterparts. For the most part, they perform these rituals in large, desert temples located near small, sacred, surface settlements.

The two innermost planets are small and barren, and possess exceedingly thin atmospheres. The outer world is less than 3,000 miles (4,800 kilometers) in diameter. The inner is called 'Ja'Lut', which means 'most joyous'. Because Ja'Lut's atmosphere is frequently lit by her sun's solar flares, she seems to be a world aglow. Both planets are known for their unusually erratic orbits.

Origins of Alpha Aries Society

The ancestors of the people of Alpha Aries came from the Andromedan and Lyran constellations. The people of Japos Da'La, while sharing the same basic perspectives on the formation of their galactic society as the Epsilon Eridanians, had very different cultural priorities. Instead, they saw themselves primarily as artistic beings, the chosen creators of what they referred to as 'living art'.

On Joo'Doo, they established a society that was meant to function as the embodiment of art on a grand scale. The Alpha Arians discerned that art comprised subjects of taste, style and imagination, and included sculpture, painting, literature, dance and drama. Their unique galactic society, therefore, emphasizes these many different aspects of their culture. To the peoples of Japos Da'La, art is, in fact, the highest living expression of being human, and a way to honor the Creator's greatest gifts – the soul and the physical universe to which we all belong.

Thus, the galactic human society inhabiting Alpha Aries is totally unique. It almost resembles a living theatre, filled with dynamic, ever-changing living art. The people of Japos Da'La perceive their galactic society in this way, as a vibrant work of art composed of many equally superb pieces. In this wonderful, richly creative environment, each citizen is capable of using a special technique of artistic creation. The people of Alpha Aries call this creative process their 'living logic'. Our astronomers classify their star – Alpha Aries – as the primary star in the Aries constellation. The peoples of Japos Da'La see themselves in that way, and they are content.

Galactic Society of Japos Da'La (Alpha Aries)

The Alpha Aries people created their own unique, nine-clan galactic society (see Chart 4 below: 'Hamal' Alpha Aries Main Governing Council). This modified model was in keeping with the original six tribes that, in the traditional Lyran/Sirian model, are called the Spiritual Warrior; Administration; Science; Science

'Hamal' Alpha Aries Main Governing Council

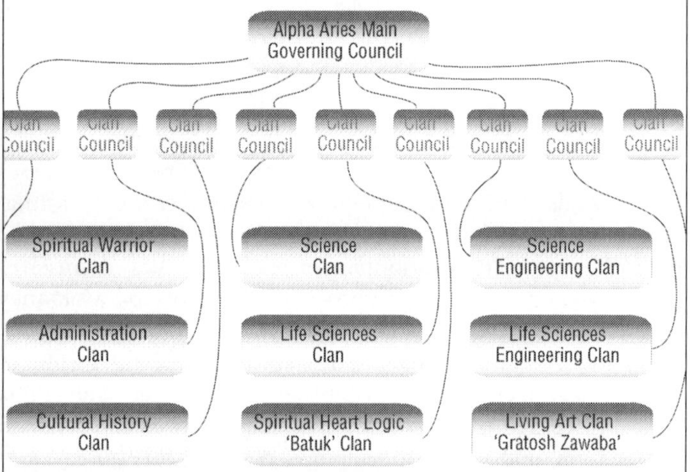

Chart 4

Engineering; Life Sciences; and Life Sciences Engineering clans. In a departure from this classic Lyran/Sirian example, the people of Japos Da'La added three more groups. According to the model derived from the people of Jadok-san (Epsilon Eridani), the first clan deals with the concepts of creating cultural unity within a multiculturally diverse society. This 'Cultural History' clan is a modification of the cultural tradition and history families that are part of the 12-clan Andromedan model.

The second clan, unique to the Epsilon Eridani 8-clan prototype, is known as the Spiritual Heart Logic ('Baruk') clan. This group develops techniques that allow various tasks to be carried out holistically. That is, this second clan's most crucial task is to preside over the development and use of 'the spiritual logic of the heart'. To the adaptations made by the peoples of Jadok-san, the galactic society of Alpha Aries added a third clan. It consists of teachers and counselors who provide instruction in their society's core value – living art – or, in their language, 'gratosh zawaba'.

Following the classic model, each of these clans forms its own main clan governing council, which, in turn, sends representatives to Alpha Aries' main governing council. Here, we notice yet another point of contrast in the people of Japos Da'La. Whenever this governing council is in session, distinguished liaisons from the Spiritual Heart Logic and Living Art clans act as special presiding referees, assisting members of the main governing council in solving problems or difficulties as they arise.

Clearly, both the Alpha Aries and Epsilon Eridani peoples have found a way to incorporate dissimilar components from the Lyran/Sirian and Andromeda models. This ingenious aptitude has brought them acclaim throughout the Milky Way Galaxy. In effect, the people of Epsilon Eridani and Alpha Aries have applied Andromeda's talent of creating unity out of diversity, and combined it with two invaluable attributes of their Lyran ancestors - an immense spiritual capacity and a deeply communal, yet personal, sense of spiritual loyalty to the Great Blue Lodge of Creation. And, by applying the Epsilon Eridani spiritual logic to their art, they have also fashioned an enlightened society celebrated for its creativity and its ability to present the nuances of any subject in an extraordinarily joyful way.

For this and other reasons, the Alpha Aries people are famous, galaxy-wide, for what they refer to as 'living art' – for applying intuitive logic to the arts, and for using that reasoning to create a specific situation and represent it in a positive way so that everyone will fully grasp its nuances. The Alpha Aries people are hailed as exceptionally gifted artisans and logicians; a quality this society deems its greatest achievement. Often, the living artists of Alpha Aries are called upon to put this 'living art' to use in other sectors of the Galactic Federation of Light. Throughout the galaxy, galactic human societies applaud the prodigious talents of the people of

Japos Da'La, and appeal to them whenever necessary.

Description of Inhabitants

On Alpha Aries (Hamal), there are two major species of human. The first group resembles the original Lyran/Sirian and Andromedan human colonist. Male physiques vary from perfectly formed and muscular to a rare, child-like body type. In height, males range from 6 feet, 6 inches to 7 feet, 4 inches (1.98 to 2.24 meters). Japos Da'La women are extremely curvaceous and stand between 6 feet, 2 inches and 6 feet, 8 inches (1.88 meters and 2.03 meters) tall. Their hair varies from blond to light brown, and their eyes from pale blue to navy or dark green. Their skin comes in many colors: red, orange, green, ivory or light blue.

The second, a human hybrid, sprang about two million years ago from the union of dinosaurians and humans. A series of large-scale attacks by dinosaurian forces from the constellation of Orion resulted in the capture of several fleets of Andromedan colonists. After the Anchara Alliance forces from the Star-Nation of Bellatrix had carried out experiments on the colonists, they freed the Andromedan fleets, which continued on to Alpha Aries. There, the dinosaurian/human hybrids were honored as full-fledged members of the Alpha Aries Star-Nation.

The hybrid Hamalan has scaly skin and unmistakably cat-like eyes of red, brown or lemon yellow. The body, legs, neck and arms are more muscular than those of a human, and a number of thick, vein-like swellings run their length. Each hand and foot has 3 long, thin digits that end in a small claw. Males stand between 7 and 8 feet (2.13 to 2.44 meters) tall, while females range from 6 feet, 10 inches to 7 feet, 7 inches (2.08 to 2.31 meters) in height. Neither species requires more than three hours of sleep.

The costumes of the Alpha Aries people are most unusual. Unlike the filmy, flowing, short and ankle-length gowns adorned with the ribbons and insignia of their Lyran/Sirian or Andromedan ancestors, the people of Japos Da'La have chosen far different apparel. The traditional Alpha Aries outfits consist of a billowing, ankle-length skirt in a bright color that identifies one's clan. Sheer outer blouses, either waist-length or ending just above the knee, feature an open shoulder, usually on the left. Special graphic designs on the blouse indicate individual rank and honors or achievements.

The Alpha Aries outfit worn on Galactic Federation spacecraft is a two-piece jumpsuit, much like their traditional costume. The pants are relaxed in fit, and the shirt extends just below the waist. This jumpsuit bears the clan color codes, as well as special graphics to denote rank and official honors. Boots are integral to the costume; they merge into the pants and appear as a continuous unit.

All personnel of star-nations belonging to the Galactic Federation of Light are required to wear their official uniforms while on call and, especially, while on duty. In all other cases, they are permitted to wear the clothes of their distinctive cultures.

The people of Japos Da'La are known throughout the Galactic Federation for their expertise as artists, innovators and scientists.

There are two spoken languages. The human language is gentle and melodious, while the hybrid language tends to be more guttural and coarse.

Ships of Alpha Aries (Hamal)

Two types of Alpha Aries ships are part of the first contact fleet that monitors Mother Earth each day. The first is a low orbit to upper atmosphere command mothership. At 10,000 feet (slightly over 3.0 kilometers) long, it is small, and shaped like a double lens. It serves as the carrier for 2,000 science liaison officers who co-ordinate the preliminary analysis of data from the sector quadrant to which this mothership is assigned.

The second type, a special defense observation craft, resembles a rounded equilateral triangle with three equal sides, each approximately 240 feet (72.96 meters) long. This ship monitors black operation bases belonging to your secret government. Occasionally, it takes part in special operations to neutralize or shut down special craft or exotic weaponry when they are deployed from secret government bases.

5

The Star-Nation of Eta Hercules

Frequently, during my 'retraining' in the late 1980s, Washta would remind me that each human star-nation was a distinct society that expressed the astounding diversity of galactic human culture. A case in point is the Star-Nation of Eta Hercules. Like the peoples of Alpha Aries, the Eta Hercules Star-Nation is renowned for its exceptional creativity, its beautiful art and its talent for providing creative solutions to any possible problem. By relating spiritual science to the creative arts, the people of Eta Hercules have given rise to art with a distinctive purpose. They use this art to solve any problem or express the nature of any difficulty encountered by any podlet in the Eta Herculean 12-clan society. This experience gave me graphic proof of the actual operation of fluid dynamics within a specific galactic society.

Eta Hercules is yet another example of the many possible variations that can exist in class, custom and creative focus within a human galactic society. Eta Hercules is celebrated throughout the Galactic Federation of Light as one of the finest examples of the ways artistic pre-eminence and a detailed use of 'spiritual logic' can be combined. Together, they produce a truly unique and powerful perspective on the best ways to gather and interpret the great gifts bestowed by the Creator upon humanity.

Status and Location

The Star-Nation of Eta Hercules was first accepted into the Galactic Federation of Light nearly 2.4 million years ago. Originally, Eta Hercules had been one of a series of strategically located defense colonies settled 2.5 million years ago by Galactic Federation of Light human colonists from the Andromedan Confederacy, and human star-nations located in the constellation of Lyra.

The constellation of Hercules, one of the five largest in your night sky and a major summer star-group in your Northern Hemisphere, is located between the constellations of Draco (Greek for 'Dragon') and Ophiuchus (Greek: 'Serpent Bearer'). It is best known for its great globular cluster (M-13), which formed more than 11 million years ago. You will find the star Eta Hercules by looking for the four stars that comprise the 'keystone' in the constellation of Hercules: Eta Hercules is in the upper northwest corner, pointing toward the constellation of Bootes (Greek: 'Herdsmen') and its brightest star, Arcturus (Greek: 'Bear Guard'). Eta Hercules is nearly 112 Light Years from Earth.

Eta Hercules Solar System

The solar system of Eta Hercules consists of six planets. As is usual in this galaxy, the smallest is closest to the sun and the largest farthest away. The innermost planet in this system is half the size of your Earth. Her thin atmosphere glows from constant discharges from her sun, Butok ('Bright One'). Perpetual electrical storms light this planet, turning her atmosphere into a collection of rare, charged gases that reduce it to a mix of principally methane and nitrogen. The only life forms able to survive in such a caustic environment are chains of very primitive bacteria and algae.

The next world is more amenable to life. Nearly the same size as Earth, this sphere's atmosphere is similar to your own. However, unlike your Earth, this planet possesses a hot climate and semi-arid topography. The shorelines of her two continents are covered mainly by lofty coastal mountain ranges, which contribute, in turn, to the existence of broad interior deserts. These landmasses are surrounded by five small, shallow, interconnected seas; a high mountain range extends down one continent's center. Life here is extremely diverse: reptilians, amphibians, birds, bats and small, shrew-like mammals comprise, in part, the land's varied ecosystem. In its seas swim a multitude of species: among them, primitive, armored fishes, crab-like creatures and assorted, rudimentary aquatic arthropods. The Eta Hercules people treat this semi-arid world as an elaborate, on-going study by their life scientists in biological diversity. Plant and animal life unheard of elsewhere in their solar system or in other parts of this galaxy exist here in abundance.

The remaining outer planets in the Butok solar system are 'gas giants' similar, in many regards, to the large planets of other systems, including that of your own Sun. Still, differences do exist. These planets not only spin much faster than your Jupiter, Saturn, Uranus or Neptune, but their atmospheres possess anomalies more akin to the giant red spot found on Jupiter. These include interconnected large spots that look like giant, multi-colored ink blots. The fifth (outer) world of this solar system has a very large and beautiful ring system that is easily the equal of Saturn. This ring system exists because, in the last seven billion years, several comets and other stray chunks of space debris occasionally passed too close to this planet's small, inner moons. The impact set a chain of events in motion that drove the moons too close to their world and caused them to explode. The outcome was a series of three multicolored rings.

Description of Home World

The Eta Hercules' home world, called 'Shom-Fes' ('the Holy Place') in their language, is the third planet in this solar system. Of her solar system's twenty moons, Shom-Fes has four. Like other planets, she is hollow and has a double-layered firmament and a global, semi-tropical climate. She is nearly one and one-half times bigger than Earth, with four continents and seven oceans. The largest continent, called Q'fuir Daj ('high ridges') in Eta Herculean, is famous for the high saw-toothed mountain ranges that extend down through her interior. The blue seas' floor contains enormous canyons, like those of Earth, which are almost as deep as Shom-Fes' great mountain range is high.

Origins of Eta Hercules Society

The ancestors of Eta Hercules originated in the constellations of Andromeda and Lyra. While they shared perspectives on the formation of galactic society similar to the people of Epsilon Eridani and Alpha Aries, the cultural and artistic priorities of the inhabitants of Shom-Fes were somewhat different. Humans embody a higher emotional condition, a state of grace and compassion. Whereas the people of the Alpha Aries feel that the highest expression of that compassion is in art, those of Eta Hercules believe that it is communicated best through science.

Here, we are discussing the spiritual science emphasized over and over again in our weekly messages. How do we define art? Or science? And in what ways do they converge? How do we create a society that is artistic, that is living drama, an animate expression of the artistic self that, at the same time, is guided by logic? How do we take art on the one hand, and logic on the other, and marry the two?

On their primary home world, the Eta Hercules people gradually established a society that would serve as the embodiment of art and spiritual science on a grand scale. For the individual Eta Herculean, art included subjects of taste, style and imagination, while spiritual science contained a natural flow around which this ever-growing art could be structured. To the peoples of Butok, art and natural logic are the dual expressions of being human and represent ways to honor the Creator's greatest gifts – the soul and the physical universe to which we all belong.

The galactic human society that sprang from Eta Hercules is entirely unique. Indeed, the galactic society of Butok demonstrates a society's ability to unite two such totally distinct concepts as art and logic. What are the best qualities of each? How can they be communicated to their society? To what wonders does that society give form? By examining the community's creations, we can understand how it manifests its wonders to their highest possible level. Finally, in what way can its different components be merged? This is the decisive point of our discussion, and the basis of the Eta Herculeans' social contract.

Galactic Society of Eta Hercules

The Eta Hercules people created their own unique eight-clan galactic society, which was based upon the retention of the original six clans of the Lyran/Sirian model. But, in a departure from the classic Lyran/Sirian example, the people

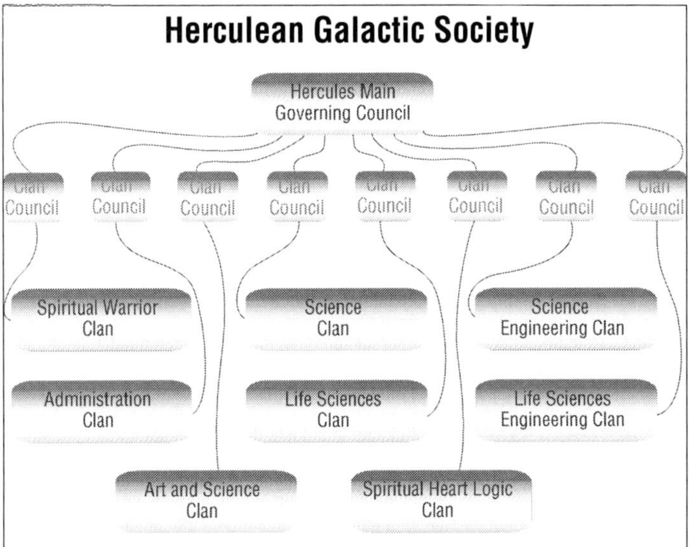

Chart 5

of Shom-Fes added two additional clans (see Chart 5 above, "Herculean Galactic Society"). The first clan creates concepts and refines techniques so that a variety of tasks can be performed holistically. That is, their crucial mission is to preside over the development and application of 'the spiritual logic of the heart'. For that reason, they are called the Perkoh or 'Heart Logic' clan. The second is called the Art and Science (Da-Sang-koh) clan, and is unique to Eta Hercules. Its purpose is to guide society by demonstrating the best expression of 'living art' through various forms of logic, all of which comprise the infinite diversity called human consciousness or, even better, the Consciousness of the Creator.

Mirroring the classic model, each of these clans forms its own main clan governing council. In turn, they send representatives to Eta Hercules' main council. Here, we see yet another contrast to the original Lyran/Sirian model. During sessions of this governing assembly, distinguished liaisons, belonging to the two 'new' clans, act as special presiding referees to assist members of the main governing council in solving any difficulties that may arise.

Clearly, the peoples of Shom-Fes have succeeded in adding

new, useful components to the Lyran/Sirian model. This astounding aptitude has brought them acclaim throughout the Milky Way Galaxy. The Eta Herculean reflects upon how a society can unite two such totally distinct concepts as art and logic. What are the best qualities of each? How are they communicated to their society? To what wonders does that society give form? By examining its many and varied creations, we can understand how the community manifests its marvels to their ultimate possible extent.

For these and other reasons, the Eta Hercules peoples are renowned, galaxy-wide, for their perfect melding of art and spiritual logic to create a unique and shining example of a galactic human society. Galactic human societies throughout the galaxy acknowledge the unrivalled skills of the people of Shom-Fes, and are delighted to call upon them whenever required.

Physical Description of Inhabitants

Eta Hercules humans resemble the original Sirius B humanoid colonists. Men's bodies vary from perfectly formed, muscular physiques to child-like builds and range from 6 feet, 6 inches to 7 feet, 4 inches (1.98 to 2.24 meters) in height. Women are extremely voluptuous and stand between 6 feet, 2 inches and 6 feet, 8 inches (1.88 meters to 2.03 meters) tall. Hair is blonde to light brown and eyes are light blue to green. Eta Herculean skin tones are extremely pale, light red or light blue. Like their Sirian kinfolk, they require only two hours of sleep per day.

The clothing of the Eta Herculeans resembles that of their Sirian ancestors. The people of Shom-Fes have adopted a style that incorporates the same gauzy, flowing, short or ankle-length costumes. The classic Eta Hercules outfit includes a traditional Sirian gown topped by a special, sheer outer blouse that extends to just below the waist. Their garments, like those of the Sirians, take the colors of their clans, and are decorated with ribbons and other symbols of rank or high honor.

A two-piece jumpsuit is worn aboard Galactic Federation spacecraft. The pants fit tightly, while the top, like one of their more popular traditional outfits, ends just below the waist. It, too, adheres to clan color codes and is embellished with the special ribbons and epaulettes that designate rank and commemorate distinctions. Boots are integral to this costume and are designed to merge into the pants, creating a seemingly continuous piece.

Herculeans are renowned for their undisputed skills as artists, diplomats, negotiators and Galactic Federation Liaison Counselors. They excel at bringing together groups of very different sentient Beings to assist them in achieving their goals as peacefully and amicably as possible.

The language of the Eta Herculean Star-Nation is syntactically very close to Polynesian. However, later waves of Andromedan colonists eventually produced a series of variations in pitch that are very similar to Chinese in style and sound. The result is a composite language, largely unique and known for its sweet and musical tones.

Ships of Eta Hercules

Two types of Eta Hercules ships are part of the first contact Earth fleet. The first, an all-purpose scout ship, is used to constantly monitor your beloved planet's harmonics. It is ball-shaped, with a small, lens-like, circular wing attached to its middle and a diameter of more than 100 feet (30.4 meters).

The second type is a small, low orbit to upper atmosphere command mothership that resembles a cigar with a small bulge in its middle. It is 20,000 feet (slightly more than 6.0 kilometers) long. It serves as the carrier for 5,000 science liaison officers who co-ordinate the preliminary analysis of data from the sector quadrant to which this mothership is assigned.

6

The Pegasus Star League

Often, Washta would explain to me Sirius-B's leadership role in the colonization and history of the Pegasus Star League. Located in the constellation of Pegasus, this grand union of star-nations consists of hundreds of members. Together with the Andromedan Confederacy, the Pegasus Star League forms one of the Galactic Federation of Light's original 14 Regional Federation Councils. The Star-Nations of Pegasus were first accepted into the Galactic Federation of Light approximately 3.78 million years ago. Their many members are as close to Mother Earth as 35 Light Years or as far away as 400 Light Years.

My first meeting with a group from the Pegasus Star League occurred when I was about seven. A Pegasus mothership came to Earth to study the political, spiritual and technological status of Earth's humanity. Along with the Andromedans, the Pegasians were known throughout the Galactic Federation of Light as great scientists, technicians and healers. Many of our technological scanners, power system monitors, and computer components and their programming were the result of the creative work of individuals or groups from the Pegasus Star League.

Washta would give me frequent lessons, laden with examples, telling how, nearly one million years ago, the accumulated knowledge of the Andromedan Regional Federation Council saved the Galactic Federation from ruin. Like their Andromedan neighbors, Pegasians are deeply dedicated to ending the perpetual cycles of galactic war through the use of their technical and healing skills. Washta instructed me in the nature of Pegasian society: he inspired me with his many breathtaking lessons and stories about the history of the galaxy and told me how humanity, originating on Vega, crossed this vast galaxy and formed colonies as close as Sirius-B, and as far away as some member star-nations of the Pegasus Star League.

Pegasian Society

The Pegasians pride themselves on being one of the oldest members of the Galactic Federation of Light. As part of the Andromedan Regional Federation Council, they chose to honor both their constituents' diversity and the sheer size of their joint Regional Council by deciding that more than one solar system should serve as their primary headquarters.

The outcome of their decision was a rotating system whereby each constituent member of council is given an opportunity to serve as host of the Regional Council meetings. Every few thousand years, the Regional Council switches the location of its headquarters. According to their logic, this rotation permits every Council member able to provide a potential meeting-place to accommodate the meetings of the entire Regional Council and its various staffs.

In this way, they nurtured the deep loyalty, Love and inner joy that endure to this day. The Pegasians and the Andromedans are justifiably proud of their achievements. Through the application of their inner joy, they have been able to make significant advances in scientific knowledge and are, in fact, among the leading human scientists in the Galactic Federation of Light. The Pegasians see themselves as equal partners on a regional council that views their successes as proof of their potential, and they are eager to bring that promise to every aspect of the Galactic Federation of Light.

Their co-operative efforts are lauded throughout the Galactic Federation of Light for doing just that – demonstrating their work and function, displaying their joy and its uses in transcending group diversity, exhibiting the ease with which they release and reveal their full creative abilities and their freedom in effecting enormous changes for the individual, the planet and the Star League.

They have also shown that these cultural differences, when

worked at, can actually strengthen any culturally distinct group. Pegasian liaison teams are famed throughout the Galactic Federation of Light for their wondrous capacity to explain and express their joy and, out of it, to create unity. For this reason, the Pegasians are major participants in the planning of your first contact.

Cultural Nuances of the Pegasian Star League

The types of clan structures encountered throughout the Pegasus Star League differ widely from sector to sector. The most common prototypes are the Lyran/Sirian one, which consists of six clans, and a modified version, which has up to eight. The Pegasian use of these galactic society prototypes is unique, since most of their galactic societies contain sub-cultures that have retained their own unique languages and traditions.

Of these, the crucial element is their cultural liaisons and counselors. While star-nations such as Eta Pegasus use a Lyran/Sirian model, the two inhabited home worlds in this solar system each possess a rich layer of unique subcultures. Each world maintains liaisons that function as semi-official interpreters for the totality of cultures that exist on that planet. In addition, a special inter-world cultural liaison board provides creative solutions to any problems that may arise. When this system is interfaced with advanced translator technology and peoples' natural telepathic abilities, it allows free communication between individuals and groups. What results is a constant stream of information that, by making positive use of its differences, allows this multi-faceted society to create many revolutionary innovations every day.

Yet another way for this to be achieved lies in the habitable planets that comprise the Mu Pegasus solar system. These home worlds adopted a modified Lyran/Sirian model that uses 8 clans, rather than the Lyran/Sirian six. This model contains clans devoted not only to culture, but also to counseling and liaison: the latter two developed because the Pegasians found it easier to have a separate system in which to train individuals in these important specialties. Each clan serves as a repository for specific wisdoms. The other six clans can make use of these areas of expertise, or, if one of the six clans cannot solve a particular problem, it can be entrusted to one of the two clans that seems most capable of solving it.

By embracing the 8-clan system, Mu Pegasus is perceived as a star-nation that contains many of the most outstanding scientific research groups in the galaxy. Her reputation is due, mainly, to the extent to which their modified 8-clan system officially addresses their broad diversity. This system, modeled on prototypes developed originally by the Eta Hercules and Alpha Aries star-nations, has been dispersed through sectors of the Pegasus Star League.

Pegasus Star League Solar Systems and Description of Some of their Home Worlds

The home worlds of Pegasus vary from water worlds, similar to Mother Earth, to semi-arid spheres. Those on which we intend to concentrate – planets in the multiple stars of Eta Pegasus and the bright yellow giant of Mu Pegasus – are located between 117 and more than 215 Light Years from Earth. The constellation of Pegasus is an immense cluster of more than 1,000 stars that is positioned between those of Cygnus (Greek for 'Swan') and Aquarius (Latin: 'Water-Carrier') in the winter and autumn skies of the Northern Hemisphere. The star-nations of this League are situated between 35 and 400 Light Years from Earth.

The Home Worlds of Eta Pegasus

Let us begin with the home worlds of this bright yellow giant and her two companion stars, familiar to your astronomers as Eta Pegasus but known also by her Arabic name, Matar ('Fortunate Rain'). Humans first colonized these stars, located in the middle of the 'neck' of the Pegasian 'horse', nearly 4 million years ago.

The largest Earth-like water world in the Pegasus Star League, which her inhabitants call Erkha ('Homeland'), is one of three planets orbiting the central star of Eta Pegasus. Erkha is noted for her boundless oceans, teeming with many different living species, and for her polar night skies, resplendent with luminous, pastel auroras that encompass the entire color spectrum. And, in the seven oceans and seas that surround this world's seven continents, live the largest aquatic cetaceans in the Pegasus Star League.

Approximately two million years ago, a special group of clan liaisons and counselors met on this beautiful world. Here, they formulated a modified 8-clan system, which added a counselor/liaison clan and a cultural history clan to the original Lyran/

Sirian model. In doing so, they wished to emphasize the concept of joyous passion that had become so important to the people of the Pegasus Star League.

The project began after a three-day chanting ritual performed by a group of 24 master liaisons and counselors. These administrators, having examined the future of their diversified society, were able to find the answer to a recurrent problem that earlier had perplexed Andromeda but that they wished, now, to solve in their own unique way: how to design a new program for the proper training and administration of all of Pegasus' liaisons and counselors.

The solution, though similar to that originally devised by the famed Andromedan innovator, Toudok, had some fresh and inspired variations: immersion of individuals, such as newborns, in a combined clan that makes these noble professions a priority. This clan would also embody the pure, creative joy that was the underpinning of her galactic society. As in Toudok's case, their heart reasoning told them that the existence of such a clan can encourage souls that were to be incarnated as counselors or liaisons to seek out this new clan for their embodiment. They also discussed the necessity for a new clan, totally devoted to the study and preservation of their home world's rich history and varied cultures.

Furnished with these concepts, they arrived at a new model for galactic society. Having quickly given reality to these ideas, the administrators of this plan were able to solve many complex societal problems. Their modified Lyran/Sirian prototype sped across the length and breadth of the Pegasus Star League.

While the central star of this cluster of three initiated the 8-clan system, the inner of the two companion stars encircling her contained worlds of legendary beauty, as well. The two inner planets of this inner companion sun contain water worlds, alive with subterranean volcanoes that erupt in the mountain regions of several large islands located in the widest of her three oceans. Here, too, are found multi-colored pools of boiling mud and still-hot igneous rock formations. Humans from Sirius-B colonized this system's second planet, where they found a world of turquoise seas, blue-violet skies and many small island-continents scattered sporadically across her surface.

The significance of this world, which they call Grosna-Ja

('Where Joy has come'), lies in her adoption and modification of the Erkhan 8-clan model to suit her own needs. Here, on sumptuous lands covered with forests of fantastic orange pine trees, some rising 500 feet high, and swarming with large, deer-like or other woodland creatures, a new procedure for administering a main star council was born.

Formerly, main star councils in the Pegasus Star League had taken a particular clan council's advice and simply given an issue swift and uncritical approval. With this assembly, an open forum was created in which the decisions of each clan council could be thoroughly and rationally discussed. At the same time, other groups had an opportunity to review a clan's decision and determine its relevance to their own issues. Taking part in the forum were counselors and liaisons highly familiar with the means whereby the decision had previously been reached. Through this uncompromising new process, many precedents were set, allowing a gratifying resolution to be achieved for all involved.

The Home Worlds of Mu Pegasus

The other important star system is known as Mu Pegasus or, in Arabic, Sadabari ('Excelling One'). This solar system, located approximately 117 Light Years from your planet, contains one large water world and a smaller one nearly twice the size of Mother Earth. A colony dedicated to advancing the principles of spiritual science was founded here nearly 3.1 million years ago.

The colonists first established their headquarters inside the smaller water planet, close to the yellow sun that they called Lahabihm ('Living Essence of Light'). The climate of this world, named Jamadok ('Place of Great Inner Joy'), was predominantly semi-tropical. Strange, ferny trees and ginkgo-like ones grow here, creating never-ending forests of orange, blue, purple, red and brown trees, which extend to the edges of astonishing, rainbowy beaches. Multi-colored mountains as tall as Earth's Himalayas rise on the two largest continents. Exotic birds and large, even worm-like mammalian and reptilian life forms populate these gorgeous locales.

The two scientist colonies quickly realized that their home worlds were a rare treasure, spilling over with incomparable beauty. In this habitat, the spiritual scientists near Lahabihm developed new technologies for material replicators and for new types of energy and propulsion systems. In the course of their work, they discovered methods which, combined with studies provided by the famed scientific research centers in Pi Andromeda, were pivotal in improving the use of physicality's healing energies to restore all sentient Beings. These breakthroughs quickly established the Pegasus Star League as a major center for scientific research and healing.

We have discussed only a very few of the thousands of home worlds that make up the Pegasus Star League. Each one possesses a distinct cultural tradition and a unique history. Those we have just described are among the most noted examples in this widely diverse star league. The rest are equally delightful and, in their own way, alluring. The inhabitants of these worlds are intensely proud of their homelands. We have described them only briefly. What remains, you will hear about from the galactic humans of the Pegasus Star League themselves.

Pegasian Galactic Society

Like the Andromedans before them, the inhabitants of Pegasus were able to take the measure of their society and decide that they wished to create a community of people that was greater than that from which they had sprung. Like the Andromedans, too, they were endowed with a natural aptitude for science and its applications – a logical analysis of how everything in this universe was intuitively created. They decided, therefore, to examine how they could apply these principles to frame a greater and worthier society.

The peoples of the Pegasus Star League have created a society that is widely considered to be one of the most joyous of any planetary group. As a result, the various Pegasian star-nations have been able to become a powerful liaison group in the Galactic Federation of Light. They have learned how to suggest ways that will reveal and communicate the expertise and essence of each Being at their highest levels. The Pegasians are also among the most influential liaisons in the Science and Exploration (S&E) fleets and take great pride in this particular aspect of their society. The ways in which all of the many aspects of Pegasian galactic society come together – their different councils and the clans, sub-clans, pods, podlets – manifest joy, which enriches their natural abilities for creation and innovation.

Physical Description

Three major species of human co-exist in the Pegasian Star League. The first is much like the Sirian human in height and appearance, and is subdivided into the same white and blue skin types. The second is a thinner human whose skin is red or orange. The final species is a hybrid of the dinosaurian and the second humanoid.

The first species resembles the original Sirius-B human colonists. The men's physiques vary from perfectly formed and muscular to child-like. They stand from 6 feet, 6 inches to 7 feet, 4 inches (1.98 to 2.24 meters) tall and have blonde to light brown hair with light blue to green eyes. The women are extremely voluptuous and vary from 6 feet, 2 inches to 6 feet, 8 inches (1.88 meters to 2.03 meters) in height. Their skin is either chalk-white or light blue.

The second human species bears a slight resemblance to the first in height and/or body type, with two major exceptions. First, both skin and hair are light red or dark orange. Second, the eyes are more feline in shape, while the iris is red or navy blue. This group originated from the more distant stars in the Lyra constellation.

The human hybrid third species has scaly skin and striking, cat-like eyes of red, brown or lemon yellow. The body, legs, neck and arms are more muscular than those of a human and thick, vein-like swellings extend along their length. Hands and feet have 4 long, thin digits, with each ending in a small claw. Males stand from 7 to 8 feet (2.13 to 2.44 meters) tall while females range in height from 6 feet, 10 inches to 7 feet, 7 inches (2.08 to 2.31 meters).

Pegasians are noted throughout the Galactic Federation for their talents as innovators, scientists and diplomats. Depending on their species, they need only one and one-half to three hours of sleep.

There are two distinct Pegasian languages. One language is musical, while the other is guttural and coarse.

Ships of the Pegasus Star League

Three types of Pegasian ships maneuver in or near Earth. The first, a defense ship, is used to guard the scouts that habitually monitor Mother Earth and act as security attachment for those defense scout ships that monitor secret government underground bases and their unconventional technologies. This ship resembles a round-cornered equilateral triangle. Each of its three sides is approximately 74 feet (22.56 meters) long.

The second is an all-purpose scout ship. It is used primarily as part of the Earth observation fleet that constantly monitors your beloved planet. It is oblong in shape, with an average diameter of about 85 feet (25.9 meters).

The third type, a low orbit to upper atmosphere command mothership, resembles a double lens. This very small atmospheric command mothership is roughly 1,300 feet (402 meters) in length. It serves as a carrier for 350 science liaison officers who coordinate the preliminary analysis of data from the sector quadrant to which this mothership is assigned.

7

The Pleiadean Star League

From my early childhood, Washta told me that, since ancient times, a joint command, consisting primarily of the Sirian Star-Nation and the Star League of the Pleiades, had observed and indirectly guided the peoples of Mother Earth. Both groups had enjoyed a long history overseeing this solar system: some decades ago, Earth's scientists uncovered an ancient memorial to their efforts on Mars. Other signs of their protection include the many megalithic structures spread across this planet. In reality, these primeval monuments are only one indication of the profound influence they have had on many ancient civilizations.

Washta made a point of always honoring the Pleiades' impact on the progress of Mother Earth's inhabitants. As a result of his high regard, I was able to revel in many delightful visits with the scientists and scholars of the Pleiades.

One of my first visits occurred when I was nearly six, when Washta introduced me to a delegation of planetary scientists from a large Pleiadean mothership cloaked approximately 100 miles (161 kilometers) ahead of us. This group had originated from the star that we call Electra. I was struck by their remarkable resemblance to us. Even their height was similar: dressed in vivid blue jumpsuits, they were slightly shorter than Washta, with the same merry twinkle in their equally blue eyes. We entered one of their mothership's main conference rooms to find them immersed in a lively discussion with a knot of Sirian scientists on possible future levels of Mother Earth's volcanic and seismic activity. Both groups paused in their conversation to honor Washta. He, in turn, introduced all of them to me, giving me my first chance to inquire about the Pleiades.

Out of this and many later discussions aboard the Sirian mothership, I was able to learn much more about the Pleiades Star League and its extraordinary history. The Pleiades consists of many advanced galactic societies that have joined together to form a splendid star covenant. Now, with much joy, I introduce you to them.

Status and Location

The Star League of the Pleiades was welcomed into the Galactic Federation of Light more than 300,000 years ago. Originally, the Pleiades had been part of a series of strategically located defense colonies settled 400,000 years ago by Galactic Federation human colonists from the Andromedan Confederacy and human star-nations in the constellation of Lyra.

Located in the autumn and winter night sky of your Northern Hemisphere, the constellation of Taurus (Greek for 'Bull') contains a major star-cluster called the Pleiades, which can be found by first sighting the three stars that form the belt of the constellation of Orion (Greek: 'Hunter').

Visually follow these stars upward and you will quickly distinguish Taurus' major star, the bright orange Aldebaran whose Arabic name means 'Follower'. Look just above and to the right of Aldebaran, and you will see the seven bright stars that form the Pleiades star cluster (M-45).

These seven brightest stars, Alcyone; Merope; Sterope; Maia; Tageta; Celaeno and Electra, are only the most well-known of the more than 250,000 stars that belong to this immense star cluster. In all, 200 planetary systems (star-nations) have united to form this renowned Star League, which is between 200 and 500 Light Years from Earth.

Origins of Pleiadean Society

The ancestors of the Pleiadean Star League originated in the constellations of Andromeda (Greek: 'Daughter of Cassiopeia') and Lyra (Greek: 'Lyre'). While sharing the same basic outlook on the formation of their galactic society, the people of the

Pleiades had cultural and artistic priorities far different from those of their forebears. The Pleiadeans came to believe that humans embody a higher emotional condition, a state of grace and compassion that is communicated best through science. It was important that this science focus on Creation and its relation to the human condition.

On their home worlds, the Pleiadeans, like their Andromedan forebears, constructed a society that was the embodiment of art and spiritual science on a grand scale. To the peoples of the Pleiades, art and natural logic are the dual expressions of their humanity, and represent a recognition of the Creator's two greatest gifts – the soul and the physical universe to which we all belong. This results in a thorough understanding of the cosmos and her inner workings.

The galactic human society originating in the Pleiades looks at science and art in their own unique way and evaluates ways in which a society can unite two such totally distinct concepts as art and logic. What are the best qualities of each? How are they communicated to their society? By examining these questions, the Pleiadeans learned how their community manifests its wonders to their highest possible level. This is the decisive point of our discussion, and the basis of the Pleiadean Star League's social contract.

Pleiadean Galactic Society

The model of clan structure in use throughout the Pleiadean Star League is the Andromedan/Pleiadean prototype (see page 58, Chart 6). It contains twelve clans and is extraordinary because Pleiadean galactic societies include a number of distinct subcultures that have retained their unique languages and traditions. The most significant element is this society's cultural liaisons and counselors, who serve as semi-official interpreters for the cluster of cultures on each world. In addition, a special interworld cultural liaison board provides creative solutions for any problems that may arise.

When this system interfaces with advanced translator technology and the Pleiadeans' own natural telepathic abilities, it enables each individual and group to communicate freely with one another. The result is a continuous flow of information that incorporates these differences and makes possible the many startling innovations to which this highly diversified society gives form each day.

We have chosen two examples to show you how this society operates. The first is the binary star system of Asterope and the second, the 8-planet system of Celaeno.

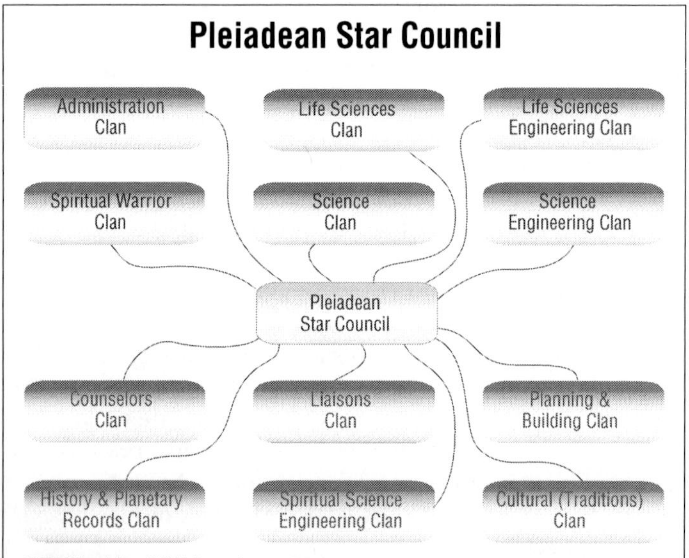

Chart 6

Both of these star-nations adopted the aforementioned Andromedan/Pleiadean prototype. This model includes clans that are dedicated to counselors and liaisons, and to culture. These three clans developed because they found it easier to operate a separate system for the education and training of such esteemed professionals. Each clan acts as a repository for specific insights, which can be put to use within the other nine clans. Alternatively, whatever difficulty cannot be solved by one of the nine clans can be submitted to any of the three specialist clans that seem most capable of resolving it.

The 12-clan system allows members of the Pleiadean Star League to be perceived as star-nations that comprise many of the most successful scientific research groups in the galaxy. They attribute this reputation to the extent to which their modified 12-clan system formally addresses their broad diversity.

Solar Systems and Description of Several Home Worlds

The Pleiadean home worlds range from water worlds, like those of Mother Earth, to semi-arid realms. We intend to concentrate on planets within the multiple stars of Asterope (21 and 22 Tauri), and the faint blue star known as Celaeno or 16 Tauri. They are located between 350 and 400 Light Years from Earth.

The Home Worlds of Celaeno

Let us begin with the home worlds of the faint blue star that your astronomers refer to as 16 Tauri. This star was first colonized nearly 400,000 years ago by humans who named her Kajer ('Blue Soul of Light'), and contains one of the largest water worlds in the Pleiadean Star League. Those who live on this world call her Sirah ('Wise Giver of Joy'). Kajer is the third planet orbiting the central star of Celaeno. She is noted for her vast oceans, teeming with multiple life forms, and for her polar night skies diffused with intense and luminous auroras.

These auroras are unusual in that they contain soft pastels, which represent every color in the spectrum. On Kajer, there are six continents surrounded by seven large seas. Two of the largest continents even contain distinctive inland seas. Only here, in Andromeda and on Sirius-B, are large silver spinner dolphins to be seen.

The next home world is a hot, semi-arid planet. Her two continents are largely desert-covered and surrounded by three small seas. A high mountain range extends down the center of the larger continent, and there are a series of mountain ranges on each coast. Although a variety of species lives here, amphibians and certain types of small dinosaur-like creatures dominate the land and a variety of crab-like creatures rule the seas. The people of 16 Tauri use this planet as a laboratory in biological diversity. Plant and animal life found nowhere else in their solar system exists here, in abundance.

The remaining outer planets in the Calaeno solar system are so-called 'gas giants' similar, in many ways, to the large planets of your Sun's outer solar system. The eighth, or outer, world of this solar system contains a ring system that the Pleiadeans consider to be the most beautiful in the galaxy. This ring system was the result of a collision between several comets and erratically orbiting space debris with the planet's small, outer moons. A sequence of events occurred that propelled the moons too close, causing them to explode and culminating in the formation of the series of three multi-colored rings.

The Home Worlds of Asterope

Asterope (21 Tauri and her dwarf companion, 22 Tauri), yet another binary star system, is more than 370 Light Years from Mother Earth. Her smaller star is blue-white and generally similar in appearance to Sirius-B. On this compound body, a colony, dedicated to advancing the principles of spiritual science, was founded nearly 200,000 years ago. The two scientist colonies quickly realized that their new home worlds were abundant sources of treasure, filled with intense energies. In this rich environment, they formulated new technologies for interstellar travel, propulsion and energy production.

The larger star (21 Tauri) is home to three different-sized water worlds, one of which is at least three times the size of Mother Earth. The smaller star is very similar to the main home world of 'Akonowai' (Sirius-B). Washta sees 22 Tauri as proof of how the sacred, spiritual energies of the Great Blue Lodge were spread throughout the Milky Way Galaxy.

The Pleiadeans came to feel that this solar system (21 Tauri) and her third planet were very sacred and erected a great temple here. It was similar in size and location to that found on Sirius-B. The priest and priestesses from the Spiritual Warrior clan of Sirius-B come here regularly to perform sacred ritual with their Pleiadean counterparts. The sacred blue dolphins of Sirius-B are brought here as well, to swim in the sea next to the temple and to participate in the same rituals.

The fourth planet, the next water world in this solar system, is famous for its prestigious university and research institution. This inner world facility often sends distinguished scholar/representatives, who have researched virtually every form of human galactic culture, to the main Galactic Federation of Light cultural center in the Vega system.

Originally, the dwarf twin of Asterope contained a nine-planet solar system. In the course of the galactic wars, however, her solar system was entirely destroyed. Today, this small blue companion serves as a monument to those former worlds, and to the urgency for galactic peace.

We have examined only a few of the many Pleiadean home worlds. Much remains for you to learn from the galactic humans of the Pleiadean Star League themselves.

Descriptions of the Pleiadean People

Pleiadeans resemble Earth humans. Most often, aboard ship, they wear conventional, multi-colored Galactic Federation of Light jumpsuits. However, Pleiadeans also have traditional clothing, which varies from a style of ancient Greek gown to the pants and shirt sets very much like those of the ancient Vikings. Pleiadeans are usually either one of two basic Earth human types.

The first type is a Caucasian, whose features vary from the so-called 'Nordic' (blonde hair, blue eyes, pale skin) to a 'Mediterranean' type (dark to light brown hair, gray to brown eyes, tanned-looking skin).

The second looks typically Asian, with dark hair, dark, almond-shaped eyes and skin that can range from very pale to dark brown.

The eyes of all Pleiadeans are slightly larger than those of Earth humans. Their thin lips are very pale pink, while their ears are fitted slightly lower on the side of the head and are somewhat smaller in size. Hands and feet are delicate in appearance, with long fingers and toes.

The men vary in height from 5 feet, 10 inches to almost 7 feet (1.8 to 2.12 meters). The women's heights extend from 5 feet, 7 inches to almost 6 feet, 4 inches (1.58 to 1.93 meters). Pleiadean woman are noted for their alluring energies and their large-breasted figures. Pleiadeans require about 2 hours of sleep per day.

In the Galactic Federation ofLight, Pleiadeans, like Andromedans, are noted for their mastery of all forms of scientific endeavor. Together with Andromedans and Pegasians, Pleiadeans usually comprise the core of most S&E fleet science liaison teams/boards. They also play a key role as special cultural advisors in the many Galactic Federation of Light medical teams assigned to assist Earth humans' transformation into fully conscious Beings of Light.

Pleiadean languages vary from a dialect resembling Earth's Germanic tongues (German or Swiss-German) to a smoother and more lyrical variant spoken mostly in star-nations located in and around the star, Maia.

Pleiadean Ships

Pleiadean ships orbiting in the atmosphere around Mother Earth range from conventional, saucer-shaped scout ships with a diameter of 35 to 57 feet (10.6 to 12.2 meters), to cigar-like, small atmospheric command ships that measure up to a quarter-mile (402 meters) in length. The purpose for using these older types of beamships was to provide an observation fleet that was not too technologically advanced. The Pleiadeans felt that, since Earth's society was still rather primitive, a display of the Galactic Federation's newest ships was not necessary.

In space, the Pleiadean Star League operates two types of motherships. The first is a chain of large, cylindrical vessels, up to five miles (8.1 kilometers) long, joined by large tube-shaped connectors. These motherships, which served as science auxiliary ships for many S&E (Science & Exploration) fleets, usually housed a fleet of about 700 support scout and command ships. A second mothership, shaped like a flattened sphere, is as large as a small moon. Used for distance surveillance of a solar system, it is supported by a fleet of between 4 and 6,000 ships.

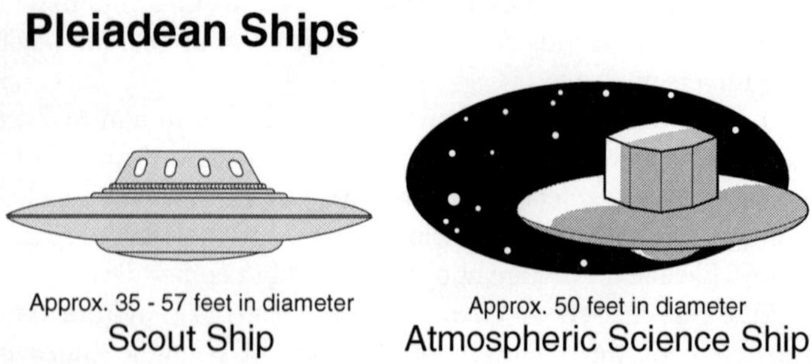

Figure 3

8

The Star-Nation of Sirius-B

My earliest remembrances of Washta, my Sirian guide and mentor, brim over with the bright and spiritually alive energies of Sirius. Each time I returned to the Sirian mothership, I felt those energies enfold me. Sirians take pride in their spiritual legacy but are humbled by the great accolades conferred upon them by the Galactic Federation of Light. Here on Sirius, the Blue Light of the Blue Lodge of Creation resolved to install its sacred presence in this galaxy. This spiritual heritage was imparted to me throughout my childhood and, for that reason, my knowledge and love of Sirius run very deep.

This chapter is dedicated to explaining this wonderful star-nation to you. In the course of her millions of years of existence, Sirius has served as a beacon in this galaxy for Love and Truth, and represents an unwavering commitment to the Four Basic Laws of galactic society and the sacred decrees of Heaven. In writing this account, I admit to a degree of favoritism to the one star-nation that I know to be my ancestral home. With the greatest of joy, therefore, I hereby present to you the wondrous assemblage of Beings that comprise the Sirius Star-Nation.

Status and Location

The Star-Nation of Sirius was welcomed into the Galactic Federation of Light nearly 4.3 million years ago. Originally, Sirius was settled by a sentient species of Lions called the Pschat ('Warriors of Heaven'), who had colonized Sirius-A more than six million years ago. When our settlers from the constellation of Lyra (Greek for 'Lyre') first arrived, we appealed to the Pschat and to the Galactic and local Spiritual Hierarchies. With their combined approval, we were able to establish our initial settlements on Sirius-B and, later, to colonize Sirius-C and Sirius-D.

In the winter night sky of the Northern Hemisphere, you can see the constellation of Canis Major (Latin: 'Great Dog'). Find the belt of the constellation of Orion (Greek: 'Hunter'), and follow its three stars down until you spot a brilliant blue star. That star, Sirius (Alpha Canis Major), is the brightest star in the sky, and sits at the top of Canis Major. She is a multiple star and is positioned approximately 8.3 Light Years from Earth.

Sirius-B Solar System

The solar system of Sirius-B consists of six planetary bodies, the smallest closest to the sun and the largest farthest away. The system's innermost planet is one-quarter the size of your Earth. She experiences constant electrical storms, which have altered her atmosphere to a thin mixture of hydrogen and nitrogen, intermixed with helium and other noble gases. In this thin, inhospitable habitat, the only life forms able to survive are a series of complex bacteria and algae. The next two planets – the third and fourth from our Sun – are inhabited.

The remaining outer planets in the Akonowai solar system are 'gas giants' similar, in many respects, to the large planets of your Sun's outer solar system. However, differences do exist: these planets spin much faster than your Jupiter, Saturn, Uranus or Neptune, and also contain some very unusual primitive, multi-cell life forms. Moreover, their atmospheres possess other anomalies, similar to Jupiter's giant red spot. This solar system's two outermost worlds contain a system of rings equaling that of Saturn in size and complexity. These ring systems came into being in the last eight billion years when a number of comets, large asteroids and other space debris passed too close to both planets' small outer moons. The collision caused a string of events that drove the moons into the other's path, resulting in an explosion that created a series of multi-colored rings.

Description of Sirian Home Worlds

The third planet with two moons, first settled over four million years ago, is called Atarmunk ('Holy Place of the Atar'). The Atar is a golden, eagle-like bird, six feet tall, which we celebrate for its valor, wisdom and loyalty to its mate. The Spiritual Warrior clan is named for it. A large nest of Atars regularly sits atop the main temple. More than 600 million people inhabit a succession of specially built, subterranean communities on this world.

For the most part, the surface of Atarmunk remains unspoiled. A series of temple sites located on its surface is surrounded by small, permanent communities of between six and 10,000 individuals. These settlements support the temple site and constantly monitor the major node that is located at the exact center of each. Ritual, including chanting, dance and spiritually animating music, is performed each day.

At the main Atar temple site is a small spaceport meant for the performance of certain diplomatic rituals, which involve the arrival of special dignitaries from other member star organizations in the Galactic Federation of Light. Owing to the presence of the Great Blue Lodge, these ceremonies take place almost every day. After the arrival ceremony, a special ritual called the Aktaiwa (Summoning) is performed to prepare the personage for a session with the Council of Nine. This meeting is held at a special stargate located between the third and fourth planets in our solar system. The gate opens with a large explosion of purple, followed by a light blue flash.

The fourth planet, named Muktarin ('Land of the Blue Seas'), looks much like your own. In its oceans live highly sentient, aquatic Beings who resemble the whales and dolphins of your Earth. They are this planet's main guardians. In Muktarin's oceans, a number of temples have been constructed. There, each day, these Beings, called the Makudeem ('sacred ones'), participate in divine ritual.

On Muktarin stands the headquarters for the Sirius-B Galactic Federation mission, which includes our diplomatic, liaison and defense operations. We do not allow any large starships or their fleets to enter our solar system: only a fleet of specially designated scout ships is permitted. The Sirians do not take stewardship of the Sirius-B system lightly. We are fully aware of its legendary sacredness, and of how many yearn to come here.

Still, we understand that we are only honored guests and that we must conscientiously pay homage to the wishes of the holy ones who rule this realm. Hence, we limit the number of visitors to Sirius-B in order to honor the requests of the sacred heavenly Councils that preside here.

Origins of the Sirius-B Galactic Society

The ancestors of the peoples of Sirius-B sprang from the constellation of Lyra (Greek: 'Lyre'). On their primary home world, the Sirian people established a galactic society, which they intended to function as the embodiment of creativity and spirituality on a grand scale. For Sirians, creativity and the full expression of the individual's unique talents is life-affirming. For that reason, they adopted the Lyran model and significantly enlarged it by raising the positions of counselor. This brought about the formation of liaison boards and the creation of a system of inspired solution finding called 'fluid group management'. This innovative tool was conceived and first used about 3.7 million years ago by members of both the Administrator and Spiritual Warrior clans. Over time, this technique has been refined and taught to many other developing human galactic societies across the Milky Way Galaxy. By applying this method, the galactic society of Sirius-B developed new training technologies for its clan counselors. This, in turn, led the various clans and the Main Governing Council to reassess their training programs and use of liaisons.

The galactic human society born nearly 3.7 million years ago on Sirius-B is entirely unique. Indeed, she has become the core source of insight on how human galactic societies operate. Accordingly, this model was renamed the 'Lyran/Sirian prototype' (see page 67, Chart 7: Lyran/Sirian Prototype of Galactic Society). In examining its creation and operation, we are able to understand how the Sirian community manifests its wonders to their highest possible level. Finally, in what way can its different components (clans, creativity, freedom, as well as its collective and individual sovereignty) be merged? This is the decisive point of our discussion, and the basis of the Sirians' social contract.

Lyrian/Sirian Prototype of Galactic Society

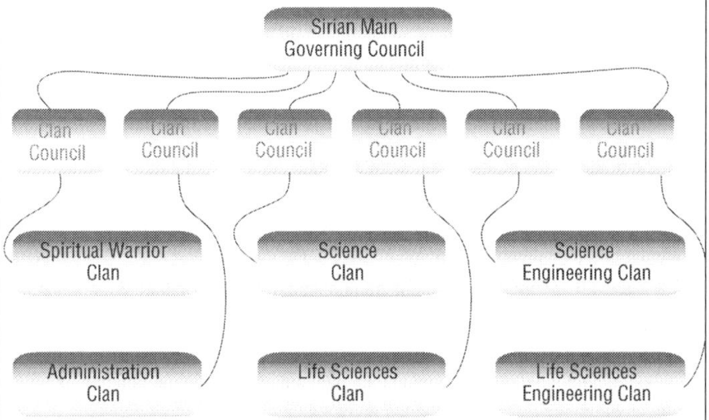

Chart 7

Galactic Society of Sirius-B

The Sirian Star-Nation is a galactic human society. She has been a model for many other human star-nations in the Galactic Federation of Light and consists of six major clans: Atar; Shiratar; Pukman-ya; Shik-da; Dubasnak-ya and Dubasnak-ya-men. On Earth, they could be referred to as the Spiritual Warrior; the Administrator; the Science; the Science Engineering; the Life Sciences; and the Life Sciences Engineering clans. Each one is further separated into sub-clans, pods and podlets. The working forces that support these clans are fluid group dynamics and the Four Sacred Laws of galactic society. Clans are intertwined to form communities. Every individual on Sirius B sees her- or himself as a sovereign, creative Being of Light. Each has come to fulfill certain talents and a life mission. This does not prevent her or him from suggesting a creative solution to any community or global problem. In fact, the Sirian galactic society welcomes and greatly honors such ideas.

The nature of galactic society is truly organic; a living organism with fluid or mutable shape, it is based on the dynamic of flow and tied to society's natural rhythm. This rhythm is determined by the natural resonance of the planet and its many inhabitants. It is fluid because the concept of a definite hierarchy is absent:

everyone in the society contributes effectively to its open dynamic. Yet this organism is graceful and elegant in its inner growth and in the spread of its all-embracing compassion. It fully nurtures all of the sentient Beings in its midst.

Nurturing the individual is a cardinal focus of galactic civilization. From the moment of birth to adulthood, parents and all other podlet members engender in each person feelings of self-esteem and social worth. The very fact of your existence, and the enduring contribution you have made to the podlet simply by entering into physicality, are always consistently recognized. Each child is constantly reminded that, at the right divine time, she/he will begin to bring forth creative innovations that can enhance the podlet and the entire galactic society.

Intention and its manifestation are a primary result of this dynamic. Consequently, an air of creative innovation and inspiration is continually present. Part and parcel of this vast dynamic field is the realization of each person's full potential.

Galactic society exists to encourage and enhance the complete achievement of one's divine life purpose. In this realization, the individual flowers fully, as does the entire society. It is this remarkable dynamic that keeps galactic society so open to change and to reinventing itself, as necessary.

Another case in point is the Sirian language. It is contextual in nature. For example, the word 'selamat', which means condition, precedes words in a greeting or salutation to emphasize the word or phrase that follows. 'Selamat Ja!' means 'may a condition of Joy or Oneness be present'. This can be further reinforced by the word 'Jarin': '-rim', '-rin' or '-ran' signifies 'ultimate'. Thus, 'Selamat Jarin' means 'Blessings'. We see Joy as the natural state of all sentient Beings – in fact, the word for the Creator is 'Ja Ta' or 'Joy of Heaven'. Water is 'wa ta' or 'thing of Heaven'. 'Sa' means 'one', both as a number and as an individual – for example, 'sa bha', or 'one soul' and 'Washta sa', or 'Mister Washta'. The Sirian language contains nearly the same number of consonants as do most of your Earth languages. It also contains five major vowels, which are strung together to form words. Because verbs and nouns are given equal weight, our sentence structure will seem strange to you.

These words can be broken down into a number of basic proto-words. Normally, these consist of a consonant combined with a vowel. For example, the word for the main continent of Muktarin is 'Sa-ka-ra' or 'soul of female creativity'. 'Ra' is the principle of female creativity: 'ka' refers to the body guardian or its soul: and 'sa' denotes the entirety of anything. This same principle is found in your words. The Anunnaki realized, at an early stage, the power of language to unite or divide a population. Therefore, they scrambled their proto-word codes and made the meanings of proto-words in your many languages very different from one another. Ancient Lemurian closely resembles Sirian, as well as the language of Vega – the origin of all humans in this galaxy. The languages used by many of Earth's Pacific Ocean peoples come closest in meaning to the proto-words of galactic Sirian.

Physical Description of Inhabitants

The bodies of men on Sirius B range from perfectly formed, muscular physiques to child-like figures and vary from 6 feet, 6 inches to 7 feet, 4 inches (1.98 to 2.24 meters) in height. Women are extremely voluptuous and stand between 6 feet, 2 inches and

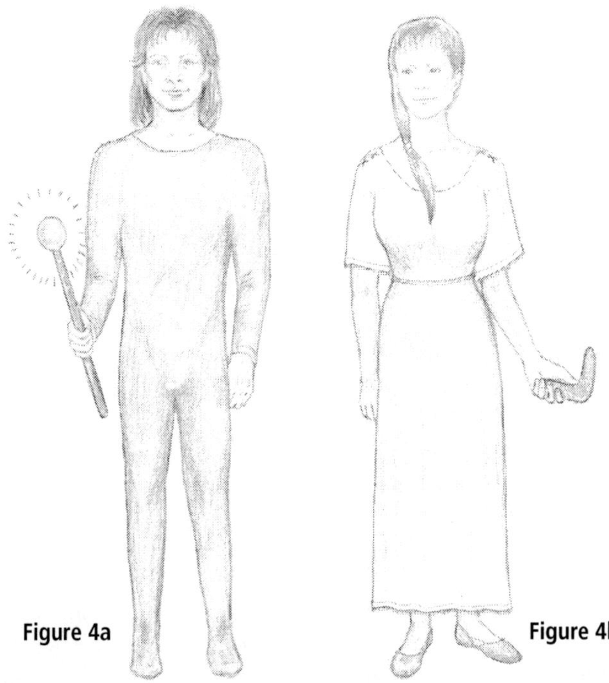

Figure 4a

Figure 4b

6 feet, 8 inches (1.88 meters and 2.03 meters) tall. Sirian hair is blonde to light brown, and eyes are light blue to green. Their skin tones are extremely pale, light red or light blue. Sirians require only two hours of sleep per day (see page 69: A typical child-like male or typical female Sirian).

The Sirians are noted for their sheer, flowing, short and ankle-length gowns for men and similar gowns, possibly longer, for women. The colors of these garments indicate the individual's clan, while ribbons and other decorations signify rank or high honor.

The jumpsuit is the distinctive dress worn aboard Galactic Federation spacecraft. The trousers are shaped close to the body, while the top is specially fitted to join seamlessly with the pants. It, too, is color-coded to each clan, and displays the special ribbons and epaulettes that bespeak rank and insignia. The boots, which are an integral part of this costume, merge with the pants to form a visually integrated unit.

Sirians are renowned for their undisputed skills as diplomats, negotiators and Galactic Federation liaison counselors. They excel at bringing together groups of dissimilar sentient Beings to enable them to achieve their goals as peacefully and amicably as possible.

Ships of Sirius-B

Three types of Sirius-B ships serve as part of the first contact Earth fleet. The first, an all-purpose scout ship, operates primarily in the observation fleet that regularly monitors your beloved planet. It is ball-shaped, with a small, lens-like circular wing attached to its middle, and a diameter of more than 100 feet (30.4 meters).

The second is a supply ship, which transports equipment and personnel to and from the first contact fleet in near-Earth orbit. Resembling a large bell with a semi-spherical object attached to its underside, this ship is 200 feet (67 meters) in diameter and carries a crew of 8. It can ferry up to 30 passengers, or supplies weighing up to 5 tons (4,500 kilograms).

The third type, a special defense observation craft, resembles a rounded equilateral triangle whose three sides each measure about 70-110 feet (22.25-33.53 meters) long. This ship is used to monitor black operation bases of your secret government. Occasionally, it takes part in special operations, with the purpose of neutralizing or shutting down special craft or exotic weaponry that are deployed from secret government bases.

Sirian Ships

Approx. 200 feet in diameter
Supply Ship

Approx. 100 feet in diameter
Science Scout Ship

Approx. 70 - 110 feet in length
Defense Ships

Figure 5

Part II

The Cetaceans

An Introduction from the Cetaceans

Cetaceans, like most fully sentient mammals, became the dominant species on home worlds similar to those that favored humans, and in solar systems that contained wondrous, lush water worlds. There, over a period of many millions of years, land cetaceans flourished and developed their own unique forms of society.

Many such land and aquatic cetacean star-nations exist in this galaxy. However, owing to the particular importance of Nu-Ceti, it was decided that our specific star-nation should be featured as a prime example of Cetacean civilization.

Nu Ceti, unlike most mammalian star-nations, has upheld our grand tradition as galactic merchants, innovators and historians. Detailed records of our far-reaching journeys across this galaxy gave the Galactic Federation and her many predecessors a better understanding of the immense sentiency within this galaxy. It also allowed them to gain a basic appreciation of the many dark empires with whom we all share this most beautiful galaxy that we call home.

Nu Ceti's home world is famous for a number of native plants and animals that our ancestors exchanged, long ago, for other merchandise on your world: among them, potatoes, citrus fruit and cats. Until approximately 5,000 of your years ago, Nu Ceteans were hailed, among other Cetacean civilizations, as this galaxy's greatest explorers and historians. Then, compelled by the immediacy and savagery of several wars, we secluded ourselves on our home world.

At that time, our various clans and merchant/explorer classes joined to form a new, united star-nation government. Since then, we have focused on our scientific skills and have been able to develop many significant environmental and cloaking technologies. These discoveries resulted, decades ago, in a hostile incursion by the Draconian Empire, which led, indirectly, to our return to the Galactic Federation.

The rest, as they say, is history. May you enjoy this description of our star-nation and know, in your hearts, that we Love you and wish, some day, to freely walk among you. Besides – yours is the best garlic (one of our greatest delicacies) in the galaxy!

9

The Star-Nation of Nu Ceti

I retain the deepest love and most cherished memories of the next star-nation. In the late 1980s, my contact with Washta was once again taking shape and, through a set of very unusual circumstances, I met a member of this marvelous Nu Ceti star-nation. It would be the first time I had encountered a citizen of another world without Washta's guidance. I learned that his name was Gor-tan Shara'a (his family nickname was Gor'i), and we quickly became friends. At that time, his uncle was Prime Director of Nu Ceti's governing council. Owing to the primitive (at least for Nu Ceti) technology available to him, Gor'i's long journey to Earth took him slightly over 10 years. Nonetheless, he arrived to observe and learn how Earth had fared since Nu Ceti ceased their merchant expeditions to other worlds nearly 5,000 years before.

As a result of Gor'i's discreet inquiries, he and I met in the fall of 1987. Out of that encounter grew my first long-term friendship with a land cetacean from another world. His nearest earthly relatives are aquatic cetaceans, in particular the many species of toothed whales, such as dolphins and Orcas. Gor'i is well-known for his practical jokes and puns, and for his perfectly whimsical takes on the foibles of human civilization. His remarks would move me to gales of laughter; often, I would laugh until tears streamed down my cheeks.

Gor'i is highly intelligent, fun-loving and extremely resourceful.

He was clever at solving whatever plumbing and electrical malfunctions occurred in my home. But that same quick intelligence was also accompanied by an intense curiosity that would often put me in ticklish situations. He loved to take items such as glasses or clothing and watch my reaction when I discovered them missing. His whoops of laughter at my sudden frustration would show me that he was responsible. Yet, although in many ways he is very child-like in temperament, his wisdom about life and society is very profound.

By the early 1990s, Gor'i had researched and made contact with the Galactic Federation First Contact fleet. Those meetings eventually led to his appointment as a 'special' Galactic Federation ambassador. For nearly two decades, we have enjoyed each other's company. Therefore, with the greatest of pleasure and with Gor'i's assistance, I introduce you to his home world.

Present Status and Location

Nu Ceti, a distant minor star with an Earth-like white/yellow Sun, is positioned in the constellation of Cetus (Greek for 'Whale'). She is approximately 810 Light Years from Earth. Cetus is located in the Northern Hemisphere, between the constellations of Aries, Pisces and Eridanus, in the southern part of our autumn and winter skies. Nu Ceti is situated in the western half of the constellation Cetus, next to the much brighter star of Mu Ceti.

For almost 2.5 million years, the Star-Nation of Nu Ceti belonged to the Galactic Federation of Light. About 5,000 years ago, Nu Ceti withdrew from the Federation and reverted to her previous status as a neutral star-nation. Nu Ceti's original inhabitants were land cetaceans whose technology was much sought-after by both sides in the course of the various galactic wars.

Even after the Treaty of Anchara marked the end of war, the Nu Ceteans delayed until they felt sure that peace would be permanent. Once they had gained that reassurance, they rejoined the Galactic Federation of Light.

Nu Ceti Solar System and Description of Home Worlds

The solar system of Nu Ceti contains eight planets. In the Nu Ceti language, the star known as Nu Ceti is called Ca'W"iP"'aa (meaning 'Giver of Light') with ' standing for a simple glottal stop and " representing a quick click of the tongue. The outer two planets in this solar system are huge gas giants, similar in size and appearance to your planets Uranus and Neptune. Next in your journey inward toward the bright yellow/white star of Nu Ceti are two semi-arid worlds. Each is approximately one-half the size of Neptune and Uranus (about 13,000 miles or 20,800 kilometers in diameter). The fourth planet is the home world for the Nu Ceti Star-Nation.

In size and appearance, the Nu Ceti home world is very Earth-like. This planet, which her inhabitants call Cem"L'am, has a diameter of 8,100 miles (13,000 kilometers), a width only 300 miles greater than Mother Earth. Like Mother Earth, she has seven continents, seven major seas and four large oceans. Unlike Mother Earth, most of the islands found in those bodies of water are quite small.

Nu Ceti's biggest island, which somewhat resembles Australia, is located in an archipelago to the northeast of the main continent in her largest southern sea. At its widest, this island is only 200 miles (320 kilometers) across. Its narrowest section is about 60 miles (100 kilometers) long. Most of the remaining islands, which are usually found in Nu Ceti's southern hemisphere, are no more than 25 miles (40 kilometers) wide.

Like Mother Earth in her fully conscious state, this world's atmosphere contains a two-tiered firmament, which supports an ecosystem famous for its broad diversity of life forms. Among its flora and fauna are varieties such as those found on Earth: foods such as garlic, citrus fruits and potatoes: animals that resemble domestic cats, dolphins and whales. The inhabitants of this world are immensely proud of their vast forests and broad meadows, which abound in many different plant and animal species.

On Nu Ceti's northern continents, mountain ranges tower almost as high as Mother Earth's Himalayas. Unlike your Himalayas, however, even the tallest peaks of these long mountain chains are rarely snow-capped, and alpine forests rise almost to their summits.

This home world's climate is semi-tropical and only slightly cooler at its poles. Like all worlds, Cem"L'am is hollow, with an inner world populated, even for this ecosystem, by some very strange creatures. The inhabitants of the Star-Nation of Nu Ceti, who number just above 600 million, live in a grid of special crystal cities that are dotted throughout its interior.

The third planet in this solar system, a smaller water world about the size of Mars, is 4,000 miles (6,400 kilometers) in diameter. The tallest mountains on her two continents are part of very long coastal ranges, making her interior resemble the semi-arid regions of your central India. This planet is particularly noted for her extremely hot, dry surface environments. The more arid climate on these continents makes it much easier for the many species of lizards and other reptiles to be the dominant form of land animals. The four large oceans that surround her landmasses teem with an assortment of creatures probably similar to those that existed during Mother Earth's late Paleozoic Age.

The two innermost planets are small, barren worlds whose atmosphere is very thin. They are known for their extremely cratered surfaces. The larger, outer sphere is less than 1,000 miles (1,600 kilometers) in diameter. To a great extent, the smaller, inner planetoid has practically no atmosphere. What remains is sometimes set aglow by her sun's solar flares, making the entire planet seem on fire. The Nu Ceti people have observed this same phenomenon in the past, in several other solar systems across this galaxy.

History of Nu Ceti

For a very long period in their history, the Nu Ceteans enjoyed their status as one of the galaxy's pre-eminent merchant star-nations. They traded with all sides and, owing to the value of their wares and their participation in a general treaty of non-interference, maintained, until approximately 5,000 years ago, a state of lucrative neutrality. By that time, the wars had reached very close to Nu Ceti's location in the constellation of Cetus.

Suddenly, the Nu Ceteans found that they could no longer perpetuate the illustrious 'star-faring' traditions that they had struggled to establish throughout the galaxy. Consequently, they cut themselves off and, for almost 5,000 years, essentially prohibited anyone from leaving their star system or from traveling within 300 Light Years of Nu Ceti.

They take great satisfaction from the fact that, during their period of galactic commerce, they exchanged many goods with the then-primitive civilizations of Earth.

The Nu Ceteans are immensely proud that some of Mother Earth's most basic commodities – all citrus fruits and forms of potatoes, as well as a few other tubers – came, originally, from Nu Ceti. Gor'i tells me, in fact, that garlic is the Nu Ceteans' favorite tuber. And, although Nu Ceti introduced it to us, the garlic we cultivate has come to be the finest in this galaxy. Nu Ceti also introduced to this planet what we know today as the domestic cat.

The Nu Ceteans feel greatly honored that they were able to achieve these feats. Their histories consist mainly of large navigational charts, annotated by massive diaries and containing detailed descriptions of the many diverse cultures with which they are so familiar. They take pride in their encyclopedic knowledge of the Milky Way Galaxy and her peoples. Appropriately, they have enshrined these countless artifacts, with their accompanying logs, in a series of museums dedicated to the many distinct epochs that are described in their voyages of trade and discovery.

Society of Nu Ceti

Nu Ceteans are essentially land cetaceans. In many ways, their culture, based upon pods and podlets, resembles that of Earth's Orcas. By nature, it is predominantly matriarchal rather than patriarchal. At the peak of Nu Ceti society stand the counselors. Together, they comprise a regional assembly that joins with other similar bodies to form a ruling council. And, while this body enacts basic laws, the society itself is governed according to long-held traditions in which they take great pride. Nu Ceteans originated as night hunters and farmers, and their entire cultural focus is agrarian.

The people of Nu Ceti, and their nearby neighbors on Mu Ceti, are very proud of their culture and of their own scientific and galactic discoveries. Nu Ceti culture differs from that of a conventional galactic society in the formation and operation of its pods and podlets. Although similar in many meaningful ways to a traditional galactic society, in many others, Cetean culture is unique.

One of the most important of these is the matriarchal system that rules their society. For many generations, the Beings of Nu Ceti have traced their descent through their mothers. They also chronicle their histories from that perspective. Moreover, they revere all other galactic societies that also are rooted in matriarchy.

On Nu Ceti, after a couple has birthed all of their children, they participate in a ritual similar to marriage. They consider such a ceremony to honor the complete and sacred state of family. Every member of the pod or podlet, not just the parents, raises a family's children. Nu Ceteans treat their children and their extended family – the individuals belonging to each pod or podlet – with the utmost respect.

Politically, the Nu Ceteans were neutral in this galaxy for long periods of time and, for that reason, kept very much to themselves. Approximately 30 years ago, during the final, uneasy truce of the seemingly endless succession of galactic wars, an armada of ships from the Anchara Alliance's Draconian Empire, in search of an extraordinary cloaking device, destroyed the Nu Ceteans' main planet. Prior to this assault, they had been forced to relocate to another, specially hidden planet far from their home solar system. During the attack, Gor'i was compelled to flee toward Earth. His remarkable adventure led him, eventually, to our meeting in the mid-1980s. Recently, the Nu Ceti people, with the help of the Galactic Federation, were able to re-establish their shattered home world and return, victoriously, to their much-beloved home.

Nu Ceti's re-entry into the Galactic Federation of Light is yet another example of the topic under discussion: the binding together of the former Anchara Alliance and other neutral star-nations with the core confederacy for the forces of Light, to form a stronger, more effective and truly Galactic Federation of Light.

Physical description of Nu Ceteans

A highly sentient land Cetacean inhabits this star-nation. The Nu Cetean is a small, short-tailed, bear-like Being, covered with multi-hued brown fur that varies in color from dark chocolate to very light tan.

Although its head is shaped like a bear's, the Nu Cetean has a large, snout-like mouth and very powerful jaws. Sharp gums contain two upper and lower teeth that it uses for tearing or ripping its food.

Its large, prominent, black eyes are very light-sensitive, indicative of its former nocturnal life-style. With human-like ears located on the sides of the head, its sense of hearing is acute.

Because the Nu Cetean is a biped, it has a highly developed center of gravity. Its two muscular arms end in paw-like hands that contain four stubby fingers each. Its legs are very muscular and it has two long, wide feet that each end in three stubby, clawed toes.

These Beings, male and female, stand between 3.75 and 5.5 feet (1.14 to 1.67 meters) tall. This species requires only one to two hours of sleep per day.

Nu Cetean men typically wear flowing, knee-length gowns: those worn by the women are longer. For both, the color of their attire corresponds to their respective pods or podlets, and their clothes are often adorned with ribbons and other insignia indicative of honor or position.

Aboard Federation spacecraft, Nu Ceteans wear jumpsuits. The top is loose and styled so that it joins seamlessly with the pants. It, too, conforms to the color codes of each pod or podlet, and is decorated with ribbons and epaulettes consistent with the wearer's rank and commendations. The boots, which are an integral part of the outfit, are designed to merge into the pants, thus appearing as a single, continuous unit.

Nu Ceteans are renowned for their undisputed skills as negotiators and Galactic Federation Liaison Counselors. They excel at bringing together very different groups and assisting them in achieving their desired goals as peacefully and amicably as possible.

The inhabitants of Nu Ceti are well known for their skills in designing some of the most advanced light-beam technology to equip Galactic Federation exploration fleets. They also are considered some of the galaxy's best pilots, navigators and philosophers.

To our ears, the language of the Nu Ceti land Cetacean is similar to Chinese, with the addition of a series of special, very high-pitched tones, some clicks and occasional guttural sounds.

Ships of Nu Ceti

Two types of Nu Ceti ships are part of the first contact Earth fleet that regularly monitors your beloved planet. The first, an all-purpose scout ship, is primarily used as part of the observation fleet that continuously watches over Mother Earth. This craft is recognizable by its distinctive, straw hat-like shape, and extends from 40 to 55 feet (12.16 to 16.72 meters) in length.

The second, an orbital mothership, is usually very large and blimp-like. It measures between 1 and 12 miles (1.6 and 19.2 kilometers) in diameter. This small mothership serves as a carrier for 500 science liaison officers, who co-ordinate the preliminary analysis of data from the sector planetary quadrant to which she is assigned.

Some Parting Words from our Relatives Mother Earth's Cetaceans

We are your Earth-bound ET's. Like others with whom we share this galaxy, we have lovingly watched over you. We have undertaken this task simply to guide you on your return journey to Spirit. During the past 13 millennia, we have witnessed how the great care and Love that you have shown to Mother Earth and your fellow creatures was influenced by the dark, and have seen you rage helplessly against this world. Yet, despite such manipulation, our hearts knew that this great Love that the Creator had instilled in you lay there, dormant and unrealized.

Now, the divine hand of consciousness is rousing you from your long slumber. In these extraordinary times, many of you have risen in support of us and, by dint of your inexhaustible will, have changed the false opinions that many had held of us. For this, we send you our thanks. Moreover, we are aware that your passions have ignited an ember in your long-smoldering Love. This is only the beginning of a sacred process that will lead you back to your true and fully conscious selves.

In our hearts, we know that what has begun can only accelerate. Those with whom we share this galaxy have come to join us in the fulfillment of this grand and divine mission called first contact. The time has come when we shall meet and reveal our sacred True Selves to you. Be ready and willing-hearted to emerge from this cocoon that is your present moment, into a new and more glorious reality! In this, we await your final awakening as you join with us in forming our new star-nation!

Given in Love and in Joy
Mother Earth's Cetacean Nation

Part III

Equians

An Introduction from the Equians

Like all mammalian societies, our Equian civilization was born on beautiful water worlds scattered throughout this sector of the galaxy. The most famous of these societies developed many millions of years ago, on the star that you know as Arcturus.

Here, amid the finest healing energies known in the Galactic Federation, was created the star-nation that we know as Hadmos Sankh. This exquisite water world is acclaimed for her natural beauty and her capacity for rejuvenating the physical body and bringing untold joy to one's soul.

Little wonder that the race of Beings bred on this extraordinary world came quickly to be known as the most admirably gifted healers in the galaxy. Equians are extremely dedicated to perfecting the art of revivifying all of life, from individuals to entire star-nations. This profound desire has brought us to your galaxy and enabled us to apply our healing skills to all who truly need it.

By the time the first inhabitants arrived on Arcturus from Andromeda, they had already established colonies on constellations ranging from Cygnus to Eridanus. Our Equian ancestors' pursuit of the perfect haven for their healing arts ceased when they discovered Hadmos Sank.

Here, the energy we had sought for so long pervaded every breath, and every thought. Consequently, we founded a great and noble civilization here, dedicated to carrying out the sacred principles of Equian society. You know its fully sentient citizens simply as Arcturians.

As you read this brief passage about us, we ask you to be fully mindful that, each day, we lovingly assist your heavenly guardians in transforming you. At the same time, we help you to achieve transformation through whatever spiritual, mental and emotional healing you may need. We care very deeply that you reach your destined goal, and are eager for you to join us in healing this entire galaxy through the use of Love.

10

The Arcturus Confederation

The most interesting Beings I ever met during frequent childhood visits aboard the Sirian mothership were the tall, horse-like and very matter-of-fact Arcturians. An ancient species, the Arcturians' sentient culture had observed the rise and fall of many galactic 'situations', and watched many star-cultures come, go or be transformed. Their healing team members, who were stationed aboard the Sirian mothership, taught me about time and its role in releasing the divine plan to this galaxy. The energies exuded by these wise Beings were instantly calming. Their manner of speaking left listeners in a positive and enthusiastic frame of mind.

Integral to their sacred essence was the art of healing. Their message, eagerly conveyed, was that Earth and her people were to be healed and their deep wounds cleansed. Earthlings would learn the ways of harmony and the reciprocal joys of compassion. Life is a blessed experience: at its heart lies a free sharing of knowledge. That commonality forms the heart of the Galactic Federation's philosophy of Light, which is about to shine its full and infinite Love upon this planet.

The Arcturians' consummate dedication to this mission of Love is apparent in their whole-hearted participation in the Galactic Federation of Light's revised medical team program. The core of each team consists of selected members of the renowned Arcturian healing teams who, for millennia, have been helping your Ascended Masters to move humanity toward its Ascension – a return to full consciousness. To the Arcturians, first contact will bid you welcome into this new and magnificent reality.

Present Status and Location

In the late spring and early summer skies of the Northern Hemisphere, the constellation of Bootes (Greek: 'Shepherd') is located between Ursa Major (Latin: 'Big Bear') and Virgo (Latin: 'Maiden'). Arcturus (Greek: 'Bear Watcher'), or Alpha Bootes is the brightest star in the Bootes constellation, a glittering orange giant approximately 37 Light Years from Earth. After Sirius, Canopus (Greek: 'Helmsman'), or Alpha Carina and Alpha Centauri, Arcturus is the brightest star in the Heavens and sits, pointed toward Spica (Latin: 'Ear of Wheat'), the brightest star in the constellation of Virgo.

The Arcturus Confederation (known to its inhabitants as the Confederation of Hadmos Sankh) was a charter member star-nation of the Galactic Federation of Light. Arcturus is one of the star-nations that comprise the Arcturus Federation Regional Council. Arcturus, one of 24 members of the Galactic Federation Regional Council, is seated next to your own future district assembly, the Sirian Regional Federation Council.

Arcturian Solar System and Description of Home Worlds

The solar system of Alpha Bootes contains eight planets. Like most solar systems in this galaxy, the four outer planets are huge 'gas giants', similar in size and appearance to your planets Saturn, Uranus and Neptune. Orbiting at the center of this solar system is a semi-arid world that is approximately one-third the size of Neptune and Uranus (about 9,800 miles or 15,700 kilometers) in diameter.

This planet is of particular significance because she supports a chain of dedicated colonies, originating on the Arcturian home world, which is constantly in use. The planet's drier climate is much more congenial to colonists and to the pilgrims, who arrive from Hadmos Sankh to take part in their consecrated planet-keeping rituals. For the most part, they celebrate these ceremonies in large, desert temples adjacent to small, sacred colonies located on major planetary nodes. Enveloped in this special, positive energy, they are able to increase their legendary healing powers. The rituals performed here sustain this intensified energy, enabling the Arcturians to achieve almost impossible feats of healing on the individuals and societies who enter their sacred circles.

The planet next closest to their sun serves as home world for the Arcturus Confederation. She is the third planet from Ya'Ju'r known to her natives as Hadmos Sankh.

At first glance from space, the home world of Hadmos Sankh closely resembles your planet. Unlike the Earth, however, she contains eight large continents surrounded by nine oceans and is nearly 9,000 miles (14,400 kilometers) in diameter. This mother world possesses a three-tiered firmament, which supports an ecosystem remarkable for its wide variety of life forms.

The home world's climate is semi-tropical and cooler only at her poles. Like all planets, Hadmos Sankh is hollow, with an inner world populated, even for this ecosystem, by some very exotic creatures. The inhabitants of the Arcturus Confederation, who number 950 million, live in special crystal cities scattered throughout her inner-planet realm.

The two innermost Arcturian planets are small, barren worlds that possess little or no atmosphere. Both are well known for their extremely erratic orbits, which cause them to frequently criss-cross one another. The outer is less than 2,000 miles (3,200 kilometers) in diameter. The inner is slightly more than 1,500 miles (2,400 kilometers) in diameter.

Arcturian Galactic Society

The people of Alpha Bootes created their own unique, eight-clan galactic society, based upon the original, six-clan human Lyran/Sirian model. In a departure from this classic example, the people of Ya'Ju'r added two additional clans. The first, called the Sak He'Maat or 'Healing Logic' clan, develops techniques that allow certain restorative procedures to be performed in a more holistic way. That is, this tribe's crucial task is to preside over the development and use of the healing arts. The second, called the Medical Records or Lik'Co'Sat'Duk clan, is also unique to Arcturus. Its purpose is to guide society by demonstrating that the healing arts are a living, organic Being that can assist people in carrying out their sacred work.

A traditional human galactic society consists of a governing council and, beneath it, a series of clan councils. Below them is a vast system of six, eight or twelve clans, which are divided according to function, e.g. medical, administrative or spiritual clans. Arcturian society is different from others in that it is governed by a true ruling council. The organization of their clan system is slightly different, as well: clan councils are set up as 'healing' or 'grace' modules.

Each module is based upon finding within its members a way to express grace and create an energy pattern that allows that same grace to be expressed within a given group. The Arcturians use this clan system-equivalent as a means by which to express grace.

Between each group, Arcturians maintain liaisons whose purpose is to unite the different aspects of grace, creating what they refer to as 'grace synthesis modes'. Grace modes allow planetary healing to be sent out into the galaxy, into other dimensions, and throughout the Universe. At this point, the process becomes what they call their 'core'. By transmitting different aspects of grace mode to other parts of physicality, the Arcturians are able to create grace and allow it to heal those groups and others.

The Arcturians believe that their highest purpose is to use their gift for providing divine grace to heal each aspect of physicality, allowing them to realize their maximum potential. In such a way, through the power of loving care and healing, all of physicality can become open to the sum-total of its knowledge and wisdom.

The philosophy underpinning the Arcturian culture is a belief that the foundation of a fully conscious Being exists in her/his capacity to heal another – that is, the power to bring another species or individual of that species to a point where they feel at peace and free of stress. The Arcturians produce these circumstances through a process that they call 'divine healing grace'. They are skilled practitioners who have learned how to create and maintain such a condition. They consider it one of their missions as fully conscious Beings, and strive to maintain an ever-expanding galactic state of divine healing grace.

Arcturus' Role in Creating an Expanded Galactic Federation

For the Arcturians, part of first contact has been the supervision of the Galactic Federation Medical Teams. This involves creating a situation in which grace is felt and becomes one with the processes of healing and transformation. For that reason, when dealing with an Arcturian healing group, you feel embraced in Love and compassion and enfolded in the energy of grace. Grace becomes an energy, a sense that all is well and comfortable, or 'in grace'. Arcturian society is primarily concerned with divine comfort and divine nurturing. That is what they have been doing for a long, long time – working to create a successful galactic society that is solidly rooted in creating and giving this divine grace to others.

During the past few years, the Arcturians have applied their skills to all of the many reptilian, dinosaurian and insectian groups who, while not fully comprehending the exact nature of the Galactic Federation, still are eager to transform their societies from tyrannical to galactic. Through participation in the Arcturus Confederacy's different healing activities, these former Anchara Alliance foes are learning to become more a part of the Galactic Federation of Light. Such interactions have helped to impart to them the concepts of divine grace and its use in healing the various afflictions in their societies. As a result, the former Ancharans are able to examine major issues, such as trust, and their apprehension in confronting the approaching transcendent change in new and more constructive ways.

The Arcturians' ability to exhibit and openly express grace, and their skill in demonstrating the creation of useful healing modalities, provided effective solutions to many potentially complex situations within the former Anchara Alliance's far-flung empires. This factor helped the Galactic Federation of Light forge ahead dramatically in unifying the many divergent members of the Anchara Alliance who had joined the Galactic Federation in the last seven or eight years.

Numerous cultural exchanges have made substantial contributions in helping to overcome these feelings of deep unease. Arcturian healing teams have trained many Anchara Alliance star empires in the optimal techniques for proceeding with the much-needed changeover. In addition, healing study groups that these former galactic foes sent to Arcturus have given them a better understanding of the steps required to change their societies. These sessions focused on the importance of retaining certain cultural nuances in the process of carrying out a re-evaluation, with grace, of your entire society.

Description of the Arcturians

Arcturians are a highly sentient mammalian species that looks very much like a horse (see Figure 6a, 6b, 6c, below: A typical Arcturian). They have a rather tall, slender body with a somewhat stylized horse's head. Arcturian skin color ranges from a vanilla shade to a very dark brown. A mane grows on the back of their neck and head, and they have an extremely thin tail that only slightly resembles that of a horse.

Their arms, legs and bodies seem very muscular, and their hands end in fingers that are very long, supple and extremely thin.

Figure 6a

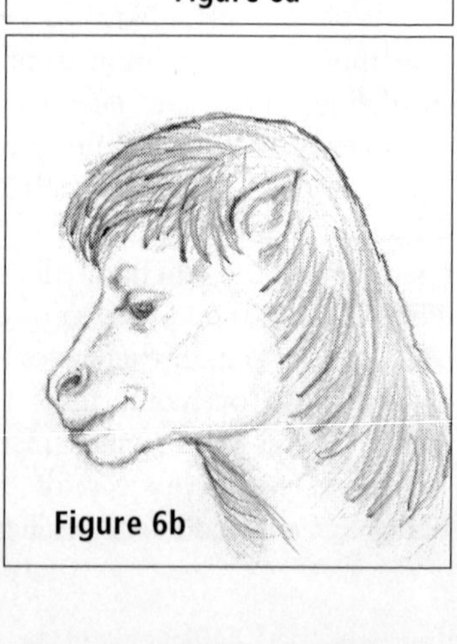

Figure 6b

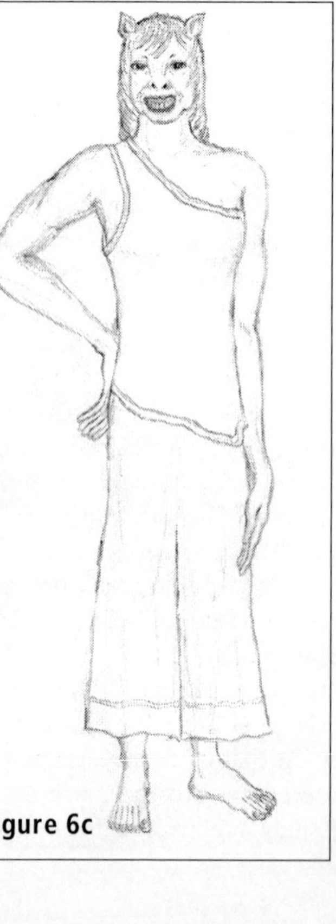

Figure 6c

Arcturian eyes are much bigger than those of Earth humans and are either pale blue or dark brown in color. In some ways, their ears correspond to those of a horse, but are smaller and more rounded than their earthly counterparts.

Arcturian males stand from 7 feet to almost 8 feet, 6 inches (2.31 and 2.64 meters) tall. Female heights vary from just below 7 feet to about 8 feet, 2 inches (2.11 to 2.49 meters).

The clothing of the Arcturians is noticeably different. The people of Ya'Ju'r adopted flowing, ankle-length, harem-style pants in the bright colors that identify their clan. Matching sheer outer blouses bare one shoulder, most often the left, and are either waist- or knee-length. Instead of ribbons or epaulettes, a series of special graphic designs on the blouse, along with its color, serve to indicate the wearer's office and honors.

Aboard Galactic Federation spacecraft, Arcturians wear a one- or two-piece jumpsuit. The two-piece design more closely resembles the ancestral Arcturian costume. Pants are relaxed in fit, while the top extends just below the waist like a popular, traditional Arcturian style. Like the off-duty outfit, the jumpsuit takes the colors and graphic designs of the wearer's clan. The boots, a necessary component of the uniform, are designed to merge with the pants as a seemingly continuous unit.

The Arcturian diet consists of food resembling creamed vegetables, or multi-colored salads. The people from this Confederation usually require only 1 to 3 hours of sleep a day.

Arcturians are celebrated in the Galactic Federation for their mastery of healing and for their marked proficiency in science and philosophy.

Arcturian Ships

Two different Arcturian craft belong to the first contact fleet that monitors Mother Earth regularly. The first, an all-purpose scout ship, is diving bell-shaped, and has a diameter of 80 to 90 feet (24.4 to 27.4 meters). It is part of the fleet that observes your planet every day.

The second is a low orbit to upper atmosphere command mothership. Small, lens-shaped and over 1,000 to 3,000 ft. (304.8 to 914.4 kilometers) long, it serves as carrier for 40,000 science liaison officers who co-ordinate the preliminary data analysis for the sector quadrants to which this mothership is assigned.

Arcturian Ships

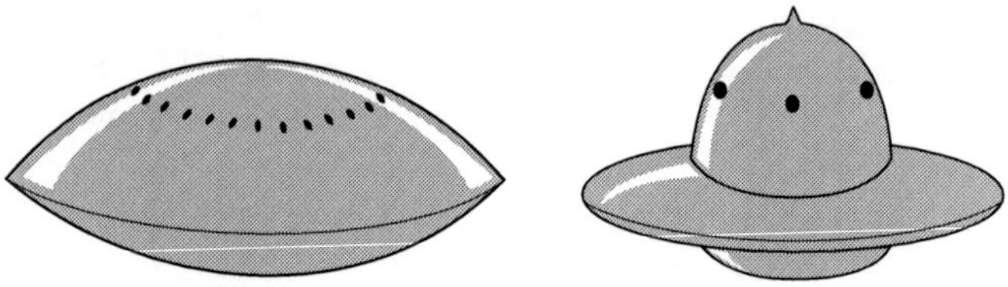

Approx. 1,000 - 3,000 feet in diameter
Mothership

Approx. 80 - 90 feet in diameter
Multi-Purpose Ship

Figure 7

Part IV

Dinosaurians ~ Reptilians

An Introduction from the Dinosaurians ~ Reptilians

The Dinosaurian/Reptilian hybrids that settled the constellation of Draco nearly 25 million years ago originated from a number of 'hatcheries'. These egg-nurturing colonies, founded more than 35 million years ago by Dinosaurian empires loyal to their dark creator-god, Anchara, were scattered throughout the constellation of Sagittarius.

Since the Dinosaurians and related Reptilian Beings generally lacked Light Bodies and, therefore, fully integrated souls (because Anchara wished only faithful, robot-like servants), they were settled into hatching environments in the constellation of Draco. There, they would prepare themselves to conduct the sweeping attacks by which they intended to expand the ways of Anchara across further sectors of the galaxy.

Within Draco (later the heart of the Draconian Empire), the worlds chosen for these settlements resembled, for the most part, the semi-arid habitat of their former Sagittarian home worlds. We found that this mixture of shallow oceans, barren landscapes and occasional flora-laden regions was most agreeable to our bodies and our temperaments.

When we selected planets for future settlements, we tended to choose those that closely resembled our own worlds. These colonies, often secured by force, were designed to serve as the eventual main bases for our administrative personnel and as birthing and training sites for our renowned security forces.

One example of this process is the prime Draconian Empire colony established on the bright blue star, known to your astronomers as Bellatrix, in the constellation of Orion. Because these home worlds bear a close resemblance to our former homes in Sagittarius, we felt that they provided a suitable location and were most satisfactory for our purposes.

Now, our many colonies, together with our major bases and administrative zones, have been freed to become a cluster of new star-nations. The star-nations that we have chosen for this book are prime examples of what we once were, and show how we are transforming and reaching for the Light. Please enjoy the next three chapters, in full understanding that those you once feared are eager, now, to alter their ways; master their soul body integration; acquire Light Bodies and freely share of their arcane knowledge and advanced technologies.

11

The Star-Nation of Bellatrix

Often, Washta would describe to me the almost incomprehensible horrors of the galactic wars, which had lasted for many millions of years. At the heart of these conflicts were the Draconian Empire and its many territories. One such was the League of Orion and its chief ruling star-nation, Bellatrix. The Bellatrician rulers were notorious for their vicious and tyrannical hold over the League, which had attacked and taken control of Earth's solar system on several different occasions. The last major assault occurred about 1,000,000 years ago, devastating your solar system and leaving Mars and Venus in their current states.

On Earth, the League destroyed the first colony of Hybornea. Then, approximately 900,000 years ago, the Galactic Federation returned and expelled the Orionites and their dark allies from your solar system. Your trans-Martian water world was destroyed and the Asteroid Belt created.

In the mid-1990s, the League of Orion and the former Anchara Alliance, under direct decree from their creator-god, ended their hostilities. Finally, the time had come for the Federation to welcome these previously virulent enemies as its allies. For this reason, it is imperative that you begin to understand them and their adjustment to their own new realities. The Star-Nation of Bellatrix is the first former foe about whom we can learn, and whom we can prepare to receive as one of our galactic neighbors.

Present Status and Location in Galaxy

The Star-Nation of Gamma Orion (Bellatrix) was accepted into the Galactic Federation of Light nearly eight years ago. Previously, it had belonged to the League of Orion and was that sector's headquarters for the former Anchara Alliance. Originally, Bellatrix (Latin: 'Warrioress') had been settled as an armed outpost of the Draconian Empire close to 25 million years ago.

The inhabitants of Bellatrix refer to their home world as 'Hakkos'Q'Dak'Laq' ('Great Blue Light'). The third-brightest star in Orion, she is located approximately 245 Light Years from Earth.

On a winter night in the Northern Hemisphere, you will recognize the constellation of Orion (Greek: 'Hunter') as a distant group of larger-magnitude stars. Orion's familiar shape is often used as a guide by which to find other stars and star clusters in the night sky. It is positioned between the constellations of Taurus (Greek: 'Bull') and Canis Major (Latin: 'Big Dog'), and just below that of Auriga (Latin: 'Charioteer').

The easiest way to find her is simply to look for the famous Belt of Orion. This row of three bright stars is located at the very center of the constellation. Just to the right and slightly above Orion's Belt, you will see a bright blue star, which you know as Bellatrix.

Bellatrician Solar System and Description of Home Worlds

The solar system of Bellatrix contains eight planets. The outer four are huge 'gas giants' similar, in size and appearance, to your planets Saturn, Uranus and Neptune. At this solar system's center is a semi-arid planet that measures about one-half the size of Neptune and Uranus (approximately 15,000 miles or 24,000 kilometers) in diameter. The planet next closer to their sun serves as home world for the Gamma Orion Star-Nation. Known to its inhabitants as 'Juk'HiqKal'Bhk', it is the third planet from Hakkos'Q'Dak'Laq.

At first glance from space, 'Juk'HiqKal'Bhk' seems very un-Earth-like in appearance. It is a planet nearly 11,000 miles (17,600 kilometers) in diameter and, unlike Mother Earth, consists of four very large continents surrounded by three oceans. The

Bellatrician mother world has a one-layer firmament, which supports an ecosystem that is recognized for its wide variety of reptilian, amphibian, dinosaurian and other strange aquatic life forms.

The climate here is semi-tropical and cooler only at its poles. Like all planets, Juk'HiqKal'Bhk is hollow, with an inner world whose population, even for this ecosystem, consists of some exceedingly strange creatures. The inhabitants of the Star-Nation of Bellatrix, numbering 1.2 billion, live in special, large cities that are scattered throughout her home world's interior.

The highly oxygenated atmosphere of this large water world is noted for its blue/orange tinge. Her skies swarm with billions of large, bird-like creatures and an enormous reptilian that resembles a bat. One continent is famous for its wide meadows of red and orange grasses. The next two landmasses are well known for their broad mountain ranges, thick jungles and vast inland seas. The last continent, which looks vaguely like a large foot, contains an inland sea that is connected to the oceans by two narrow straits located near its southeastern rim.

Bellatrix's hybrid dinosaurian/reptilian species has chosen the semi-arid world of B'Kuab'KQln on which to establish their most sacred sites. Her drier climate is reminiscent of their original home worlds on Sigma and Eta Draco. To honor these worlds, they perform rituals in large desert temples located near small, sacred surface settlements.

The two innermost planets are small and barren, with the thinnest of atmospheres. They are known for their exceedingly erratic orbits. The outer one is less than 3,000 miles (4,800 kilometers) in diameter. The inner, often lit by its sun's solar flares, seems like a burning sphere.

Description of Bellatrician Society

The culture of the Bellatrician Star-Nation is highly unusual, and notable for a ruling class that came to dominate its entire society. That society is in the midst of a transition to a more traditional, galactic way of life. The core of Bellatrician society is comprised of a ruling council that includes the elite from every sector of its population. This council, which is in charge of Bellatrix's day-to-day activities, elects a chief ruler, a King or Queen, who serves in that capacity for a period of twenty years (see page 98, Chart 8:

Bellatrician Prototype of Anchara Alliance Society).

Beneath this ruling council is a group similar to your planet's royalty. They served as regional rulers who supervised the day-to-day administration of the ten distinct political districts within their sphere of influence. Bellatrician royalty more closely resembled your nobility (princes, dukes, counts, et cetera). Using their immense influence as Gamma Orion's regional heads, they oversaw its many pressing socio-political activities. This involved the negotiation of important economic contracts and scrutiny of every detail of their region's economy. Their diligence enabled them to attain a very rarefied and powerful status.

Bellatrician Prototype of Anchara Alliance Society

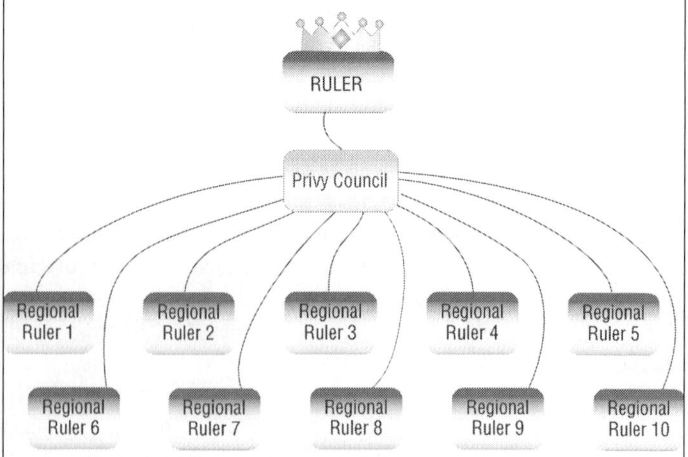

Chart 8

Clearly, Draconian society, like many others in the former Anchara Alliance, was extremely hierarchical and tyrannical. At its top were rulers appointed by the Empire's major governing group. They were the chief administrators for Orion and its many surrounding constellations, and formed one of the major working groups overseeing this sector of the galaxy.

Deciding that the groups that had controlled their society's daily operations should change their political direction, the Bellatrician ruling council established new hierarchies of government. Whereas membership previously had been based upon

Empire bloodlines originating on Draco nearly 25 million years ago, it was now based upon merit.

For the first time, the Bellatricians are creating a much more democratic society. According to the new system, each group is permitted to argue its points when reporting any findings and suggestions to the Grand Council. The Grand Council makes a decision based upon the conditions existing within the society. An action plan is formulated, which is then sent back to the various working groups for implementation.

For now, the hereditary ruling group has maintained its power on the Grand Council. Eventually, members of the various working groups will be permitted to become part of the now-hereditary Grand Council.

Now, too, the League of Orion Councils has divided Orion into regions, thus wresting exclusive power from the Bellatricians' grasp. This has helped to foster a belief throughout Orion that change truly can occur. The League of Orion is shifting, and is no longer as belligerent. They are beginning to open themselves to peace, and to the transformation of their societies. The extent of their accomplishments is truly remarkable.

Bellatrix's Former Role in Anchara Alliance

As I have mentioned, the Bellatricians acted as the chief administrators for the Draconian Empire in this sector of the galaxy. This subdivision included outposts in the constellations of Orion, Taurus, Eridanus (Greek: 'River'), Auriga and Trianglum (Greek: 'Triangle'). Occasionally, the Bellatricians even served the Anchara Alliance as overseers of important secret projects. A case in point was their dealings with Earth's 'secret governments' and the former overlords of your world – the Anunnaki. The task escalated in importance when the Draconian Empire informed your 'secret governments' that their overt acts to counter various secret treaties were emphatically most unwise. Moreover, their continued misdeeds could provoke an escalating level of aggression between them. Thus, with the help of their Altairian 'friends', the Bellatricians acted as diplomatic intermediaries between the three groups from the 1950s until the 1990s. Their efforts resulted in a new series of clandestine treaties that were intended to resolve difficulties and ensure that the interests of each party were served. The Bellatricians undertook this assignment again, in the mid-1990s, when the Anchara Alliance suddenly approached the Galactic Federation of Light for a treaty that would ensure a permanent galactic peace.

Because the Draconian Empire did not trust the Galactic Federation's emissaries, they asked the Bellatricians and the Altairians to barter this arrangement. The Treaty of Anchara remains the basis for acceptance of former empires of the Anchara Alliance into the Galactic Federation of Light. But their role did not stop there. During the past half-decade, the Bellatricians and the Altairians have worked hard, in co-operation with a number of other star-nations, to assist the formerly dark sectors of this galaxy in making their peace with the Light.

Physical Description of the Bellatricians

The predominant species inhabiting Bellatrix is a dinosaurian/reptilian hybrid that first migrated from the constellation of Draco (Greek: 'Dragon') and Sagittarius (Latin: 'Archer') approximately 25 million years ago.

The body of Bellatrix's dinosaurian/reptilian hybrid is typically very scaly and bony. The upper head is surrounded by a large, bony crest, and the eyes are large and set forward, just above and to either side of a very small nose. The mouth is distinguished by thin lips that extend from one side of the head to the other.

The ears are non-existent, their only indication being an extra-smooth, 3-inch (7.62 cm) circle on either side of the head, just behind the eyes. The eyes are large, red or dull yellow, and resemble those of Earth's reptiles. The skin has a crocodile's scaliness and can be green, yellow, brown or red. A small, bony crest that runs up the middle of the back is connected to the larger crest on the top of the head.

This Being is a biped. It has thin 'hands' with six long, clawed fingers and feet that have five toes ending in stubby, razor-sharp claws. Its tail, which is very short and thick like a crocodile's, reaches only as far as the feet. The male is shorter than the female: Bellatrician males stand between 8 and 10 feet (2.44 and 3 meters), while the females range from 8.5 to 10.25 feet (2.6 to 3.12 meters) in height. This species requires between 5 and 8 hours of sleep per day.

The clothes of the Bellatricians are very different from those of most others in the former Anchara Alliance. The Beings of

Hakkos'Q'Dak'Laq adopted an array of spectacular, rainbow-colored garments entwined with flowing, multi-hued gowns. Ribbons or epaulettes inscribed with special graphic designs and colors are worn on the shoulder of the outer blouse to indicate the individual's rank and insignia.

Aboard spacecraft, Bellatricians wear relaxed-fit, two-piece jumpsuits. The top half is waist-length and zips to the pants as if it were one piece. The jumpsuit also takes the color codes and special graphic designs that designate rank and conferred honors. The boots, which form an integral part of the uniform, merge with the pants and usually appear to be an undivided unit.

Bellatricians are renowned for their great skills in diplomacy and leadership. For the past six million years, they have been in charge of all the former Anchara Alliance's forces for this sector of the Milky Way Galaxy.

The Bellatrician language is very coarse and often guttural. It is marked by frequent growls and hisses.

Bellatrician Ships

Bellatrician scout ships, which can resemble either dewdrops or beetles, measure approximately 40 feet (12.2 meters) in length. Smaller motherships range from 1 to 400 miles (1.6 to 640 kilometers) long and look like large tadpoles, while larger ones are more like stacks of round bread loaves. The larger motherships are very self-sufficient and usually keep only to deep space.

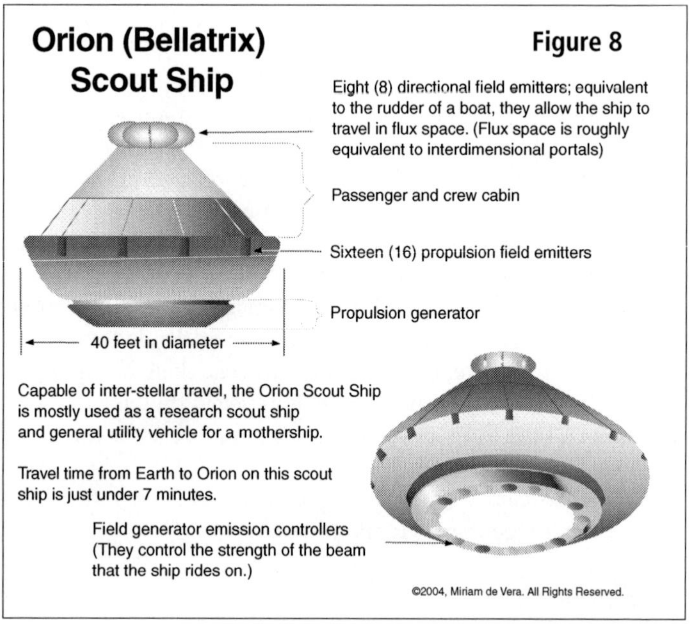
Orion (Bellatrix)
Scout Ship
Figure 8
Eight (8) directional field emitters; equivalent to the rudder of a boat, they allow the ship to travel in flux space. (Flux space is roughly equivalent to interdimensional portals)
Passenger and crew cabin
Sixteen (16) propulsion field emitters
Propulsion generator
40 feet in diameter
Capable of inter-stellar travel, the Orion Scout Ship is mostly used as a research scout ship and general utility vehicle for a mothership.
Travel time from Earth to Orion on this scout ship is just under 7 minutes.
Field generator emission controllers (They control the strength of the beam that the ship rides on.)
©2004, Miriam de Vera. All Rights Reserved.

12

The Star-Nation of Eta Draconis

Many times, Washta would instruct me in the unutterable horrors of the various galactic wars and how, despite countless truces, they had lasted for many millions of years. At the root of these wars were the Draconian Empire and its many close allies. The chief architects and strategic planners in charge of waging these galactic wars were the rulers of Eta Draconis. Using many annexed empires as their foot soldiers, they waged a seemingly endless series of wars across all sectors of this galaxy, which had been occupied, at various times, by forces of the Galactic Federation and its predecessors.

The Eta Draconians were famed for their brilliant strategies and for the creative means by which they administered these wars and kept the conflicting forces of the Anchara Alliance together. Their diplomatic skills became legendary throughout the whole of the Alliance. Their notoriety followed them everywhere. Soon, they were providing societal models for every evil empire with which their masters, the dark lords of the Draconian Empire, were associated. Because of the power granted them by the rulers of Eta Draconis, these dark lords became, very quickly, the most powerful component of the Anchara Alliance.

In the mid-1990s, under direct decree from their dark creator-god, Anchara, the Draconian Empire and its imperial allies (such as the League of Orion) ended their prolonged hostilities. The rulers of Eta Draconis commissioned a series of diplomatic task forces whose mission was to work with suitable counterparts and negotiate a treaty. The outcome was the Treaty of Anchara, which the peoples of Eta Draconis used to dissolve the Draconian Empire and create a new advisory body known as the Draconian Regional Federation Council. As a result, they entered the Galactic Federation of Light as a separate star-nation.

Now, this formerly fierce foe is one of your new galactic neighbors. For that reason, it is important to learn about them and how they adjusted to their own altered realities.

Present Status and Location

The Star-Nation of Eta Draconis formerly belonged to the Draconian Empire. She served as main headquarters for the Draconian diplomatic corps, which was spread throughout the Anchara Alliance.

The Beings of Eta Draconis also acted as overseers of the Draconian Empire. The Empire's 'gem' was, of course, Orion. In order to maintain a powerful hold over the Empire, her rulers encouraged heavy, selective immigration from the star-nations of the Draco (Greek: 'Dragon') constellation to that of Orion (Greek: 'Hunter') and their other dependencies. Eta Draconians considered your solar system part of their Empire, as well. They became a member of the Galactic Federation of Light about seven years ago.

Eta Draconis, a giant yellow star with a dwarf star companion, is often paired with Zeta Draconis. In Arabic, both are called Aldhibain ('Hyena'). Eta Draconis is part of the body of the constellation of Draco. It is located between the constellations of Ursa Major (Greek: 'Big Bear') and Ursa Minor (Greek: 'Little Bear'), which contain the Big and Little Dipper respectively. You can see Eta Draconis by looking above the double star Gamma Ursa Minor that forms the farthest outer edge of the 'Little Dipper'. Eta Draconis is approximately 88 Light Years from Earth.

Solar System of Eta Draconis

The solar system of Eta Draconis consists of eight planets, with the four smallest closest to the sun and the largest farthest away. Of the two innermost planets in this system, one is one-eighth the size of your Earth, while the other is only slightly larger. The innermost planet's extremely thin, highly ionized atmosphere glows dimly owing to constant discharges from her sun, Qart'Lu'Takr'Rw ('Sacred Light').

The next world is more congenial to life. She is nearly the same size as Earth and has an atmosphere similar to your own. Nonetheless, this planet is hot and semi-arid, with two large continents covered mostly by high, coastal mountain ranges and enormous deserts. Shallow seas and drying seabeds surround her continents. Five miniature seas are all that remains of a once-large, integrated ocean. Evaporation has left a mere 40 per cent of her sea floor submerged. The rest has become a bewildering maze of dry, desolate canyons, low mountain ranges and muddy, salty ooze that dries to a hard, metallic luster.

Life on this planet is abundant and diverse. While a predominantly reptilian population inhabits her lands, her dying seas support schools of giant, plated ancient fish and tiny crustaceans. Flora and fauna unique in the Eta Draconis solar system, and this galaxy, flourish here.

The three most remote planets in the Qart'Lu'Takr'Rw solar system are 'gas giants' that have much in common with your own solar system's large, outermost spheres. Unlike them, however, these worlds rotate far more rapidly, and they are surrounded by uniquely beautiful ring systems.

These outer planets display other atmospheric anomalies such as Jupiter's conspicuous giant red spot. The ring systems that encircle them are equal to those of Saturn or narrower, like those of your Uranus or Neptune.

Description of Home Worlds

Eta Draconis' two main home worlds are hot and semi-arid. The first, called Sam'Kech'Qlah ('Amazing Dry Place') is a large, dry planet, measuring approximately 9,500 miles (15,200 kilometers) in diameter. Twelve moons revolve around Sam'Kech'Qlah: the largest, three-quarters the size of Earth's moon, is surrounded by a thick, life-sustaining atmosphere.

The second home world, called Seck'Ha'Lak'Bekn ('Wondrous Wet Land'), is more abundant in water. She is the same size as the first planet but has only five continents, four of which are as dry and barren as those found on Sam'Kech'Qlah. The fifth landmass contains a huge, inland sea that makes the interior less desolate. A chain of rivers flows toward this mini-ocean from the mountain range that rims its northern shore. Forests, consisting of exotic tree ferns, conifers and primitive, deciduous trees and bushes, stretch down, in unbroken vistas, to the beaches' edge. Red or blue mountains, streaked with purple, soar above her continents. Amid such extravagant natural settings, many strange and wonderful life forms – insect, amphibian, dinosaurian and reptilian – make their homes. And here, on this world, stands the sacred cultural capital of the Eta Draconians - the site of her most sacred temples and institutions of higher learning.

Changes occurring in Eta Draconis' Society

The rulers of Eta Draconis were their Empire's diplomats and overseers, who saw it as their glorious obligation to maintain this domain. The task of negotiating the Anchara Treaties had been one of their primary responsibilities. Suddenly, the Draconian rulers, realizing that they had a duty to ensure that this peace process could be achieved, used their enormous influence to guarantee its success.

This decision had an incalculable effect on the social order. As with most of the other societies that belonged to the Anchara Alliance, theirs was exceedingly hierarchical and tyrannical. The ruling elite wished to change the living conditions of the so-called lower castes, who were poorly treated and lived in very spartan circumstances. Ancharan societies have an innate capacity for developing their natural abilities to the utmost and for reshaping things in their own style. Therefore, after comparing galactic culture to their own on Eta Draconis, they decided that they had to create a reptilian, dinosaurian and Ancharan concept of Galactic society.

Rather than a clan system, they decided to implement a governmental structure that retained the well-known Eta Draconian efficiency. That is, a task was assigned and completed, successfully and on time. They also agreed to abolish their Ruling Councils. Eta Draconis, in fact, was actually the first dinosaurian society in the Anchara Alliance to eliminate these Councils, which previously had been their elite governing body. They replaced them with a parliament whose members had been part of the original dynamic councils. These new groups, in turn, would unite to form the major Ruling Council.

No longer was there a succession of dictators who addressed the people of Eta Draconis directly from Thuban (Alpha Draconis), the Empire's major ruling star-nation. Throughout all of Earth's history, Thuban has been the most dreaded place of the galaxy. Now, however, the Beings of Eta Draconis no longer feared them, nor did they consider them the primary representatives of their planet, of the Anchara Alliance, or even of the Draconian Empire. Instead, they decided to take advantage of the special opportunity created by the Treaties of Anchara to institute a galactic society, in accordance with the traditional concepts first promulgated by Anchara.

They issued a series of decrees to the former Draconian Empire. Through diplomatic channels, they presented these decrees to the major Councils of the Empire and, using their connections, set out to transform it. Their purpose was to assemble, within the Galactic Federation, a united group that adhered to the dictates of Anchara. For them, the crucial element was change. A fresh new breeze, based upon heart and the Light, was sweeping through the former home worlds of the vast Anchara Alliance. Using their influence, they began to initiate an exhaustive series of changes. It is an extraordinary story. Consequently, the Eta Draconis Beings, as a group, have entirely changed the way members of the Anchara Alliance perceive each other and the Galactic Federation. In fact, they are actually the ones most responsible for the new synthesis unfolding now throughout these formerly dark realms.

Physical Description of the Eta Draconians

The inhabitants of the Eta Draconis star system are a dinosaurian/reptilian (shape-shifter) hybrid that migrated from the constellation of Cepheus (named for a mythic king of Ethiopia in an ancient Greek tale) approximately 35 million years ago.

Typically, their bodies are very scaly with occasional, prominent ridges and crests. The top of the head is crowned by a large crest that rims the forehead and stretches down the back.

Large eyes are set on either side of a very small nose. They are either brown or dull yellow, and resemble those of Earth's snakes. Thin, dark lips, extending from one side of the head to the other, trace the edges of the mouth.

The ears are large, circular masses covered by very smooth

membranes more than 7 inches (17.8 cm) in diameter. They are located on either side of the head, just behind the eyes.

The skin has the rough scaliness of a reptile; it glistens like that of a crocodile, alligator or toad and is green, yellow, brown or red. A narrow ridge running up the middle of the back is connected to the larger ridge on the back of the head. This Being is a biped. It has thin hands with three long, clawed fingers and four-toed feet that have short, very sharp, claws. The tail is very large and narrow, like a reptile's, and extends just beyond the feet.

Eta Draconis males are shorter than their females. Males stand between 7.5 and 8 feet (2.28 and 2.43 meters) tall, while female heights vary from 8.25 to 9.5 feet (2.51 to 2.89 meters). These Beings normally require 5 to 6 hours of sleep per day.

The clothes of Eta Draconis' inhabitants resemble most others in the former Anchara Alliance. The Beings of Qart'Lu'Takr'Rw wear an array of spectacular robes overlaid with sheer, multi-colored blouses, similar to those worn by the inhabitants of Bellatrix. Epaulettes marked with special graphic designs and command colors adorn the shoulders of the outer robe to designate the individual's rank and commendations.

Aboard spacecraft, the Beings of Eta Draconis wear a relaxed-fit, two-piece jumpsuit. The waist-length top is attached to the matching pants, creating what appears to be a one-piece outfit. The jumpsuit, silver or gray, is embellished with the color codes and graphic designs that signify rank and conferred honors. Boots are an integral part of this uniform, and merge with the pants in a seemingly undivided whole.

Eta Draconians are celebrated for their extraordinary talents in diplomacy and for their remarkable aptitude for mind control. A chameleon-like capacity to change their skin's look, feel and color is integral in their use of brainwashing. In such a way, they can actually induce large groups of another species to believe that they are one of them.

During the past 25 million years, the Eta Draconians have also been the Anchara Alliance's main diplomatic arm for this sector of the galaxy. As part of this responsibility, they undertook the indoctrination of all the Draconian-governed star systems in this galaxy.

The language of Eta Draconis is very guttural, with bellows and frequent hisses.

Ships of Eta Draconis

Some Eta Draconis scout craft resemble large beetles, while others have the traditional, large-domed saucer shape. These scout ships extend between 50 and 600 feet (15.2 and 182.4 meters) in length. Motherships vary from 10 to 20,000 miles (16 to 32,000 kilometers) long and look like either a most unusual stack of large eggs, or a very large sphere.

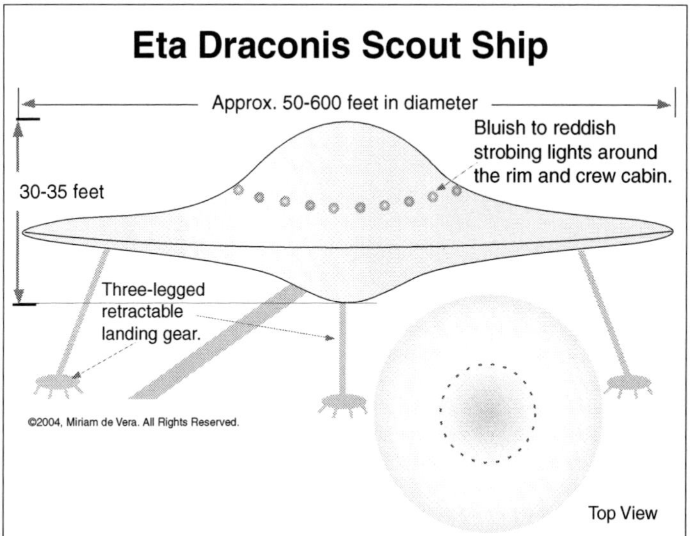

Figure 9

13

The Star-Nation of Sigma Draconis

As Washta described the appalling nature of the various galactic wars, he would often mention the exceptional bravery and masterly strategies implemented by the fleets of the Draconian Empire. The rulers of Eta Draconis appointed fleet commanders who most often were native to Sigma Draconis. The Sigma Draconian rulers and their advisors, in fact, were acclaimed throughout the Anchara Alliance for their unparalleled military leadership and epic gallantry in battle. As a result of their fame, they became the pre-eminent officer corps in the Empire. Such notoriety also enabled them to hone their skills for 'policing' and controlling states dependent upon the Draconian Empire, and they vanquished the inhabitants of their dominions with the same fierce enthusiasm that they displayed in battle. For this reason, the citizens of Sigma Draconis were feared by every member of the Anchara Alliance.

Eventually, their expertise in war also led them to become the galaxy's major developers of military weaponry and armed spacecraft. Indeed, military engineers from Sigma Draconis were soon assigned to distribute their advanced weapons technology to every corner of the Anchara Alliance. The Sigma Draconians' acquired power created a dark society that became increasingly fond of its ever-growing militarism. Sigma Draconians became objects of suspicion. Secretly, the Eta Draconians worried whether the Sigma Draconians (if, by some remote chance, Anchara made a solemn declaration of peace) would ever become its true proponents.

In the mid-1990s, by direct decree of their dark creator-god, Anchara, the Draconian Empire and all of its dependents ended their prolonged hostilities. The rulers of Sigma Draconis commissioned a succession of special military emissaries to travel to every sector of the Anchara Empire to ensure that this path to peace was honorably observed. Even when some more distant empires balked at the opportunity to declare peace, the Sigma Draconians, demonstrating their loyalty, even organized successful campaigns to cut short any Alliance rebellion against peace.

That diligence for peace became the new enthusiasm of the rulers of Sigma Draconis. Once all hostilities had ceased, they immediately issued orders for all Sigma Draconian-led fleets to return to their home worlds. There, they were either disbanded or sworn in as members of the newly integrated Galactic Federation Science and Exploration (S&E) fleets. Only recently committed to the ensuing Treaty of Anchara, the Beings of the Star-Nation of Sigma Draconis took part in the dispersal of the Draconian Empire. And, soon after sharing in the creation of the new Draconian Regional Federation Council, they entered the Galactic Federation of Light as a separate member-star-nation.

Now that this formerly fierce foe has been embraced by the Galactic Federation, it is time for you to learn about them and their adjustment to their own new realities. The Star-Nation of Sigma Draconis is only one of many about which you can learn as you prepare to receive your galactic neighbors.

Present Status and Location

The Star-Nation of Sigma Draconis belonged, previously, to the Draconian Empire, serving as the principal source for the officer corps of the Empire's military and police forces.

The Beings of Sigma Draconis were also the main engineers and suppliers of weapons and defense systems for the Draconian Empire. The prime 'gem' of the Draconian Empire was, of course, Orion. In order to secure the continued flow of Sigma Draconis' goods throughout the Empire, its rulers encouraged heavy, selective immigration from the star-nations of the constellation of Draco to those of the constellation of Orion and their other dependencies. Sigma Draconis also considered your solar system to be part of their Empire. They became a member of the Galactic Federation of Light about seven years ago.

Sigma Draconis is a type K orange star, located in the body of the constellation of Draco (Greek: 'Dragon'), which is situated between the constellations of Ursa Major (Latin: 'Big Bear') and Ursa Minor (Latin: 'Little Bear') – the Big and Little Dippers, respectively. To find Sigma Draconis, observe the Big Dipper and distinguish the stars, Dubhe and Merak, which form the Big Dipper's upper edge. Then look across to Polaris, at the outer edge of the Little Dipper's handle, and the first star you will see, along the line from the Big Dipper, is Sigma Draconis. It is 18.8 Light Years from Earth.

Sigma Draconis Solar System

The solar system of Sigma Draconis contains twelve planets, with the two smallest worlds closest to the sun and the largest farthest away.

The third inner world is almost the size of your Earth or Venus. Like Venus, she is widely known for her thick, very corrosive atmosphere, a result of her exploitation by the rulers of Sigma Draconis as a testing site for weapons destined for use in galactic wars.

The next world, fourth from Sigma Draconis' sun, is more amenable to life. Barely larger than Earth, she is surrounded by an atmosphere similar to your own. This hot, semi-arid planet contains four large continents whose surface is covered mostly by high coastal mountain ranges and interiors containing vast deserts. Eight shallow, miniature seas surround her four principal landmasses. This planet's biological diversity makes her a living laboratory for the Beings of Sigma Draconis.

The six remaining worlds in the Qart'Ku'Sarq'Rp solar system are gas giants similar, in many ways, to the large planets of the sun's outer solar system. The difference lies in their rotation, which is far faster than your Jupiter, Saturn, Uranus or Neptune, and in their vivid planetary rings.

Description of Home Worlds

Sigma Draconis consists of two main home worlds: a very hot, semi-arid sphere and a lush water world. The first is a large, dry planet, fifth from the sun, called Dosk'Qech'Qlah (the 'Marvelous

Dry Place'). She is 10,000 miles (16,000 kilometers) in diameter and has seven moons, the largest of which has a thick, livable atmosphere and is the size of Earth's moon. A headquarters was established on this moon 1,000 years after its solar system was first inhabited, and quickly became the military command center of the Sigma Draconis government. The home world below is fairly typical of others located throughout the constellation of Draco.

Since this planet resembles many of the chief home worlds in the Draconian Empire, she has become a ritual center. Temples are scattered across her continents. A large city, dedicated to the performance of ritual, is situated near the main temple site. This complex, known as Khr'Qalt'Jo'Ghrm ('the Way of Holy Rituals'), occupies both banks of the longest river on the largest of this world's five continents. Military leaders of the Draconian Empire came here to entreat Anchara's help in achieving victories in the many galactic wars.

The second planet, called Seck'Lak'Daq'Bekn' ('Wondrous Water Land'), is a true water world. Slightly larger than the first home world, she contains seven continents. While three are as dry and barren as those on Dosk'Qech'Qlah, the other four contain huge inland seas that make the interior seem less bleak. A chain of rivers flows from central cordilleras toward these seas to rim the mini-oceans' shores. Red mountains, smudged in shades of gray and blue and streaked with purple, encircle the capital. These gorgeous environments are home to extraordinary dinosaurian and reptilian life forms. The capital city of the Sigma Draconians, located at the southern edge of the very largest inland sea on the most extensive continent, is a bustling urban center of temples, government buildings, military command complexes and institutions of higher learning.

The Importance of the Anchara Treaty to this Galaxy and to Sigma Draconis

Traditionally, Sigma Draconians were the chief warriors of the Draconian Empire. These Beings are typical Dracos, and resemble giant demons. Over the millennia, they were the Draconian Empire's ultimate warriors, controllers and manipulators. Together with the Beings from Alpha Draconis, the Sigma Draconians were the essence of an immensely powerful dark energy that, for millions of years, surged back and forth in mighty wars across this galaxy. Theirs is a tradition that limited conscious Beings such as we have learned to fear.

In reality, much of what occurred during those wars is captured in our genetic memory. Take, for example, the Star Wars Trilogy. Beings such as Sigma Draconians, Alpha Draconians, Bellatricians, Rigelians and Mintakans spoke volumes about the dark side. These Beings all knew and understood war, with its related feelings of superiority, limitation and hate. Now, it has all faded away. What remain are formerly restrictive, authoritarian societies that are beginning to see themselves from a new perspective.

Consider how the Treaty of Anchara and, prior to that, the Decrees of Anchara, have changed our galaxy. Recognize that all of the beings that once elicited our instinctive abhorrence are no longer to be feared, but embraced. It is important for us to change our concepts regarding these Beings. Understand that this immense galaxy is coalescing, and that an uncertain peace can become permanent as a result of our actions here on Earth. Realize, too, that these magnificent Beings are frightening to us, now, only in memory and perception.

Creating a new Sigma Draconis Society

We do not want merely to examine these Beings and what they represented. Instead, it is important for us to see them as part of the great Galactic Brotherhood and Sisterhood that is uniting to form a new Galactic Federation of Light and a new galaxy of peace. Because our world suffered incalculable limitations and cruelties at the hands of the dark, we continue to be possessed by vexing memories of the incidents that took place here. We must allow our positive energy to surround these many different Beings. We need to let go and reflect upon our coming change, and upon the new Light that is diligently transforming the entire galaxy.

As we move into our next phase, we are growing into full consciousness. In the same way, while not all dinosaurian/reptilian Beings such as the Sigma Draconians inhabit Light Bodies, they are beginning to disclose them as a result of our work here on Earth. These Beings are allowing the changes to be revealed to us in their true light. In fact, we on Earth are a microcosm of this cosmic macrocosm. These members of the former Anchara Alliance are also changing, and will gradually develop the capacity to manifest Light Bodies. Their societies will never be the same. By what we are doing and creating, we are helping to fashion societies that will empower us all to change and move forward.

The warriors are withdrawing, dismantling their immense fleets and transferring segments of those fleets to the Galactic Federation for exploration purposes. In effect, they are converting them from vessels of war to ships of peace.

Physical Description

This star system's major species is a dragon-like dinosaurian/reptilian hybrid, which first migrated to Sigma Draconis from the constellation of Sagittarius approximately 25 million years ago.

The inhabitants of the Sigma Draconis Star-Nation are dinosaurian/reptilian hybrids that closely resemble dragons and typify the conventional Earth concept of demons. They are characterized by extreme scaliness and, for us, are frightful to look at.

Like Earth's reptiles, the large red or dull yellow eyes of the Sigma Draconian are set forward just above and to either side of a very narrow snout. Its mouth consists of thin lips that extend from one side of the head to the other. The teeth are large and clearly those of a predator, while the ears are small and scaly.

The skin has a crocodilian scaliness and is green, yellow, brown or red. The body is long and lanky, and a scaly crest stretches down the center of its back. On the back, also, is a set of bat-like wings.

This Being is a biped. It has thin hands that end in six long, clawed fingers. Its feet have five toes tipped with small, razor-sharp claws. An arrow-like point marks the end of the long, thin tail. Its body and breath reek of brimstone. The male is shorter than the female. Sigma Draconis males stand between 9 and 10 feet (2.74 and 3 meters) tall, while the females range from 9.25 to 11 feet (2.81 to 3.34 meters) in height. Beings from Sigma Draconis usually sleep between five and eight hours a day.

The clothes of the Sigma Draconians resemble most others in the former Anchara Alliance. The Beings of Qart'Ku'Sarq'Rp chose a series of long, uniquely layered garments lined with flowing, multi-colored blouses. Epaulettes inscribed with special graphic designs and the colors of command are worn on the shoulder of the outer blouse to indicate the individual's rank and commendations.

Aboard spacecraft, Sigma Draconians wear relaxed-fit, two-piece jumpsuits. The waist-length top half is fastened to the pants, creating what seems to be a one-piece outfit. Usually silver or gray, the jumpsuit complies with the color codes and special graphic designs that define rank and insignia. Boots are integral to the total outfit, and are designed to merge with the pants as a single unit.

Sigma Draconians are recognized for their outstanding leadership and military skills. For 35 million years, they led all the forces of the former Anchara Alliance in the Milky Way Galaxy.

Their language is extremely coarse and guttural, with many different growls and hisses.

Ships of Sigma Draconis

Sigma Draconis scout craft resemble either birds or beetles. Their scout ships extend from 100 to 600 feet (30.5 to 182.4 meters) in length.

Their motherships measure between 1 and 40,000 miles (1.6 and 64,000 kilometers) long, and look like large tadpoles or snakes.

Part V

Amphibians

An Introduction from the Amphibians

We are a class of highly sentient Beings who have served two different spiritual masters in this galaxy. In the beginning, we all were spiritual Beings turned toward the Light, joyfully living on our warm, swampy planets. Then, tens of millions of years ago, a malevolent scourge called the forces of Anchara advanced across this galaxy, capturing or occupying many of our worlds.

Soon, we were divided. Some continued to serve the Light, while others, transformed by the evil of their new oppressors, chose to serve Anchara's dark ambitions. This enforced partition persisted through a seemingly endless succession of galactic wars that lasted for millions of years. Now we, a sundered people, are again becoming one. Using our wondrous restorative energies and superlative technologies, we intend to heal others in this galaxy of the wounds that these wars have caused. We invite you to join us in this sacred quest!

Our worlds are intensely beautiful. They are yet another type of water world that exists across the length and breadth of this most incomparable galaxy. Even though our ships have explored the galaxy's every corner, still, our hearts prefer our own sweltering native lands.

Our solar systems are somewhat different from those that you inhabit. The size of our suns varies from diffuse, multicolored giants to ones much like yours. Yet, our worlds share common topography – our joyous swamps, wetlands and broad, rolling meadows. The unusual flora and fauna that surrounds us is known for its water-loving nature and for the great, obscuring mists that constantly unroll over us. In these environments, we have flourished, built our societies and been exemplary stewards of our worlds.

To you, these lands may be a little too hot, somewhat eccentric, perhaps even a bit much. Yet we invite you, someday, to visit our worlds and learn more about us. Until then, rest assured that we Love you and are doing everything in our power to ensure that your transformation is a success.

Therefore, enjoy these chapters about us and, in short, grow to know us better. Each of these three star-nations forms a selected cross-section of the vast history that we have just begun to reveal to you. Each chapter, too, will give you a better understanding of who we really are. We are eager for the unforgettable day when we shall walk freely among you!

14

The Star-Nation of Mintaka

Washta's history lessons would include frequent, vivid descriptions of the horrors of the many galactic wars. His teachings particularly emphasized the participation of the League of Orion, an ally of the Draconian Empire that was governed by the Star-Nation of Bellatrix. The Star-Nation of Mintaka was one of the League's most important centers for science, Orion culture and exploration. During the galactic wars, the chief advance scouts and explorers for the League and the Draconian Empire originated from Mintaka (Delta Orionis). Their task was to discover the presence and positions of any enemy fleets in this sector of the galaxy, and to determine the legal status of any sentient star-nations that blocked their fleets.

The people of Delta Orionis were acclaimed for the scientific, yet creative, ways in which they carried out their assignments. The precision with which they located even the most cloaked Galactic Federation fleet was celebrated throughout the Anchara Alliance. Soon, as a result of their fame, they were supplying advance-scouting technology to every dark empire allied with their masters, the dark lords of the Draconian Empire.

In the mid-1990s, under direct decree from their creator-god, Anchara, the Draconian Empire and its imperial allies (such as the League of Orion) ended their protracted hostilities. The Draconian Empire sent Mintaka's rulers to determine the best locales for the momentous diplomatic sessions that would lead to the drafting of the Treaty of Anchara. Consequently, the peoples of the Mintakan Star-Nation dismantled the League of Orion and created a new regulatory body known as the Orion Regional Federation Council. In due course, they joined the Galactic Federation of Light as a separate star-nation.

Now, this formerly fierce foe is yet another of your galactic neighbors. It is important, therefore, to learn about them and their adjustment to a new set of realities. The Star-Nation of Mintaka is one more about which you can learn, as you prepare to receive your galactic neighbors.

Present Status and Location

Approximately 30 million years ago, Mintaka's amphibious inhabitants created a new civilization: it was a major star-nation in this sector of the galaxy. About 5 million years later, Mintaka was conquered by forces of the Draconian Empire and became allied with the dark League of Orion. Finally, nearly 9 years ago, the Star-Nation of Delta Orionis (Mintaka) was welcomed into the Galactic Federation of Light.

The star Delta Orionis is also known as Al Mintaka, which in Arabic means 'Belt'. Her inhabitants refer to Mintaka as 'Sha'Da'Lik' ('Great Holy Light'). She is the seventh-brightest star in Orion, and is located approximately 920 Light Years from Earth.

In the winter skies of the Northern Hemisphere, the constellation of Orion (Greek: 'Hunter') resembles a distant cluster of larger-magnitude stars. Its familiar shape often acts as a pointer by which to locate other stars and star-groups at night. The constellation of Orion is positioned between those of Taurus (Greek: 'Bull') and Canis Major (Latin: 'Big Dog'), and just below that of Auriga (Latin: 'Charioteer').

The easiest way to identify Mintaka (Delta Orionis) is to locate the famous belt of Orion. One of the three stars is Mintaka: the other two are Al Nitak (Arabic: 'Girdle') and Al Nilam (Arabic: 'String of Pearls'). They are situated at the very center of the constellation. Mintaka is the bright blue star just to the right and at the top of Orion's Belt.

Mintaka Solar System

The six-planet solar system of Mintaka (Delta Orionis) is actually located on what your astronomers refer to as Mintaka-C. It is one of the companion stars encircling the prime star, Delta Orionis-A. This system's innermost planet is one-eighth the size of your Earth. Her slowly thinning atmosphere glows from the constant discharges of her sun, Sha'Bak'Lik (the 'Holy Life-Giver').

The next world, nearly the same size as Earth, is enveloped in an atmosphere similar to your own but slightly thinner. A hot, semi-arid planet, she contains three large continents whose shores are ringed by high, coastal mountain ranges. She is widely known for her broad interior deserts and immensely varied life forms.

While the remaining three outer planets in the Sha'Bak'Lik solar system are considered 'gas giants' in many ways resembling the large planets in Earth's outer solar system, they measure less than one-half the size of gas giants revolving in your solar system, and have a much more rapid rotation.

Description of Home Worlds

Mintaka's home world, Bak'Jo'La, is the third planet from her sun. She has a diameter of nearly 9,000 miles (14,400 kilometers) and contains eight enormous continents and ten oceans. Her single-layer firmament supports an ecosystem famous for the unusual diversity of her amphibian, reptilian and other aquatic life forms.

Bak'Jo'La's climate is semi-tropical and cooler only at her poles. Like all planets, Bak'Jo'La is hollow, encompassing an inner world whose population includes, even for this ecosystem, some very bizarre creatures. The 800 million inhabitants of the Delta Orionis-C Star-Nation live in special, large cities that are scattered throughout her interior.

The highly oxygenated atmosphere of this huge water world is well known for her purple-blue tinge. Bak'Jo'La's skies teem with billions of bird-like amphibians. One of her continents is noted for vast swamps hung with red and orange mosses, and strange, bow-limbed trees whose large orange and red flowers fill the wet tracts with their rich fragrance. The next two landmasses are famous for their broad mountain ranges, dense, moist jungles and immense inland seas. The smallest continent encloses an inland sea that flows through a narrow, marshy strait to the oceans.

Because her drier climate reminds them of their original planets on Sigma and Eta Draco, the hybrid dinosaurian/reptilian population of Bak'Jo'La choose to locate its most sacred sites in the semi-arid interior of the continent of Guo'Fal'Pum ('Desert Land'). To honor their home worlds, the Mintakans celebrate rituals in a spacious desert temple situated near the small, sacred settlement that serves as their main inland capital.

The Original Nature of Mintaka Society

Mintaka's home world is a wet, swampy amphibian world consisting of water, earth and mud. The Mintakans are an amphibian species that co-exists harmoniously with reptilian and dinosaurian hybrids. Within their society, they see themselves as servants: beyond the boundaries of their own group, they assume the role of explorers, and are celebrated as such throughout the Galactic Federation. For them, explorations are conducted by probes of their subject's identity – that is, by creating and compiling psychological profiles. Highly skilled at mind manipulation, the Mintakans, over many years, have succeeded in making significant breakthroughs on behalf of the Alliance.

The Mintakans were among the most prominent of the Ancharan groups to come here and ascertain how Alliance rulers could gain control over your solar system. Although they clearly failed, their culture bears a closer, second look.

Mintakan culture revered service above all else: it was their raison d'être. With the Decree of Anchara, the Anchara Alliance came to an abrupt end. The Mintakans' concept of fealty and their use of manipulation on behalf of the Alliance shifted, very suddenly, to service in the name of the Galactic Federation of Light.

The Changing Nature of Mintaka Society

Initially, following the passage of the Treaty of Anchara, Mintakan society was in a state of total disarray, utterly uncertain what to do next. However, after having observed the people of Eta Draconis and studied the Decrees, the Mintakans decided that they would best serve the Eta Draconians by spreading the new concept of galactic society throughout the former Anchara Alliance, and helping the Galactic Federation to unite the whole of Creation in peace.

The culture of Mintaka is, primarily, one of service. Its elites, who saw fulfillment of their superiors' wishes to be their life's work, were mere servants. But the Mintakans changed. For the first time, they began to allow the different amphibian species who shared their culture to join together and become creative. And, by developing psychological profiles of them, the Mintakans learned how their society and their people function.

No longer does Mintakan society consist of mere endless knots of servants. Now, as a result of the Decrees of Anchara, they are developing clans and discovering co-operative work techniques that will change the direction and nature of their culture. For you, the most important part of this introduction to the peoples of the former Anchara Alliance lies in realizing the speed at which present events are transforming a very dark society into Beings who will be an integral part of the Light.

Physical Description of the Mintakans

For the most part, the Mintakans are an amphibian majority that co-exists with a minority of reptilian and dinosaurian hybrids. In many ways, they resemble Earth's frogs and toads, but there are significant differences. They are bipeds. Their skin, which is smooth and hairless, is typically iridescent, in colors ranging from bright red, orange and green to yellow and brown.

Mintakan eyes, unlike those of Earth's amphibians, protrude only slightly. They are large, bright red, orange or greenish-yellow in color and extend around the sides of the head. The nose, consisting of two narrow slits, sits above extremely thin lips. The open mouth is very large and frog-like. The ears are two small, round circles on either side of the head.

Whereas the large head appears disproportionate to the rest of the body, the short neck seems almost non-existent. The body, arms and legs are very muscular. Each limb has four long, thin, webbed digits, and the toes end in small claws.

Mintakan males are slightly shorter than females and stand between 7 and 8 feet (2.13 and 2.44 meters) in height. Females vary from between 7.5 and 8.5 feet (2.29 and 2.59 meters) tall. The species is also characterized by a series of three narrow, interconnected ridges that extend the length of the back and end on top of the head.

Mintakans are noted for their highly specialized expertise in psychology and mind manipulation. They have amassed an immense body of scientific knowledge and retain vast libraries of inner wisdom that date back more than 15 million years. They need four to six hours of sleep per day.

The Mintakan language, although extremely melodic, is also deeply guttural.

Ships of Mintaka

Mintakan ships are almost mushroom-like and can be identified by their large, rounded, pyramid-like domes. They measure from 45 to 80 feet (13.7 to 24.4 meters) in diameter. Motherships are massive, with an approximate diameter of between 100 and 1,000 miles (160 and 1,600 kilometers). The larger ones are extremely self-sufficient and usually keep only to deep space.

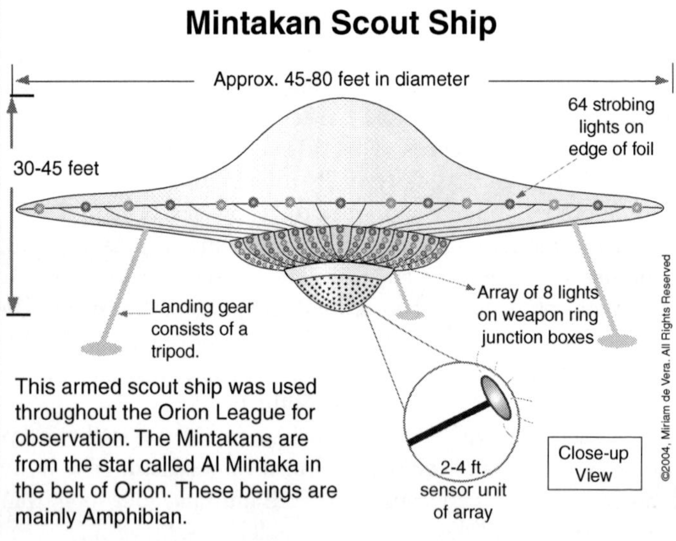

Figure 10

15

The Star-Nation of Beta Canceri (Al Tarf)

Washta would delight in giving me frequent, detailed accounts of the Beta Canceri (Al Tarf) peoples' long and storied history in the Galactic Federation. By mastering the art of creating a Light Body, these originally limited-conscious amphibians, over the course of millions of years, were able to wrest their captive star-nation from the clutches of the Anchara Alliance. In doing so, Beta Canceri became, many millennia ago, a charter member of the Galactic Federation of Light. This star-nation is located at the apex of what was a center for many long galactic war campaigns.

Indeed, one of the major points that separate the various dark Anchara Alliance empires from the member star-nations of the Galactic Federation is the whole matter of inhabiting Light Bodies. Wishing her people to be servants who lacked the power of thought, Anchara left them with the capability to have Light Bodies but did not manifest it in them. Instead, she gave these Beings limited consciousness with the capacity for deep emotions, but without the knowledge to connect with Spirit. Anchara communicated with them only by means of physical manifestation and messages to her priestesses. Therefore, the inhabitants of Beta Canceri were ripe for emotional and psychological manipulation, meted out by those whom Anchara had chosen to rule her dark domains. However, these Beings, using their natural gifts, wished to reclaim the ability to manifest their Light Bodies and become fully conscious. In the process, they rediscovered two vital facts. First: they had retained the capacity to actualize Light Bodies. Second: the complex manifestation process required the individual to transform her/his major inner perceptions and the society to collectively follow suit.

Once the Al Tarfans had attained their goal, they pledged to use their new knowledge to help liberate the oppressed star-nations of the Anchara Alliance. This pledge had caused them to join the Galactic Federation millions of years before, when they had assisted in the formation of one of its 14 Regional Federation Councils – the Gemini Regional Council. The Star-Nation of Beta Canceri was welcomed into the Galactic Federation of Light approximately 4 million years ago.

My first meeting with a group from the Star-Nation of Beta Canceri occurred when I was about six. An Al Tarf mothership had come to Earth to investigate the status of secret agendas reached between the Anunnaki, the Anchara Alliance and your secret governments. The Beta Canceri were known throughout the Galactic Federation as esteemed scientists and cultural psychologists, whose skills enabled them to understand the relationships and most probable timelines – invaluable tools for evaluating the rate at which Mother Earth's people were advancing toward their divine destiny.

During this assessment, a small group of Al Tarfans arrived at the Sirian mothership. It was one of my first encounters with non-human Beings. Sensing my apprehension, the Al Tarfans quickly transformed all of my fears to Love. After a brief discussion about the fear thresholds humans feel toward the unknown, we left the ship's recreation area. I never forgot that meeting, or my perception of the kindness and Love that flowed from those Beings.

Thereafter, Washta would often use the example of that meeting to illustrate the astonishing diversity of sentient life existing in our galaxy and throughout physicality. His spellbinding lectures and discussions on the Al Tarfans gave me an enhanced appreciation of those galactic Beings and their generous and affectionate civilizations. The key to the Al Tarfans' galactic society is the loving acceptance with which they embrace their mission, their total affirmation of the immense diversity of the former Anchara Alliance, and their utter willingness to use their gifts to enable these formerly dark Beings to manifest Light Bodies.

Status and Location

Originally, Al Tarf had been part of a chain of star-nations captured, 8 million years ago, during an attack by the Draconian Empire on this sector of the galaxy. She succeeded in freeing herself from the police forces abandoned by the Draconians more than 4 million years ago. Soon after, the Star-Nation of Beta Canceri (Al Tarf) was welcomed as a charter member into the Galactic Federation of Light.

The star Beta Canceri is also referred to as Al Tarf, which, in Arabic, means 'End'. Her inhabitants know her as Halal Baktos ('Life of Gracious Joy').

The constellation of Cancer, positioned in the winter skies of the Northern Hemisphere, is surrounded by the constellations of Gemini (Latin: 'Twins'), Leo (Latin: 'Lion'), Canis Major (Latin: 'Big Dog') and Hydra (Latin: 'Sea Serpent'). A glowing orange giant, Al Tarf is Cancer's brightest star and is located approximately 290 Light Years from Earth.

The easiest way to locate Beta Canceri is to find a triangle formed in the head of the constellation of Hydra that is immediately under Al Tarf. It is just below Pollux (Beta Geminorum), one of the bright twin stars in the constellation of Gemini.

Beta Canceri Solar System

Al Tarf consists of six planets, the smallest closest to the sun and the largest most distant. Six moons circle the Al Tarf home world, while another 32 orbit the rest of her solar system. The innermost planet in this system is about one-eighth the size of your Earth, and has no atmosphere. The next world, one and one-half the size of Earth, is more supportive of life. Called Gof Jadai ('Hot, Dry Place'), she is an oven-like planet surrounded by an atmosphere resembling your own. She has three desert-covered continents and six small seas.

The remaining outer planets in the Al Tarf solar system are so-called gas giants similar, in many ways, to the large planets in your Sun's outer solar system. However, because their speeds of rotation are different from those of your Jupiter, Saturn, Uranus or Neptune, their atmospheres contain more irregularities, such as the giant red spot clearly discernible on Jupiter.

Description of Home Worlds

The third planet in the Beta Canceri solar system is a large water world almost twice the size of Mother Earth (nearly 17,000 miles or 27,200 kilometers) in diameter. She contains four large continents surrounded by a series of interconnected oceans. Known for her extremely wet weather, this water world's highly oxygenated atmosphere can produce rainstorms of astonishing ferocity at a moment's notice. Two of her continents are famous for expanses of blue and purple grasses and their adjoining swamps, which, along the coasts, border vast rainforests. A one-layer firmament keeps the planet ice-free and her global temperature consistently semi-tropical.

Like most galactic inhabitants, the Al Tarfans choose to live below their planet's surface in crystal cities that support a population of nearly 600 million. As one of the charter members of the Galactic Federation of Light, Al Tarf acquired technology that is equivalent to any in the galaxy: it powers their cities and helps to provide their citizens with homes, clothing and food.

The Expanding Nature of Galactic Society

All of the Beings discussed in this book are our galactic neighbors. Dwelling many hundreds, or mere tens, of Light Years away, they comprise an astonishing array: reptilians, dinosaurians, amphibians and humans, as well as hybrids of all of these different species. Together, they illustrate the immensity and extraordinary diversity of our galaxy.

The significance of the Al Tarfans lies in their particular area of expertise. They are deemed the galaxy's leading experts on what we refer to as psychic phenomena. Remember that almost all of these Beings lacked Light Bodies and lived in limited consciousness. They had to learn those things that we, here on Earth, innately possess. Most of us simply lack the time to train ourselves in this hidden knowledge, or have been discouraged from manifesting the intuitive sides of our natures.

Having studied these techniques, the Beings from Al Tarf created immense repositories of knowledge, through which they were able to create a Light Body. Other peoples, using this wisdom, can also generate Light Bodies and become fully conscious Beings. Therein lies the Al Tarfans' great talent: that they were able to use this information to shape the conditions for galactic peace between the Anchara Alliance and the Galactic Federation of Light.

How Al Tarf is uniting this Galaxy

The Al Tarfans are making it possible for the Galactic Federation of Light to manifest the latent spirituality of every former Anchara Alliance member, enabling them to integrate and expand their total spiritual potential to create a whole new concept of their distinct cultures and societies. They consider this contribution to be of inestimable significance.

The Al Tarfans are taking these steps because they believe that their star-nation is an enlightened teacher. Their wisdom plays a vital role as an integral link between members of the former Anchara Alliance and the Galactic Federation of Light. In this way, the work of Al Tarf's teachers and liaisons is maintaining the galactic peace and keeping a complex integration process on course.

Physical Description

Although the Al Tarfans are, primarily, an amphibian species, they also exhibit a few reptilian and dinosaurian characteristics (see page 132, figure 11: A typical Al Tarfan). With some major differences, they resemble Earth's frogs and toads. First, they are mainly bipeds. Second, Al Tarfan skin, while smooth and hairless, is noted for its uniquely bright colors, which range across the spectrum from red, orange and green to yellow, blue and brown.

Unlike those of Earth's amphibians, Al Tarfan eyes are not overly prominent, but are large and extend around the sides of the head. They are bright yellow, blue or greenish-yellow. The nose consists only of two small slits above very thin lips. The mouth, when open, is very large, like that of a salamander. The ears are two small, round circles on either side of the head.

Relative to the rest of the body, the head seems disproportionately large. The short neck is thick and powerful, and the body, arms and legs are extremely muscular. There are six long, thin webbed toes and fingers, and the toes are clawed.

Males are slightly shorter than females and stand between 7 and 8 feet (2.13 and 2.44 meters) tall. Females range from 7.5 to 8.5 feet (2.29 to 2.59 meters) in height. Finally, Al Tarfans are recognizable by a series of small, interconnected spots that extend up their back to the top of their head. The species requires only about two to four hours of sleep per day.

The Beings of Halal Baktos have chosen a spectacular array of iridescent flowing gowns. Ribbons or special graphic designs and colors on the garment's shoulder denote rank and commendations.

Figure 11

Aboard spacecraft, they wear a relaxed-fit, two-piece jumpsuit. The waist-length top zips to the trousers, creating what appears to be a one-piece outfit. It also adheres to the colors and graphics that indicate rank and distinctions. Boots are integral to the uniform, and are designed to merge with the trousers as a seemingly undivided whole.

Al Tarfans are renowned for their outstanding psychic abilities in areas such as telepathy, telekinesis, clairaudience and clairvoyance. They are also skilled at manipulating the minds of others. They have amassed vast libraries of scientific and spiritual knowledge, dating back more than 18 million years, as well as a network of highly respected training schools that teach this inner wisdom.

While the Al Tarf language is quite musical, it contains occasional guttural tones.

Ships of Al Tarf

Al Tarf ships are almost mushroom-shaped and are noteworthy for their large, rounded, pyramidal domes. They vary between 150 and 1,000 feet (45.6 and 304 meters) in diameter. Their motherships are exceedingly large and measure from nearly 100 to 4,000 miles (160 to 6,440 kilometers) across. Larger motherships are extremely self-sufficient and usually keep only to deep space.

16

The Star-Nation of Rigel

During his history lessons, Washta was quick to examine the unthinkable horrors of the many galactic wars. Through many millions of years of hostilities, the soldiers and generals of Rigel conspicuously distinguished themselves. Like the Sigma Draconians, the Rigelians were lauded for the illustrious military leadership they provided the League of Orion. The Rigelian military and its leaders, a ruling cabal of nine senior generals, were notorious for their skilled but tyrannical control of the League's armed forces and police. When, approximately 1,000,000 years ago, the League attacked Earth's solar system, they proved their cunning in lightning strikes that decimated the solar system and left Mars and Venus in their current states of devastation.

Eventually, their expertise in war also led them to become a major developer of military weaponry and armed spacecraft. Indeed, it wasn't long before military engineers from Rigel were assigned to accompany their counterparts from Sigma Draconis to spread their advanced weapons technologies to every sector of the Anchara Alliance.

Their ingenuity produced a dark society that was becoming increasingly fond of its ever-growing militarism. It made their immediate rulers on Bellatrix (Gamma Orion) suspicious of the Rigelians' motives. Secretly, the Bellatricians worried that, by some remote chance, the Rigelians might actually seize control of the League. Their fears evaporated when Anchara made a solemn declaration of peace.

In the mid-1990s, by direct decree of their creator-god, Anchara, the League of Orion and the former Anchara Alliance ended their protracted hostilities. Now that these formerly fierce opponents are about to become our neighbors, it is time for us to welcome them into the Galactic Federation of Light. For that very reason, we must learn about them and about their adaptation to an entirely new set of realities. Rigel is only one star-nation of many about which we can learn as we prepare to receive them as our galactic neighbors.

That diligence for peace became the new enthusiasm of the military rulers of Rigel (Beta Orion). Once all hostilities had ceased, and in accordance with similar directives issued by the Sigma Draconians, they gave immediate orders for all Rigelian-led fleets to return to their home worlds. There, they were either disbanded or sworn in as members of the newly integrated Galactic Federation Science and Exploration (S&E) fleets. Then, recently committed to the ensuing Treaty of Anchara, the Beings of the Star-Nation of Rigel participated in the disintegration of the League of Orion. And, soon after sharing in the creation of the new Orion Regional Federation Council, they became a separate member-star-nation of the Galactic Federation of Light.

Present Status and Location

Rigel began as an armed outpost of the Draconian Empire approximately 15 million years ago. Later, it became part of the League of Orion and served as military headquarters for this sector of the former Anchara Alliance. Finally, eight years ago, the Star-Nation of Beta Orion (Rigel) was welcomed into the Galactic Federation of Light.

The star Beta Orion is also known as Rigel, which in Arabic means 'Foot'. Her inhabitants refer to Rigel as Hakkos'Q'Smaq 'Daq ('Great Blue Holy Place'). Rigel, the brightest star in Orion, is located about 770 Light Years from Earth.

On a winter night in the Northern Hemisphere, you will recognize the constellation of Orion (Greek: 'Hunter') as a distant cluster of larger-magnitude stars. Its familiar shape often serves as a guide by which other stars and star-groups can be located. Orion is positioned between the constellations of Taurus (Greek: 'Bull') and Canis Major (Latin: 'Big Dog'), and just below that of

Auriga (Latin: 'Charioteer').

The easiest way to find Beta Orion or Rigel is simply to look for the famous Belt of Orion. This row of three bright stars is located at the very center of the constellation of Orion. Just to the right and slightly below Orion's Belt, you will see a bright blue star. It is Beta Orion, or Rigel.

Rigelian Solar System

The solar system of Rigel (Beta Orion) contains twelve planets. Of them, the third world from Rigel is almost the same size as Venus. Her atmosphere, like that of Venus, is famously thick and stinging, a vestige of her use by Beta Orion's military as a testing site for weapons that would later be used in many galactic wars.

The next planet, fourth from the Rigelian sun, is more hospitable to life. Much larger than Earth, she is enveloped in an atmosphere similar to your own. This hot, semi-arid planet is favored with an extraordinarily varied ecosystem. Her lands are inhabited mainly by reptilians and her seas by large, crude and ancient-looking fishes, as well as by bizarre worms and an assortment of crab-like creatures. In this desert terrain, the Rigelian military has constructed scores of potential working scenarios to prepare their officers for combat operations.

The last six outer planets in the Hakkos'Q'Smaq'Daq solar system are gas giants that, although smaller, in other ways resemble the large planets of your Sun's outer solar system. However, the speed at which they rotate is faster, for the most part, than that of your Jupiter, Saturn, Uranus or Neptune.

Three of these planets are surrounded by ring systems. The rings of one, equal or far superior to those of Saturn, formed when a number of erratic comets and large space flotsam or asteroids collided with this planet's eight small, inner moons. A sequence of events hurtled these moons too close. Three of them exploded, causing a series of varicolored rings. Such an occurrence is commonplace in most solar systems of our galaxy and frequently produces some magnificent, multi-colored planetary ring systems.

Description of Home Worlds

Beta Orion consists of two main home worlds: a very hot, semi-arid planet and a lush water world. The first is a large, dry planet, sixth from the sun, called Sak'Quom'Kla'Deq' ('Sacred Desert World'). She is 11,000 miles (17,600 kilometers) in diameter and has thirteen moons, the largest of which has a thick, livable atmosphere and is half the size of Earth's moon. A headquarters, established on this moon after its solar system was first inhabited, quickly became a major military outpost of the Rigel government.

Since this world resembles many of the principal home worlds in the Draconian Empire and the League of Orion, she has become a major center for ritual. Temples are strewn across many of her continents. The main temple site, known as Khom'Boq'Dklum ('Temples of the Ancestors') and found on Sak'Quom'Kla'Deq's main nodal point, occupies both banks of the longest river on the largest of this world's five continents. Military leaders of the League of Orion came here to entreat Anchara's help in achieving victories in their many galactic wars.

The second planet, called 'Jhok'Gko'Jhlom' ('Home Land'), is a true water world. She is somewhat larger than the first home world and consists of seven continents. While two are as parched and barren as those on Sak'Quom'Kla'Deq', the other five each contain inland seas that render their interiors lush with vegetation. Purple-veined red or blue mountains encircle the Rigelian capital, which overlooks the west coast of the very largest inland sea on the planet's vastest continent. Here stands a vibrant urban center, alive with residential areas, districts for commerce and trade, temples, government buildings, military command complexes and institutions of higher learning.

The Importance and Changing Nature of Rigelian Society

The Rigelians are the Orion League's revered scientists/warriors. Soon after the Anchara Treaties were concluded, the Rigelians, realizing that war was no longer integral to their culture, set out to found a new society. After having reviewed the history of their political union and weighed their current circumstances, the Rigelians issued fresh directives based upon Anchara's new decrees for the creation of a new society.

The Rigelians decided, initially, to focus their passion for science and astronomy on the transformation of star-nations that had belonged to the Orion League. Later, they agreed, instead, to entrust this wisdom to all of the star-nations and empires that once had been part of the Anchara Alliance. The Rigelians, as former principal members of the Alliance, embraced the unique concept of a living, sacred planet.

As Beings who cherished the wonder of planets and stars, and of all life, the Rigelians resolved to find a constructive use for their veneration. They were eager to discover to what extent the complexities of galactic society could be applied to Rigel and her peoples. Rather than science warriors, they wanted to become science guardians of their planet and of every planet in the Rigelian system, and to serve as custodians of the many planets and suns in the once-vast former Anchara Alliance.

Accordingly, they initiated an aggressive campaign to give the many different Beings in the Alliance an understanding of guardianship. Guardian service has been their great gift, and they consider it of vital importance in every situation. The Rigelians are committed to ensure that these changes come to pass. They have applied the same zeal they felt for war and redirected it toward peace. In actual fact, they have become the celebrated peace warrior-guardians of the entire former Anchara Alliance.

Part of the process has involved a reshaping of their societal and governmental structure. Like most Alliance societies, the Rigelians were primarily hierarchical, controlled by an elite governing body. To follow direct orders from the Draconian Empire's major ruling council was considered an act of great respect. They applied that same attitude in carrying out the many decrees ordained in the Anchara Treaties.

All of these groups are working diligently to transform their societies from a hierarchical model to ones in which the lower castes, once treated like slaves, are given a greater voice in their society's decision-making processes. Now, in a switch of philosophical direction, the Rigelians cherish life: as guardians of other worlds and star systems, they now understand the universal need for Love.

The Rigelian social order is changing from a hierarchy based on power to one founded upon recognition of the needs, creativity and highest potential of every Being in their society. This is a dramatic reversal. The Rigelians are a prime example of abrupt changes such as these. They also exemplify the way energies unleashed by the Anchara Treaties are transforming our galaxy.

Physical Description

The predominant species in the Rigel star system is a dinosaurian/amphibian (shape-shifter) hybrid that migrated from the constellation of Cancer approximately 15 million years ago. It is marked by extreme scaliness, with a scattering of prominent ridges.

A wide crest surrounds the skull at forehead level and runs down the back of the head to the neck, where it connects to a narrow ridge that extends down the middle of the back. The eyes, average in size, are set on either side of a very small nose. The mouth is edged in thin, dark lips that stretch from one side of the head to the other. An unusually smooth hollow, 5 inches (12.7 cm) in diameter, on either side of the head and just behind the eyes, is the only indication of otherwise almost non-existent ears.

Rigelian eyes are brown or dull yellow and resemble those of Earth's amphibians. Their skin, which is green, yellow, brown or red, has both dinosaurian scaliness and the smooth shine of an amphibian.

This Being is a biped. It has thin hands with four long, clawed fingers and six-toed feet that end in short, very sharp claws. A thick, crocodile-like tail extends just beyond its feet. The male, shorter than the female, ranges in height from 7 to 8.5 feet (2.44 to 2.59 meters), while the female stands between 8 and 9.25 feet (2.6 and 2.81 meters) tall. Rigelians need from four to five hours of sleep per day.

The clothes of the inhabitants of Beta Orion resemble most others in the former Anchara Alliance. The Beings of Jhok'Gko'Jhlom chose an array of highly unique, layered robes lined with multi-hued, flowing blouses. Epaulettes inscribed with special graphic designs and the colors of command are worn on the shoulder of the outer costume to indicate the wearer's rank and commendations.

Aboard spacecraft, the outfit changes to a two-piece jumpsuit. Most often, it is silver or gray, and bears the color codes and special graphic designs that denote the individual's rank and insignia. Boots are integral to this uniform and merge with the pants in a seemingly undivided whole.

The Rigelians are renowned for their outstanding leadership skills and for their detailed knowledge of warfare and geology.

During the past six million years, they have commanded the entire military forces of the former Alliance for this sector of the galaxy. As part of this responsibility, they undertook a comprehensive geological survey of all the star systems that are a part of this galactic subdivision.

Rigelian language is guttural, with low-pitched croaks and hisses.

Ships of Rigel

Two types of Rigelian ships are part of the first contact Earth fleet. The first, an all-purpose scout ship, is used primarily as part of the observation force that constantly monitors your planet. While some craft look like ladybugs, others resemble the standard saucer shape. Both measure between 50 and 300 feet (15.2 and 91.2 meters) in length.

The second type, a deep space command mothership, varies from 10 to 12,000 miles (16 to 19,200 kilometers). Lens-shaped, it looks either like large, irregularly stacked teardrops or immense spheres. It serves as carrier for 40,000 science liaison officers who co-ordinate the preliminary data analysis from the sector quadrants to which this mothership is assigned.

Part VI

Mixed Species

An Introduction from Other Beings

The remaining groups of star-nations explored in this book are those that support mixed populations, such as the humans and sentient bears of Tau Ceti, or the humans and amphibian/reptilian hybrids of Procyon. Together, these worlds form a microcosm of the many star-nations introduced in this volume's previous sections.

And, like the other star-nations you have visited here, these, despite a few obvious difficulties, were able to join together to form working, successful star-nations. They are living examples of how a host of diverse cultures, languages and life forms can bridge their differences to create a flourishing and harmonious galaxy.

Now, this great confluence of star-nations, formed from a need to embrace diversity and a yearning to express their cultures and their joys in new ways, greets you! Our worlds are much like those you have already explored except that, here, the vast multiplicities of worlds – water, semi-arid and even swampy – coexist peacefully in a most wondrous miscellany.

Our solar systems are unique in the type of planets that exist in proximate orbit, and we have grown to love the vast range of possibilities that they represent. These solar systems also encompass a wide variety of suns: the energy that each one generates has produced the great galactic mixture that we call 'home'. Solar systems such as these form the majority in this galaxy. One sentient species or another inhabits almost every one.

We are the odd lot: worlds that, for any number of reasons, were settled by a multitude of distinct, sentient species. Yet we endured, despite wars and contradictory cultures, and, over the years, founded star-nations that truly embody the utmost in cultural diversity to build a totally unified star-nation.

We invite you, someday soon, to witness this astonishing diversity in action. Until then, please read these chapters to acquire useful and specialized knowledge of our way of life, and to appreciate the unparalleled symmetry of our multitudinous solar systems.

17

The Star-Nation of Aldebaran

Frequently, Washta would recount to me the lengthy history of the Star-Nation of Aldebaran. This grand domain, located in the constellation of Taurus, was originally a member of the Anchara Alliance, where they served as master diplomats in the Draconian Empire and the League of Orion. The Aldebaran leaders, a ruling clique of 12 senior diplomats, were honored for their unique tact and often brilliant diplomatic coups. Then, approximately 800,000 years ago, they chose to leave the Alliance and become an independent, neutral star-nation. How they did it is an extraordinary story.

Their diplomatic skills eventually led the Aldebarans to also become a major developer of foreign strategies for the Eta and Alpha Draconians. This gave them many opportunities to free themselves of the ever-present police and military forces that obstructed all those associated with the Draconian Empire. At the right moment, during a brief truce, the Aldebarans, in the presence of Galactic Federation fleets, declared their neutrality. A few millennia later – just less than 800,000 years ago – the Aldebarans became a full-fledged member of the Galactic Federation of Light.

My first encounter with a group from the Star-Nation of Aldebaran occurred when I was about nine. An Aldebaran mothership had come to Earth to confirm the status of diplomatic relationships existing between Earth's secret governments, their uneasy extraterrestrial masters (the Anunnaki) and other members of the Draconian Empire. The Aldebarans, famous throughout the Galactic Federation as superlative diplomats, governmental researchers and artists, were either human hybrids or reptilians. I was able to greet a small group of them when they arrived to exchange data with their Sirian counterparts. It was one of my first meetings with reptilians. My initial thrill of horror was replaced, soon enough, by great joy at their open kindness.

Along with the Pleiadeans and the Sirians, the Aldebarans form one of the Galactic Federation of Light's 14 original Regional Federation Councils, the Sirian Regional Federation Council.

Present Status and Location

Originally, Aldebaran was settled by a native reptilian species. Later, about 20 million years ago, it became an armed outpost of the Draconian Empire. Subsequently, Aldebaran was annexed to the League of Orion and, as such, was designated this sector's major diplomatic corps for the former Anchara Alliance. Finally, nearly 800,000 years ago, the Galactic Federation welcomed the Star-Nation of Alpha Tauri (Aldebaran) into its membership.

The star Alpha Tauri is also known as Aldebaran, which in Arabic means 'Follower of Pleiades'. Her inhabitants refer to her as Qak'Sak'Dok'Masa'Doq ('Sacred Orange Life-Giver'). Aldebaran, the brightest star in Taurus, is located approximately 68 Light Years from Earth.

On a winter night in the Northern Hemisphere, you will see the constellation of Taurus (Greek: 'Bull') just northwest of Orion (Greek: 'Hunter') and between Auriga (Latin: 'Charioteer') and Gemini (Greek: 'Twins'). Orion's familiar shape makes it a useful pointer by which to find other stars and star-groups. Orion is located between the constellations of Taurus and Canis Major (Latin: 'Big Dog'), and just below that of Auriga.

The easiest way to distinguish the bright orange star Aldebaran (Alpha Tauri) is to look for the famous 'Belt', which is situated at the very center of the constellation of Orion. You will observe Aldebaran just above and to the right of Orion, and directly in front of and below the famous Pleiades star-cluster.

Aldebaran Solar System

The solar system of Alpha Tauri contains eight planets. The

innermost world, slightly more than one-tenth the size of your Earth, has an extremely thin atmosphere filled with ionic discharges that begin in her bizarre dense, purple-blue clouds. For that reason, the Aldebarans call her Jaq'K'mLoq ('Place of Storms').

The third planet, nearly three-quarters the size of Earth, is more congenial and has an atmosphere that resembles your own. Hot and semi-arid, she contains several large continents that are blanketed by high coastal mountain ranges and vast inland deserts.

Six seas encircle these continents. On one, a soaring mountain range extends, north to south, through its heart; on another, a broad inland ocean links to other surrounding seas by way of a deep crevasse at the southernmost tip of its western coastal mountains. Here, there is a manifold variety of life. While reptilians enjoy land superiority, the seas are alive with enormous fish and other water creatures that we would find exceedingly odd. The Beings of Aldebaran reserve this forbidding world as a prison planet for exiles or criminals.

The final three, most outward, planets in the Qak'Sak'Dok'-Masa'Doq solar system are many-sized gas giants that share remarkable similarities to the large planets in your Sun's outer solar system. However, unlike your Jupiter, Saturn, Uranus or Neptune, they rotate much more rapidly. They also tend to generate odd, vortex-like windstorms, which trace constantly changing, purple-blue waves and multi-colored swirls across their outer atmospheres.

Description of Home Worlds

Aldebaran consists of two main home worlds: a very hot, semi-arid world closer to the sun and, slightly farther away, a lush water world. The first planet, second from the sun, is called Sta'Ql'kMaqt'Sqo ('Holy Lands of Ours'). She is 7,000 miles (11,300 kilometers) in diameter and has four moons, the two largest of which have a thick, livable atmosphere and are the size of your own moon. The environment on the planet below them is extremely harsh, intensely hot and uninviting.

Surprisingly, despite her seemingly barren landscape, this planet's ecosystem, her marine, insect and reptilian life in particular, is extraordinarily diverse. This is the original home world of the Aldebaran reptilians, and the seat of a flourishing and sophisticated civilization. Temple sites are scattered across her five continents. At the center of the largest continent sits the capital, which surrounds an immense cave complex considered to be the birthplace of the Aldebarans' first sentient ancestors. Beside the caves is their spacious ritual center. Known as Haq'Dkq'om'So'Grak ('Place of the Ancestors'), this site occupies both banks of this continent's longest river. Aldebaran's leaders came here to beseech their ancestors to help them.

The second home world, called Mak' Shada'lan ('Changed Water Wonder Place'), is a true water world. She was terra-formed by the Draconian Empire more than two million years ago to accommodate human hybrid Aldebarans. Slightly larger than the first home world, she contains seven continents. Although three are as dry and barren as those on Sta'Ql'kMaqt'Sqo, the variously-sized inland seas of the other four create conditions that make their interiors more verdant. On the eastern shore of an inland sea on the most extensive continent stands this world's capital - a bustling city filled with temples, government buildings, housing and shopping centers and institutions of higher learning.

Description of Aldebaran Galactic Society

Humans living in the Aldebaran planetary system enjoy a galactic society. Its reptilian society has traditionally been very hierarchical: over the years, however, they, too, have become more accessible. As a result, the Aldebaran social order and the Aldebaran Star-Nation Councils have grown much more similar to others throughout the Galactic Federation of Light. Now, they are open and based on a clan type of system. True clans did not exist as such in the earlier reptilian society. Their system, based on a hierarchical model, contained both an elite and a governing council (a subordinate group that controlled various aspects of the society). This ruling council oversaw the training of warriors, supervised the military and regulated the economy.

On the lowest rung of reptilian society was the slave class. As it opens to the Light, this group, too, has become more receptive, more capable of adopting a galactic social order. Thus, even at its bottom levels, the reptilians have grown to more closely resemble a galactic society.

Between approximately 810,000 and 850,000 years ago, the Aldebaran reptilian society, seeking a way to survive in the galaxy and declare their neutrality, broke away from the Anchara Alliance. By the time a human-crewed Science and Exploration fleet from the Andromedan Confederacy approached the Aldebarans, they were incontrovertibly neutral and no longer belonged to the Alliance. For the last three-quarters of a million years, the Aldebaran reptilian society has become very open and democratic. Over the course of time, they have introduced humans into their star-nation and, ultimately, were welcomed into the Galactic Federation of Light. Now, they take an active part in many exploration fleets and are prominent members of the liaison boards of the Galactic Federation of Light.

The reptilians of Aldebaran are extraordinary Beings. Having manifested their Light Bodies, they are enabling many other reptilian societies to understand exactly how the Galactic Federation operates. They are also demonstrating ways in which the complex process of establishing a galactic society can be achieved. Moreover, since their planetary system is one of the major gateways to the Pleiades, the Aldebarans have been influential in its settlement. In summary, we could say that the Pleiadeans have been involved, both positively and negatively, with the reptilians. This is one of their more positive encounters.

Description of the Peoples of the Aldebaran System

The sentient life forms of the Aldebaran solar system are her original inhabitants: a reptilian species and a later human hybrid species.

The reptilian Aldebaran is lizard-like, very scaly and muscular. The skin is multi-colored, in green and blue, or red and green mixed with yellow, black or purple. Eyes are large and round with reptile-like vertical slits of sky-blue, red or gold. The hands, narrower than a human's, consist of four digits and end in a short, sharp claw. The feet have five long toes that, like the fingers, end in short, curved claws. The tail is small and bulbous. The female, slightly taller than the male, has a height of just less than 7 feet (2.13 meters).

The reptilian language is guttural and contains sounds that are difficult for most humans to imitate.

The human hybrid Aldebaran has a vague resemblance to Earth humans. The male is slight in build with a well-proportioned body, head and limbs, and stands between 6 and 7.25 feet (1.8 and

2.2 meters) in height. Females, also, are strong and symmetrical. Their height varies from 5 feet, 8 inches to 6 feet, 7 inches (1.72 to 2.0 meters). Large round or almond-shaped eyes are brown, black, blue, green or hazel. Hair is blonde, brown, black or red. Skin has beige or bronze tones, and is smooth but scaly. Both species require only two to four hours of sleep per day.

Aldebarans are known as distinguished diplomats and skilled artisans. They excel at bringing together groups of uniquely different sentient Beings, and at teaching the art of creative group synergy.

The human Aldebaran language resembles German, but with an almost Chinese tone.

Ships of the Aldebaran Star-Nation

Several types of Aldebaran ships can be observed in Earth's skies. The first is a scientific research scout ship. It is disc-shaped, with a large, curved, circular flight foil attached to its underside. It has a diameter of about 65 feet (19.76 meters) and a height of nearly 40 feet (12.16 meters).

The second, a transport scout ship, is shaped like a large rod and extends between 20 and 80 feet (6.1 and 24.32 meters) in length.

A third craft, an atmospheric mothership, is shaped like a curved rod and measures from 800 feet to 2 miles (243.2 meters to 3.2 kilometers) long.

18

The Great Star Union of Centaurus

Frequently, Washta would describe the degree to which the many human galactic societies can differ in type, style and level of creativity. One example often cited by my astute guide was that of the Great Star Union of Centaurus. The inhabitants of the Centauri Union are acclaimed throughout the Galactic Federation of Light for their subtle diplomacy and highly effective liaisons aboard Science and Exploration (S&E) fleet expeditions. Unofficially, in fact, they are described as the Galactic Federation of Light's principal diplomatic liaisons and ambassadors.

I was about ten when I had my first encounter with a group from the Great Star Union of Centaurus. A Centauri mothership had arrived on Earth to determine the political and technological status of Earth's humanity. Together with the Pegasians, Pleiadeans and Andromedans, the Centaurians were acclaimed throughout the Galactic Federation of Light as outstanding scientists, liaisons and technicians. Many of Earth's specially modified scanners, computer databases, their unique components and programs resulted directly from individual or group innovations of the Great Star Union of Centaurus.

In the course of this lengthy evaluation, a few Centauri liaisons came to the Sirian mothership. It was my first introduction to hybrid human Beings. The Centauri, immediately sensing this, telepathically reassured me of their friendship and their concern for my peace of mind. Their words calmed me and allayed my initial apprehensions. After briefly discussing the true nature of my concerns and observing that fear was instilled in humans long ago in order to control them, we left the recreation area. I have never forgotten that meeting, and retain an abiding memory of their deep kindness, understanding and love.

Time and again, Washta would use this encounter as an example of the incomprehensible multiplicity of sentient life in our galaxy, and throughout physicality. His spellbinding talks and discussions on the Centauri gave me a keen appreciation of these Beings and their ancient civilizations. The key to Centauri galactic society is their innate willingness to embrace, as their mission, the immense diversity of the former Anchara Alliance, and their eagerness to assist these formerly dark Beings in fully adjusting to membership in the Galactic Federation of Light.

Location and Status

The Great Star Union of Centaurus, previously a neutral star league, had been a major arena in many battles of the galactic wars. Nevertheless, she had developed a series of distinctly different galactic societies, which she learned to use to her advantage. Centaurus also had a long history of temporary collaborations with dark star empires of the Anchara Alliance. Owing to her proximity to the headquarters sector of the Galactic Federation of Light, Centaurus has been a valued and enduring partner in the current diplomatic and cultural exchanges between the former dark empires of the Anchara Alliance and the Galactic Federation.

The Great Star Union of Centaurus, which comprises hundreds of star-nations, is located in the constellation of Centaurus (Greek: 'Centaur'), between those of Lupus (Latin: 'Wolf') and Vela (Latin: 'Sail') in the Southern Hemisphere. It is best known for its brightest star, the triple star system Alpha Centauri (also called Rigel Kentaurus). One of those triple stars, Proximi Centauri, 4.3 Light Years from Earth, is our closest known star: its other members are as far as 1,000 Light Years away. The Great Star Union of Centaurus was accepted into the Galactic Federation approximately 1.1 million years ago.

Centauri Cultural Nuances

Galactic societies in the Great Star Union of Centaurus more closely resemble those of the Aldebarans and Altairians than the Lyran/Sirian or Andromedan/Pleiadean models. The significance of the Centaurus system is that it encompasses both human and reptilian star-nations. From two societies has evolved one slightly hierarchical system, which combines the best of the other dual-clan structures. This diversity has brought together two very different civilizations – human and dinosaurian/reptilian – each living in harmony, attaining their societal potentials and, thus, manifesting the sacred prime mission of the Galactic Federation of Light.

Although the clan structures of the Great Star Union of Centaurus differ widely from one sector to another, the most common are variations of the Lyran/Sirian (six clans) and the Andromedan/Pleiadean (twelve clans) models. The Centauri melding of these prototypes into its own exclusive hierarchical system is unique, given that the majority of Centauri galactic societies contain subcultures that have retained their own distinctive language and traditions.

Crucial to this system are their cultural liaisons and counselors. While star-nations such as Lambda Centauri use a Lyran/Sirian model, each of Centauri's two inhabited home worlds contains a rich layer of unique subcultures. Each planet has cultural liaisons who function as semi-official interpreters for the totality of cultures that exist on that world. Moreover, a special interworld cultural liaison board provides creative solutions for any problems that may arise. When this system is interfaced with advanced translator technology and its inhabitants' own natural telepathic abilities, it allows free communication between individuals and groups. What results is a constant flow of information that makes positive use of any differences and allows this multi-faceted society to create many revolutionary innovations on a regular basis.

Yet another way of achieving this lies in the stars that make up Rigel Kentaurus. Their home worlds have adopted the Andromedan/Pleiadean model, which uses 12 clans instead of the Lyran/Sirian six. This model contains clans devoted to counseling and liaison, and to culture. These three clans developed because the Centauri found it easier to maintain separate systems in which to train students in these meaningful pursuits. Each clan serves as a repository of specific wisdoms. The other nine clans can avail themselves of these areas of expertise, or, if they are unable to solve a particular problem, they can consult the one clan of three that seems most capable of solving it.

By embracing the 12-clan system, Rigel Kentaurus can be perceived as a star-nation containing many of the most acclaimed scientific research groups in the galaxy. Rigel's reputation is due, mainly, to the extent to which its modified 12-clan system formally addresses its population's wide-ranging diversity. Consequently, this modified system has been dispersed throughout the Great Star Union of Centaurus.

Centaurian Solar Systems and Description of Some of their Home Worlds

The home worlds of the Centauri range from water worlds similar to Mother Earth to semi-arid realms. Those on which we intend to concentrate are planets in the multiple stars of Proxima Centari and the star, Lambda Centauri. These star-nations are located between 4.39 and 410 Light Years from Earth.

The Home Worlds of Proxima Centauri

Let us begin with the home worlds of the triple stars referred to by your astronomers as Proxima Centauri. We will concentrate primarily on the one star of this trio known as Rigel Kentaurus. First colonized by humans nearly 2.5 million years ago, she contains one of the larger Centaurian water worlds, which her inhabitants refer to as Endo. Endo is one of three planets orbiting the central star of Prima Centauri. She is recognized for her immense oceans, teeming with life, and for her beautiful skies, dazzling with nightglow.

This glow is caused by the outermost layer of the three-layer firmament, which becomes electrified from the coronal discharges from her sun. They fill Endo's night sky with a soft, pastel glow that encompasses every color of the spectrum, particularly blues, greens and violets. In her seas are whales, larger than those of Earth. These mammals calve in mid-ocean island chains located immediately north and south of Endo's equator. The calves and their mothers are honored for their ability to balance and harmonize both the water world of Endo and her inhabitants.

While the fourth planet in this solar system introduced

Centauri's modified clan system, it was the third, orbiting this same sun (that the Centauri call Yosman) that perfected it. This inner planet also encompassed worlds celebrated for their beauty. Semi-arid and volcanic, she contained multi-colored pools of hot mud and pliable rock formations that constantly move and change shape. Humans from Lyra, who colonized this planet, found a world of reddish-blue seas, orange-blue skies and many tiny continents scattered across her surface.

The Home Worlds of Lambda Centauri

This important star system, which your astronomers refer to as Lambda Centauri, also has a smaller, blue companion. Lambda Centauri's 8-planet solar system, located approximately 410 Light Years from Earth, contains two large water worlds. Nearly 1.3 million years ago, on Lambda Centauri's third planet, colonists from Andromeda and Eridanus founded a settlement dedicated to something quite dear to both of them - the advancement of the principles of spiritual science. Due to the nature of her atmosphere and the distance from her sun, her climate was predominantly tropical. Purple-veined, multi-hued mountain chains, some as tall as Earth's Himalayas, rose on most of her 10 small, island-like continents. Fascinating, sweetly singing birds, mammalian and reptilian life forms inhabited these exquisite locales.

The second group of colonists settled a neighboring water world four times larger in diameter and ascertained very quickly that this new home world was even more astounding than the first. Her atmosphere, blowing across the misshapen mountains that lay strewn across the surfaces of her continents, crackled and glowed with a brightness that filled this world with irrepressible energies. Soon, the Centauri, becoming aware of the extraordinariness of this world, erected a magnificent temple, similar in size and layout to those found on Sirius-B and in the constellations of Andromeda and Lyra. Priests and priestesses from the Spiritual Warrior clan on Sirius-B, and from corresponding worlds on Andromeda and Vega in the Lyran constellation, came here to honor this magnificent world and her great healing gift. The singing and glowing atmosphere of this world produced an exhilarating energy that vivified all. Here, soon after, the sacred blue dolphins of Sirius-B were introduced;

their world song further intensified these wondrous healing energies. Ceremonies on this world are, in fact, profoundly connected to those celebrated on the sacred home worlds of Sirius-B. The Great Blue Lodge of Creation has often told Sirian and Andromedan priests and priestesses that this sacred spot in Centaurus is one of the most unique in the Milky Way Galaxy.

The large, outer water world in this solar system is honored as one of the main repositories of historical and cultural information for the Great Star Union of Centaurus. On this watery world covered in vast inland seas, great, swampy estuaries and low-lying mountain ranges, stands a highly regarded university and research center dedicated to the advancement of the study of spiritual sciences. From this institution, distinguished scholar/representatives often travel to the main Galactic Federation of Light institute of spiritual science and culture in the Vega system, or to other influential research institutes in Andromeda. These academics, experts in the Centauri adaptations of galactic society, have trained millions of associates from across the galaxy and take great pride in the rich cultural diversity of Centaurus.

In this chapter, we have explored a handful of the hundreds of home worlds encompassed within the Great Star Union of Centaurus. Each one has a distinct cultural tradition and a unique history. The Centauri selected those we have described as fitting representatives of their worlds' beauty, uniqueness and diversity. The rest are equally splendid and, in their way, just as enchanting. The inhabitants of these worlds are intensely proud of them. To know more about the planets and their peoples, you will have to hear directly from the benevolent Beings who comprise the Great Star Union of Centaurus.

Physical Description

Human Centaurians closely resemble present-day Earth humans. The male is very muscular and well proportioned, and ranges from 6 to 8 feet (1.8 to 2.4 meters) in height. The female, also well-formed but less muscular, stands between 5 feet, 5 inches and 7 feet (1.65 and 2.1 meters) tall. Centaurian hair is blonde, brown, black or red. Skin color is either very dark brown or tan. Eyes, either almond-shaped or round, are brown, black, blue, green or hazel.

The body of the reptilian Centaurian is very scaly, lizardly and muscular, with variegated skin of either blue and green or red and green. The eyes are round and bulging, with reptile-like, vertical slits in either bright red or gold. The hands, narrower than those of a human, contain six digits, and end in razor-sharp, curved claws. The feet have five long toes, ending in the same curved claw as the hands. There is no tail. The female is slightly taller than the male, with a height of just under 8 feet (2.4 meters). Reptilian Centaurians require between 2 and 4 hours of sleep per day.

Renowned as consummate strategists and venerated Federation Liaison Counselors, Centaurians excel at bringing together groups of very different sentient Beings and in achieving their goals peacefully and harmoniously.

The human Centaurian language is guttural and resembles German, but with an inflection similar to Chinese. The Reptilian language is extremely guttural, with sounds that are difficult for humans to imitate.

Centaurian Ships

Two types of Centaurian ships can be observed in Earth's skies. The first, an all-purpose scout, is bell-shaped with a large, lens-like, circular wing on its underside. It is nearly 30 feet (9.1 meters) high, and has a diameter of approximately 45 feet (14 meters).

The second, a command mothership, is cigar-shaped with a small bulge in its middle, and measures approximately 2,000 feet (609.6 meters) long. She serves as a carrier for 350 science liaison officers who co-ordinate the preliminary analysis of data from the sector quadrant to which this mothership is assigned.

19

The Star-Nation of Sabik (Eta Ophiuchi)

Washta would tell me the detailed histories of the star-nations that he deemed important for the advancement of galactic peace and unity. One such, within the Galactic Federation, was the enduring chronicle of the Eta Ophiuchi (Sabik) people. Originally, these limited conscious reptilians had been a neutral star-nation near the outpost stations that encircle the fiercely contested Antares sector. Eventually, Sabik's reptilian society sought help from the Galactic Federation of Light, who sent a succession of colonists from Andromeda and Lyra to defend the settlement.

Over time, the humans taught the reptilians how to develop their own Light Bodies. Moreover, as the reptilian rulers grew in consciousness, they were able to adapt the rudimentary form of clan system common to all galactic societies into a modified version of the prototypical Lyran/Sirian galactic society.

Indeed, as mentioned in Chapter Fifteen, one of the major points separating the various dark empires of the Anchara Alliance from member star-nations of the Galactic Federation is the whole matter of inhabiting Light Bodies. Wishing her people to be servants who lacked the power of thought, Anchara left them the capability to possess Light Bodies, but lacking the ability to manifest them. Instead, she created limited conscious Beings with the capacity for deep emotion, but without the knowledge to connect with Spirit. Anchara communicated with them only by physically manifesting and conversing with her priestesses. In this way, the inhabitants of Eta Ophiuchi were fully susceptible to emotional and psychological manipulation, meted out by those whom Anchara chose to rule her dark domains. These Beings, however, wished to reclaim the ability to manifest their Light Bodies and become fully conscious.

The Beings of Sabik, having attained this goal, augmented their new knowledge by creating their galactic society in a most original way. As a now-combined star-nation, they joined the Galactic Federation with two missions. First: to demonstrate how such dissimilar and even antagonistic societies can come together and co-exist in harmony, with each honoring and upholding the other's cultural distinctness. Second: to prove to their Anchara Alliance kin that the complete antithesis of their warlike and vicious lifestyles was possible indeed. They pledged to use this knowledge in the cause of freeing oppressed star-nations of the Anchara Alliance. Subsequently, they joined the Libra Regional Council, one of the Galactic Federation of Light's original 14 Regional Federation Councils. The Star-Nation of Eta Ophiuchi was welcomed into the Galactic Federation of Light approximately 2.8 million years ago.

I first encountered a group from the Star-Nation of Eta Ophiuchi when I was about eleven. Under orders from the Galactic Ascended Masters Councils, a Sabik mothership had come to Earth to monitor this solar system and assess its potential for future first contact. With their flair for understanding the rela-tionships unfolding between certain elements in our planet's societies, and using details provided by the Ascended Masters, they were able to draw up the most probable timelines for first contact. Such information was invaluable in ascertaining the rate at which Mother Earth's people were advancing toward their divine destiny.

During this lengthy evaluation, a small party of Sabik reptilian liaison counselors arrived at our Sirian mothership. It was my fourth encounter with non-human Beings. The Sabik counselors, acutely aware of my uncertainty, immediately changed my every fear to joy. I have never forgotten the immensely tender love I felt from these Beings. I look forward to meeting them again in the future.

Often, afterwards, Washta would use that meeting to highlight the wondrous diversity of sentient life that exists throughout our galaxy and the whole of physicality. His captivating lessons and talks on the Eta Ophiuchians and the many other star-nations gave me a heightened appreciation of these galactic Beings and their kind and compassionate civilizations. The key to the Eta Ophiuchians' galactic society is the loving acceptance with which they embrace their mission, their earnest affirmation of the enormous diversity of the former Anchara Alliance, and their total spontaneity in empowering these formerly dark entities to manifest Light Bodies and create their own galactic societies.

Present Status and Location

Originally a society of neutral reptilians, Eta Ophiuchi approached the Galactic Federation of Light to establish a special human defense colony on their star-nation. As a result, human colonists were sent there from the Andromedan Confederacy and various other human star-nations in the constellation of Lyra. The Star-Nation of Eta Ophiuchi or Sabik (Arabic: 'Preceding'), about 84 Light Years from Earth, was admitted into the Galactic Federation of Light nearly 2.8 million years ago.

The constellation of Ophiuchus (Greek: 'Serpent Bearer') is a major summer star-group in the night skies of your Northern Hemisphere. It is located between the constellations of Hercules (Latin: 'Strong Man'), Scorpius (Greek: 'Scorpion') and Serpens (Latin: 'Snake Man'). Ophiuchus' brightest star, Alpha Ophiuchi, is referred to in Arabic as Ras Alhague ('Head of the Snake Man').

Eta Ophiuchi (Sabik) is one of the brighter stars in the constellation of Ophiuchus. To find it, spot the vivid red giant in Scorpius, Antares (Greek: 'Rival of Mars') or Alpha Scorpi. Eta Ophiuchi is located just above Antares in the constellation of Scorpius.

Eta Ophiuchi Solar System

The solar system of Eta Ophiuchi consists of eight planets. Of the two innermost planets, one is one-eighth the size of your Earth, the other slightly larger. The smaller, inner one is barren, and bakes in the blazing energies emanating from her Sun, Se'DoQ'Gwa'Loq ('Holy Essence, Giver of Great Light'). The atmosphere of the larger one is very thin – similar, in many respects, to Earth's lone moon. Like Earth's moon, too, she is blanketed with enormous craters, and sparse, shallow lakes lie far beneath her surface. However, unlike your moon, she exhibits fantastic auroral sequences at her poles and equator. These occur when electrical discharges, emanating from the two miniature moons that collect her sun's ionic ejections, occasionally hurl them toward her surface.

The next planet, hot and with an atmosphere thicker than your own, is more amenable to life. A great many life forms exist here. Among her land creatures, reptilians of varying descriptions are predominant. Many sizes and kinds of grotesque fish, as well as abundant species of crab-like creatures, govern her seas.

The three most distant planets of the Se'DoQ'Gwa'Loq solar system have many similarities to the larger planets of your Sun's outer solar system. Unlike Jupiter, Saturn, Uranus or Neptune, however, they have a much more rapid rotation.

Description of Home Worlds

Eta Ophiuchi is unique in that she contains two completely different water worlds. Reptilians live on a swampy water planet, while humans inhabit one that closely resembles Mother Earth.

The first water world, fourth from their sun, is a large sphere, 8,500 miles (13,600 kilometers) in diameter, containing six immense seas and four vast continents. Called Dak'Gugj'BoQh ('Wet, Swampy Home'), this planet has six moons, the two largest of which have a thick, livable atmosphere and are half the size of Earth's moon.

Below these six moons spins a marshy, tropical planet. Each of her four continents is surrounded by low, coastal hills that spill down to wide seaside swamps and into their deepest interior. The damp, humid conditions and heavy clouds create very long rain cycles and extremely wet continental interiors. Rivers, flowing from aquifers only an eighth of a mile (less than 200 meters) below her surface, meander through inland forests that seem more like endless swamps. Hills of varying elevations dot these wetlands, creating tropical meadows that border steaming jungles. Small, lush coastline forests that originated in narrow coastal mountain chains stretch down to the sea's edge. These features, too, produce swampy areas. The air here, rich in oxygen and other vital gases, helps to support a diverse ecosystem.

The second planet, called Ja Da Singh Lah ('Joyful Place of Light'), is a more Earth-like water world. She is home to the human colony whom the original Eta Ophiuchi invited on-planet almost three million years ago. This world, the same size as her sister planet, contains seven continents, none as marshy as those on Dak'Gugj'BoQh. The temperate and semi-tropical environments to be found on these continents are home to small and extraordinary dinosaurian and reptilian life forms that compete with larger mammalian creatures.

As in all human galactic societies, the main settlements of this hollow planet are located in crystal cities beneath its surface. Here, the human Eta Ophiuchians have established their sacred and cultural sites.

Galactic Society of Eta Ophiuchi

The Beings of Eta Ophiuchi created their own unique galactic society by modifying the original six-clan Lyran/Sirian structure and adding two more clans. In such a way, they have emulated the eight-clan structure of their original reptilian inhabitants.

As in the classic model, all of these clans form their own main clan governing councils. These councils, in turn, send representatives to Eta Ophiuchi's Main Governing Council. Here, though, a significant difference: during sessions of this latter council, distinguished liaisons from the two 'new' clans serve as special presiding referees to assist council members in solving whatever problems may arise.

As you have observed with other societies within the Galactic Federation where reptilian and human groups co-exist, the Beings of Eta Ophiuchi have succeeded in creating a star-nation that is harmonious and respectful of each other's cultures.

The reptilian group, with its long history of maintaining a clan-like system, is actually almost a reptilian version of galactic society. The Beings of Eta Ophiuchi take pride in this achievement and are eager to showcase it to others.

Their major export in the galaxy is a talent for explaining to others how easily reptilians and humans can co-exist. Now they are even able to form relationships with one another. This has resulted in frequent liaison work with the Beings of Eta Draconis, and a strong bond is developing between them. There is a powerful historical connection between the human inhabitants of the Eta Ophiuchi Star-Nation and the many human colonies located in the constellation of Hercules.

Physical Description of Inhabitants

Sentient life forms in the Sabik solar system consist of its original reptilian inhabitants and a later, colonizing human species. Let us examine the physical appearance of each in turn.

To some extent, the human Eta Ophiuchian resembles the present-day Earth human. The male is powerfully built and well proportioned. The female is shapely but less muscular. Males range from nearly 6 to almost 8 feet (1.8 to 2.4 meters) in height: females stand between 5 feet, 5 inches and 7 feet, 6 inches (1.65 and 2.29 meters) tall. Skin is either very dark brown or slightly tanned, while hair is blonde, brown, black or red. Round or almond-shaped eyes can be brown, black, blue, green or hazel. Human Eta Ophiuchi need only about two hours of sleep a day.

The body of the reptilian Eta Ophiuchian is very lizardly and muscular, and bears a close resemblance to the many reptilian species in the Orion constellation. With a height of just under 8 feet (2.4 meters), the female stands slightly taller than the male. Eta Ophiuchian skin is scaly, with patches of blue and green or red and green. Its hands, narrower than a human's, have six digits that end in a razor-sharp, curved claw: the feet, with five long toes, have the same curved claw. Eyes are round and bulging, with reptile-like, vertical slits of bright red or gold. The tail is short and slender. Reptilian Eta Ophiuchians require almost four hours of sleep per day.

Eta Ophiuchians are celebrated as accomplished explorers and astute Galactic Federation Liaison Counselors. They excel at first contact missions and at bringing together vastly different sentient beings.

The human language, like Chinese, has a singsong quality, with occasional guttural sounds. By contrast, the reptilian language is extremely guttural, with many sounds that humans find difficult to imitate.

Ships of Eta Ophiuchi

Two types of Eta Ophiuchian ships can be seen in Earth's skies. The first, an all-purpose scout, is saucer-shaped with a large, lens-like, circular wing attached to its underside. It has a diameter of approximately 45 feet (14 meters) and is about 30 feet (9.1 meters) high.

The second, a command mothership, is shaped like a very

slender cigar with a small bulge in its middle, and is close to 2,000 feet (more than 608 meters) long. She serves as a carrier for 350 science liaison officers who co-ordinate the preliminary analysis of data from the sector quadrant to which this mothership is assigned.

20

The Star-Nation of Tau Ceti

Washta, my Galactic Federation of Light guide and mentor, would delight in explaining to me the importance of Love and divine service. He said that, through devotion to the Creator and the divine plan, your True Self, your galactic society and your present physical essence are capable of fully expressing and graciously honoring your true life purpose. Thus, it is possible for you, at any one time, to determine your life's course and to make the right choices in achieving your goals. By connecting you to your creative abilities, this manifested inner purpose allows you to devise imaginative solutions to any possible problem. It also frees you to use your true talents to manifest new ideas, produce beautiful art and discover great inventions. One star-nation that has honed this process to its highest degree is the Star-Nation of Tau Ceti.

During one of his lessons, Washta introduced me to several Tau Ceti engineers, assigned as liaisons to the various work groups that oversaw the Sirian mothership's power plant and other navigational devices. They were part of an exchange program between Sirius-B and the many star-nations she had helped to colonize.

Tela, the head of this liaison group, was an engineer, trained on his home world of Tau Ceti and later on Sirius-B. He and his closeness, Jada, another group member, willingly answered my questions about Love and divine service. Our discussion centered on their Tau Ceti home world of Agada, which means 'divine Love'. Its inhabitants were taught that the divine connections with your True Self are precious and that this inner Love leads to a graceful divine Love, the 'heart' of Tau Ceti society.

The Tau Ceti civilization was centered on the creation of methods that would enhance the applications of 'divine Love' within a galactic society. 'Divine Love' could assist any galactic society in carrying out its responsibilities to its inhabitants, to its society as a whole, to its solar system and to the Milky Way Galaxy. Indeed, entire institutes, highly honored by the Galactic Federation of Light, had been established to teach methods of achieving greater resonance with this sacred process.

Status and Location

The Star-Nation of Tau Ceti, which is about 11.8 Light Years from Earth, was welcomed into the Galactic Federation of Light nearly 2.5 million years ago. Originally, Tau Ceti was a star-nation of neutral, bear-like mammals. Approximately 2.4 million years ago, they approached the Galactic Federation of Light to ask that a special human defense colony from the constellation of Hercules be located on the fourth planet of their system.

The constellation of Cetus (Greek: 'Whale') is a major autumn star-cluster in the night sky of your Northern Hemisphere. Cetus is located between the constellations of Pisces (Latin: 'Fish'), Aries (Latin: 'Ram') and Eridanus (Greek: 'River'). Its brightest star is Beta Ceti or Diphda, which in Arabic means 'Frog'.

To find Tau Ceti, a sun-like star in the constellation of Cetus, scan the southern region of the autumn sky for the bright star in Piscis Austrinus (Latin: 'Southern Fish'), Fomalhaut (Arabic: 'Mouth of the Fish'). To the immediate left of Fomalhaut is the bright star, Diphda, which forms part of the whale's head. To Diphda's lower left is another, slightly darker star: Tau Ceti.

Tau Cetean Solar System

The solar system of Tau Ceti or Lakwedak ('Light of Salvation') consists of twelve planets, with, as in most solar systems, the two smallest closest to the sun and the largest farthest away. The two innermost planets, one-quarter the size of your Earth, have no atmosphere.

The fifth planet from the Tau Ceti sun is slightly more

hospitable to life. Hot and semi-arid by nature, she is barely larger than Earth, and possesses an atmosphere similar to your own. Eight interlaced oceans surround her four spacious continents. Within her diverse ecosystem, reptiles and insects predominate on land, while a fascinating array of fishes control the seas. Strange species of flora and fauna that exist and thrive here are found nowhere else in this solar system.

The Lakwedak solar system's three outmost planets are 'gas giants' that in many ways resemble the large planets of your Sun's outer solar system. Like your Jupiter, these gas giants' atmospheres display irregularities, such as bright blue and purple spots. The tenth and eleventh worlds are encircled by a system of rings even more complex than those of Saturn.

Description of Home Worlds

Tau Ceti has two main home worlds: a lush forest planet and a true water world. The first, third from the sun, is noted for its magnificent woodlands and beautiful mountains. Known as Hashabha ('Forest Home'), she is 8,500 miles (13,600 kilometers) in diameter. Hashabha has four moons, the largest two of which have a thick, livable atmosphere and are almost three-quarters the size of Mother Earth's moon. After special scientific stations were established on Hashabha, both of these moons quickly became influential centers of science research for the Tau Ceti government.

The planet below them is lush and beautiful. Hashabha consists of five spacious continents surrounded by seven broad oceans. Rimmed by the broken remnants of many coastal mountain ranges, the interiors of her continents are covered in verdant woodlands and occasional large, grassy meadows. Rivers flow from the planet's interior aquifers to her surface and meander through huge inland forests. Still other rivers have their origins in tangled chains of mountain lakes that are part of a vast inland waterway. The air, rich in oxygen and other vital gases, supports a remarkably diverse and vibrant ecosystem.

Owing to her enormous beauty and her inhabitants' deep and boundless Love for her, this planet has become a sought-after ritual center. Temple sites are scattered across her continents. An imposing settlement on the largest continent, known as Hakhabalah ('Spiritual Navel of the World'), is located at the exact center node of the planet. Priests and priestesses of the bear-people of Tau Ceti come here to serve their world and demonstrate their immense Love for her.

The second home world, called Wa-Ta-Ma-Kka ('Spiritual Water Land'), is a true water world. She is somewhat larger than the first and contains seven continents: of these, three are almost as luxuriant as those of Hashabha. Moreover, three continents enclose inland seas that cleave their interiors, and a wide-ranging system of rivers that descends from the low-lying mountains flanking these oceans and flows toward vast interior seas. More than two million years ago, a human colony was established on this planet. A main ritual settlement on the third largest continent is crowded with temples, building complexes and schools of higher learning that concentrate on the history and culture of both Tau Ceti peoples.

Tau Cetean Galactic Society

The Beings of Tau Ceti have created their own unique eight-clan galactic society, a modification of the original six Lyran/Sirian clans: Spiritual Warrior; Administration; Science; Science Engineering; Life Sciences; and Life Sciences Engineering. In a departure from the classic Lyran/Sirian example, the Beings of Wa-Ta-Ma-Kka added two more clans. The first, known as the Cultural History clan, has to do with the creation of cultural unity within an extremely diverse society. The purpose of this clan, a modification of the cultural tradition and history clans in the 12-clan Andromeda prototype, is to make possible the bringing together of Tau Ceti's two sentient Beings. The second clan (Divine Service) develops ways to demonstrate that each task one performs is an expression of her/his divine service. That is, the clan presides over the development and application of the grace that comes of knowing exactly how the individual should manifest her/his divine service.

Mirroring the classic model, each of these clans forms its own main clan governing council. They, in turn, send representatives to Tau Ceti's Main Governing Council. Herein lies yet another difference from the traditional Lyran/Sirian model: during sessions of its governing assembly, distinguished liaisons from the Divine Service clan act as special presiding referees, enabling members of the main governing council to discover that each proposal or act is really part of their individual or collective divine service, thus solving or circumventing whatever problems may arise.

Clearly, the Beings of Tau Ceti have succeeded in amalgamating contradictory components from the Lyran/Sirian and Andromedan models. Their astonishing proficiency has brought them great acclaim from across the Milky Way. In effect, the Tau Ceteans have combined the Andromedan ability to create unity out of diversity with two remarkable Sirian traits - a wondrous spirituality and a celebrated sense of personal and shared spiritual loyalty and divine service to the Great Blue Lodge of Creation.

For these and other reasons, the Beings of Tau Ceti are distinguished for what they refer to as their gracious exercise of divine service. Galactic societies throughout the galaxy often ask the liaisons and counselors of Tau Ceti to explain their discoveries, and are extremely happy to call upon them whenever needed.

Tau Cetean Purpose

Tau Ceteans excel as navigators and pilots and have developed many types of technologically advanced ships for the Galactic Federation's Science & Exploration (S&E) fleets. The Tau Ceteans' highest mission is to understand the philosophy underlying construction of every Galactic Federation ship or vessel and the reasons for the Federation's S & E fleets, and to convey their findings to former member star-nations of the Anchara Alliance.

That philosophy is based upon Love and divine service. Therefore, every Galactic Federation of Light ship is a living, Loving Being in divine service to her crew and her divine mission. This is especially true with regard to the mission of first contact, in which the S & E fleet's tasks are to explore and work with galactic and local Spiritual Hierarchies to spread Light throughout this galaxy.

This is in stark contrast to Anchara Alliance ships, which often were either mechanical, or of an organic nature that was under their commander's complete control. Thus, ship and crew were subjected to the whims and dictates of their leader. The liaisons and teachers of Tau Ceti are endeavoring to explain these differences to former Alliance members.

Why does the Galactic Federation of Light explore? Why does

it assist star-nations in completing first contact? This course of action makes possible the expansion of the Galactic Federation of Light. It also allows even the darkest souls of the former Anchara Alliance to join the Galactic Federation and encourages them, as new members, to achieve their highest potential.

The Galactic Federation of Light knows the infinite potential of each star-nation in the former Anchara Alliance. Tau Ceteans realize that, as the Beings who have joined the Galactic Federation most recently grow toward the Light, they are prepared to offer up innovations of all kinds. The Tau Ceteans honor this point of view, and consider their participation in this process their primary concern. It is also the fulfillment of their divine service to the Milky Way Galaxy and to our Creator.

Physical Description of Inhabitants

Galactic humans of Tau Ceti bear a close resemblance to humans of the constellation of Hercules. Among Tau Ceti humans, there are three predominant skin colors: brown and reddish-brown, and dark and light shades of red and green.

The hair of brown-skinned humans ranges from light brown to copper, or black to red-orange. Eye color ranges from green and blue to brown and gray. Males are very well proportioned and stand between about 7 and 8.5 feet (2.13 and 2.59 meters) tall. Women are slightly shorter, ranging from just over 6.5 feet to almost 8 feet (1.98 to 2.40 meters) in height.

The hair of green-skinned Tau Ceti humans varies from light green to blonde or brown: their eyes may be green, hazel or steel blue. They have the same relative heights as brown-skinned humans. Red-skinned humans have red, orange or blonde hair and red, brown or dark blue eyes. They, too, are the same size as the other two Tau Ceti human types. In all cases, females are quite full bosomed.

The other mammals of Tau Ceti are huge, furry Beings with bear-like bodies covered in brown, black or light golden brown fur and small, furry tails. Their heads are shaped like those of bears, but with smaller muzzles. The teeth look more like those of a galactic human than of Earth bears. The eyes, set forward on the head and similar to those of humans, are brown, blue or black. The ears, which resemble those of Earth's bears, are positioned just above the eyes at the sides of the head.

(See Figures 12a and 12b below: A typical Tau Cetean.)

Because this highly sentient Tau Cetean Being walks on two legs, it has a higher center of gravity than bears found on Earth. Its two muscular arms have paw-like hands and five stubby, clawed fingers. Very muscular legs end in extremely small feet with five short, thick toes each. These bear-like Beings range from 9 to 12 feet (2.74 to 3.66 meters) tall. Both species of sentient Beings require only about one to two hours of sleep per day.

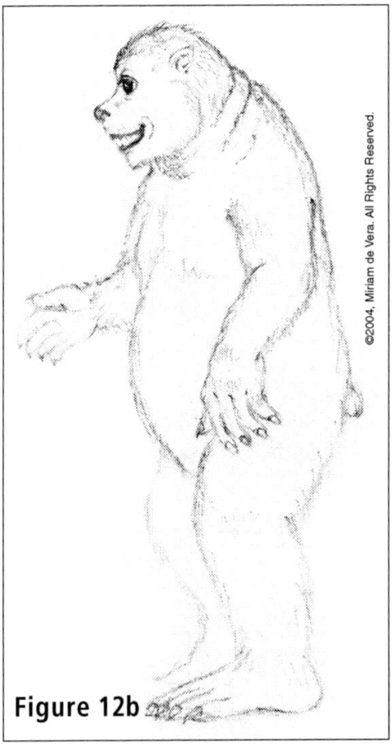

Figure 12b

Figure 12a

The bear-like Beings of Hashabha have adopted a unique series of layered robes worn over flowing, multi-colored blouses. Ornamental braiding, special graphic designs and distinctive command colors worn on the garment's shoulder distinguish rank and insignia.

The Beings of Wa-Ta-Ma-Kka have chosen a style of dress that avoids the Sirian filmy short and ankle-length clothes trimmed in ribbons and other indications of standing or honor. Instead, their traditional garments consist of sheer, billowing pants topped with gossamer waist- or knee-length shirts. Following the Sirian design, these outfits adhere to clan colors. And, instead of ribbons or epaulettes, special geometrical designs on the shoulder indicate rank and commendations.

Aboard Galactic Federation spacecraft, a one-piece jumpsuit, which adheres to Galactic Federation uniform dress codes, is worn. Normally, it is worn only when the crew consists of members of several different Galactic Federation of Light star-nations, such as on Science and Exploration (S&E) fleets assigned to a first contact mission.

The inhabitants of Tau Ceti are celebrated for their expertise in designing some of the most advanced ships in the Galactic Federation's exploration fleets. They are also considered some of the best pilots and navigators in the galaxy.

The human Tau Ceti language is very guttural and resembles German or Arabic. The bear-like Beings' language sounds somewhat the same, but with a much deeper gutturalism.

Ships of Tau Ceti

Tau Ceti scout ships are huge plasma craft, roughly 200 to 250 feet (61 to 76.2 meters) long, and are easily recognizable by their diamond-like shapes.

Their interstellar and intergalactic motherships, which usually serve as Galactic Federation of Light Science and Exploration (S&E) fleet command ships during first contact expeditions, are shaped like stacks of blood cells 20 to 50 layers high and measure between 4 and 44 miles (6.44 and 70.94 kilometers) in diameter.

21

The Star-Nation of Procyon (Pro-see-on)

Often, Washta would enthrall me with details of the inhabitants of Alpha Canis Minoris (Procyon) and their beginnings in the Galactic Federation. Originally, this was a mixed group, consisting of amphibian/reptilian refugees in flight from the pitiless galactic wars being waged in the constellation of Cancer, and a sizable human settlement from Sirius-B. These pioneers were forced to reach immediate agreements that would allow them to survive, and their new colonies to exist and thrive in safety. A series of understandings resulted, enabling the two groups of colonists to endure, and producing a string of commitments that were to serve, at a later date, as the basis for the future star-nation.

These events, which set in motion a series of precedents that involved refugees from former Anchara Alliance star empires, allowed the new Sirian colonists the chance to carry out their goal of establishing a new colony. In so doing, they were able to interact amicably with individuals and groups from the Anchara Alliance. Indeed, as a result of this prolonged collaboration, the refugees made two requests of the human colonists. First: would it be possible for their species to inhabit Light Bodies? Second: would the human colonists assist them in creating a galactic society that would enable them to express their unique culture and life style?

Over the course of two million years, these former fugitives from Anchara's dark Draconian Empire learned how to manifest their own Light Bodies. In so doing, they became, millions of years ago, one of the first realms in the Galactic Federation of Light to form a new, hybrid (amphibian/reptilian and human) star-nation.

Having succeeded in their quest, the Beings of Procyon swore to use this new knowledge to liberate the oppressed star-nations of the Anchara Alliance. This pledge, in fact, had been one of the major reasons underlying their joining of the Galactic Federation. As members, they belonged to one of the original 14 Regional Federation Councils – the Sirian Regional Council. The Star-Nation of Procyon was welcomed into the Galactic Federation of Light approximately 3.78 million years ago.

I was about ten when I first encountered a group of planetary scientists from the Star-Nation of Alpha Canis Minoris (Procyon). A Procyon mothership had come to Earth's solar system to evaluate each of its planets. Part of this assignment included the drafting of a series of timetables for each of several scenarios decreed by Earth's Ascended Masters. The Beings of Alpha Canis Minoris, renowned throughout the Galactic Federation as esteemed planetary scientists and brave explorers, designed timelines most likely to fulfill their specific objectives. In this way, Procyon's inhabitants provided information that the Galactic Federation and Sirian mothership's scientists found extremely useful in assessing how quickly Mother Earth would be able to reach her divine destiny.

In the course of this solar system evaluation, a handful of amphibian/reptilian scientists from Procyon appeared at the Sirian mothership. It was another of my early encounters with non-human Beings, and I was understandably apprehensive. The group from Procyon, sensing this, enveloped me in their benevolent and unwavering Love. We enjoyed a brief chat about Earth humans' unfortunate fear of the unknown, and said goodbye. I have never forgotten that meeting, or the sense of infinite Love that emanated from those Beings.

Time and again, Washta would use this meeting as an example of the unimaginable diversity of sentient life in our galaxy, and throughout physicality. His captivating lessons and dialogues on the Procyon Star-Nation, and others, gave me an acute appreciation of these Beings and their compassionate civilizations. The key to Procyon's galactic society is their unconditional willingness to accept, as their mission, the enormous multiplicity of the former Anchara Alliance, and their readiness to support these previously dark Beings in creating Light Bodies and fully adapting to membership in the Galactic Federation of Light.

Status and Location

Amphibian/reptilian refugees from the constellation of Cancer ('Crab') and human colonists from Alpha Canis Majoris (Sirius-B) first settled Procyon nearly 3.9 million years ago. Almost 3.8 million years ago, the Star-Nation of Alpha Canis Minoris (Procyon) was welcomed into the Galactic Federation of Light.

The star Alpha Canis Minoris is also known as Procyon, which, in Greek, means 'Before the Dog'. She is also known by her amphibian/reptilian inhabitants as 'Sak'Qok'Dapk' ('Sacred Place of Refuge') and by her Sirian human citizens as 'Lamabha' ('Light of the Soul'). Procyon is the brightest star in Canis Minor ('Lesser Dog'), and is located approximately 11.4 Light Years from Earth.

On a winter night in the Northern Hemisphere, you will see the constellation of Canis Minor to the immediate northeast of Orion ('Hunter'), and between Cancer ('Crab'), Canis Major ('Greater Dog') and Gemini ('Twins'). Orion's familiar shape often serves as a pointer by which to locate other stars and star-groups. The constellation of Orion is situated between those of Taurus ('Bull') and Canis Major ('Big Dog'), and just below that of Auriga ('Charioteer').

The easiest way to observe the bright blue star, Procyon, is simply to locate the Belt of Orion, the row of three brilliant stars at the center of Orion. Above the Belt are two of its stars, Betelgeuse and Bellatrix. They point to Procyon, which lies directly to their east. Immediately below Procyon you will find Sirius, the brightest star in the evening sky.

Procyon's Solar System

Alpha Canis Minoris (Procyon) is a binary star. Her solar system, Procyon-A, consists of six worlds, the smallest planets being closest to the sun and the largest farthest away. The innermost planet is one-eighth the size of your Earth. Her extremely thin atmosphere glows dimly because of constant discharges from her sun, 'Sak'Qok'Dapk' ('Sacred Place of Refuge'), which renew this atmosphere and also maintain her strange, aura-like glows.

The next world is more congenial to life. She is nearly the same size as Earth and has an atmosphere similar to your own. This planet is hot and semi-arid, with four large continents and eight small seas. Soaring mountain ranges extend, north to south, through the interiors of two continents. Her ecosystem is exceptionally varied: reptiles are her predominant land creatures, while her seas are governed by great, primeval fish encased in scaly armor, and by curious crab-like creatures. The Beings of Procyon-A value this desert world for its biological diversity and occasionally live here.

The final two outlying planets in the Sak'Qok'Dapk solar system are 'gas giants' that closely resemble the large planets of your Sun's outer solar system. Unlike them, however, those of Sak'Qok'Dapk have congealed atmospheres enshrouded in large, multicolored geometric shapes, and spin more rapidly.

Description of Home Worlds

Alpha Canis Minoris (Procyon-A) has two main home worlds. One, third from the sun, is called Qam'Saq'Deqq ('Safe, Beautiful Place'). A large water planet, she is part semi-arid, part green and luxuriant. She measures 9,800 miles (15,700 kilometers) in diameter, and has six moons, the four largest of which have a thick, livable atmosphere and are about the size of Earth's moon. As a planet, she enjoys a diverse and lively environment, and contains twelve interconnected seas and eight continents.

While six of the continents are largely dry, the other two are exceedingly lush and contain many large inland and coastal swamps. Their air is rich in oxygen and other life-supporting gases. Despite the predominantly moistureless landscape on six of her continents, a diverse ecosystem exists on this world, and amphibian/reptilian Beings make their home here.

The second home world, fourth from Lamabha ('Light of the Soul'), abounds in water. Known as Hawatamah ('Wondrous Wet Land'), this planet, the same size as the first, contains seven continents. Two are as dry and barren as those on Qam'Saq'Deqq. The other five, however, encompass vast inland seas that shatter the isolation of their interiors. A chain of rivers flows from the central mountain ranges that border these mini-oceans' shores. Here, at the planet's key nodal points, stand many small temple compounds.

Natural wonders – extensive tracts of giant trees, intermingled with sweeping meadows and lofty, red and blue, purple-streaked mountains – blanket the planet's interior. Astounding species of amphibians, reptiles, birds and mammals inhabit this magnificent ecosystem.

Procyon's Galactic Society

Procyon's inhabitants are skilled in the discovery and accommodation of different species and in the integration of different groups, no matter how dissimilar they may be in language and culture. The humans of Procyon-A first recognized this gift after they had successfully assimilated refugees from the former Draconian Empire into their galactic society. Their increasing expertise in this field has made it possible for the Galactic Federation to more easily integrate its highly diversified members into an effortlessly-operating whole. This, in turn, has contributed to first contacts involving a multitude of previously neutral star-nations. Therefore, and because of the skills of its inhabitants, a great many of them have originated in Procyon-A.

Physical Description of Inhabitants

The Procyon star system consists of two types of sentient Beings. The first is a pure Lyran/Sirian humanoid. Like those on Sirius-B, these individuals are either blue- or white-skinned, and are fully conscious. Procyon amphibian/reptilian hybrids are slightly taller than its humans and have green, brown or blue skin.

Galactic humans of Procyon resemble typical Lyran/Sirians. They look much like humans on Earth, with two major differences. First: their eyes, which range through shades of blue, green and brown, are much larger and more alert, while their two ears, smaller than those of humans, are joined to the head at a slightly lower level. Second: the top and back of their heads are enlarged to accommodate a greater brain capacity. Like other Lyran/Sirian humans, Procyon males stand between 6 feet, 6 inches (1.83 meters) and 7 feet, 4 inches (2.24 meters) in height. Their females are well endowed and range from 6 feet, 4 inches (1.93 meters) to almost 7 feet (2.13 meters) tall. Procyon humans require only about one to two hours of sleep per day.

Her amphibian/reptilian Beings possess lizard-like bodies covered with scaly skin. The head is almost round and in proportion to the rest of the body, while the neck is short and well defined. Wide-set bulging brown, yellow or red eyes rest on either side of a very thin, ridged nose that ends in two slit-like nostrils. The eyes move independently of each other. Ears are small, 2-inch (5-centimeter) ovals set just behind each eye: the mouth is a thin-lipped slit extending from ear to ear.

The body and appendages of the amphibian/reptilian are very muscular. It has four thin, nail-less fingers and three long, sharply clawed toes. The stunted tail looks like a small bump at the base of the spine. Females are slightly larger than males and range from 7 to 8 feet (2.13 to 2.44 meters) tall. The more compact males stand between 7 feet and 7 feet, 8 inches (2.13 and 2.34 meters) in height. Amphibian/reptilians need no more than three or four hours of sleep per day.

The clothes of Procyon-A's inhabitants are sheer, flowing, short and ankle-length robes adorned with ribbons and other symbols of rank or high office. Filmy blouses, either knee- or waist-length, are worn over the top. Following the Sirian precedent, they take the colors of their respective clan.

The outfit worn aboard Galactic Federation spacecraft is a one- or two-piece jumpsuit. Normally, the one-piece style is worn only when there is a mixed crew consisting of several Federation star-nations, as, for example, on Science and Exploration (S&E) fleets assigned to a first contact mission. This one-piece ensemble adheres to the uniform requirements of Galactic Federation dress codes.

The Beings of Procyon, well known as gifted scientists and avid explorers, have led many successful expeditions into previously unexplored sectors of this and other galaxies.

The human Procyon language is very melodious and has few guttural sounds. Amphibian/reptilian speech is much the same, but contains many more guttural nuances.

Ships of Procyon

There are two kinds of Procyon scout craft. One resembles a large teardrop and the other, a giant beetle. They measure between 45 and 200 feet (13.72 and 61 meters) in diameter.

Their deep space motherships look like either huge snowflakes or enormous jellyfish, and extend from 100 to 4,000 miles (161 to 6,440 kilometers) in length.

22

The Confederation of Fomalhaut
(Fo-mal-ought)

Washta reveled in frequent discussions surrounding the curious beginnings of the inhabitants of Alpha Pisces Austrini (Fomalhaut). Their solar system, originally a refuge, had later served as a battleground for a mixed group – a band of Pleiadean rebels fleeing the large Draconian Empire fleet that had destroyed their settlements and, 50,000 years later, a smaller cluster of dinosaurian/reptilians escaping the savagery of the galactic wars in the constellation of Orion. Finally, nearly 20,000 years ago, following a prolonged period of intermittent wars, a truce was signed. As a result of that 'truce', a series of agreements made possible the survival of both groups of colonists and solidified the 'contracts' that later would serve as the basis for a future star confederation.

With that final accord and its peaceful dénouement, precedents were established regarding refugees from former Anchara Alliance star empires, as well as from the Pleiades and the Galactic Federation. With the signing of the treaty, the two colonies became one. By embracing a societal model that combined the most delicate subtleties of each culture, the resultant neutral star-nation formed a society similar, in many ways, to that of Altair.

However, the Fomalhautans' perception of neutrality was quite different from that of the Altairians. Like Altair, they encouraged both sides to foster harmonious relations. Nonetheless, the Fomalhautans yearned to join the Galactic Federation, a longing that was intensified by the number of conflicts being waged around them. When, finally, Anchara approached the Alliance to bring an end to these pointless wars, the Fomalhautans were quick to request membership in the Galactic Federation of Light.

I had my first meeting with a group of planetary scientists from the Confederation of Alpha Piscis Austrini (Fomalhaut) sixteen years ago. Beings from their world were renowned across the Galactic Federation as highly regarded scientists and intrepid explorers. A Fomalhaut mothership had arrived here to assess the physical and spiritual status of each planet in Earth's solar system. Their assignment included the drafting of possible timetables for first contact, as well as the drawing up of a preliminary schedule for the 'terra-forming' of Mars and Venus.

Their expertise made it possible for them to design the most probable schedule for their specific objectives. Using these invaluable data, Galactic Federation scientists were able to assess the rate at which Mother Earth would advance toward her divine destiny.

In the course of this appraisal, a small group of dinosaurian/reptilian scientists from Fomalhaut arrived at the Sirian mothership on which Washta and I were passengers. This would be one of my last major encounters with non-human Beings. Sensing my agitation, the Fomalhautans engulfed me in their gracious and never-failing Love. We chatted briefly about the current state of the solar system, and then parted. I will always remember this fateful meeting with such marvelous Beings.

Later, Washta would return often to this meeting as an example of the infinite variety of sentient life, in this galaxy and throughout physicality. His memorable talks and our subsequent conversations on Fomalhaut and other similar star-nations gave me a heartfelt appreciation for these galactic Beings and their benevolent societies.

Present Status and Location

The Confederation of Fomalhaut (Alpha Piscis Austrini) is a two-member neutral star-nation that joined the Galactic Federation of Light about seven years ago. Approximately 250,000 years ago, a gang of human rebels arrived from the Pleiades to colonize her. Fifty thousand years later, a smaller dinosaurian/reptilian band from Bellatrix (Gamma Orion) arrived. For many years, the two groups waged a series of mutually destructive wars until about 20,000 years ago, having made their peace, they formed this Confederation.

The star Alpha Piscis Austrini is also known as Fomalhaut, which, in Arabic, means 'Mouth of the Fish'. Her dinosaurian/reptilian inhabitants refer to her as 'Sak'Koq'Lapq' ('Given Place of Refuge'), while the descendants of her former Pleiadean colonists call her 'Khalamah' ('Sacred Light'). Fomalhaut, the brightest star in Piscis Austrinus (Latin: 'Southern Fish') and the 17th brightest star in the sky, is located approximately 25 Light Years from Earth.

On a spring night in the Southern Hemisphere, the constellation of Piscis Austrinus is located immediately beneath and between those of Aquarius (Greek: 'Water Carrier') and Capricornus (Greek: 'Goat'). Precisely below it is the constellation of Grus (Latin: 'Grane'): beside it is that of Microscopium (Latin: 'Microscope').

To observe Fomalhaut, locate the famous magic square of Pegasus and then find the two bright stars that form the square's north-south side. In a straight line above these two, you will see a blazing white star. It is Fomalhaut.

Fomalhaut Solar System

The solar system of Alpha Piscis Austrini (Fomalhaut), like most solar systems in this galaxy, has eight planets, the smallest closest to the sun and the largest, most distant. Fomalhaut's dinosaurian/reptilian inhabitants refer to her as Mok'Qa'FpQ ('Light of Sacred Life'), while the humans living on her third and fourth worlds call her Lamadha. The innermost planet is barren and one-sixth the size of your Earth. Constant discharges from her white sun cast a dim glow that permeates her extremely thin, ionized atmosphere.

The fifth planet, nearly twice the size of Earth, is more hospitable, and possesses an atmosphere similar to your own. Hot and semi-arid, she contains eight large continents mostly blanketed in a patchwork of high coastal mountain ranges and far-flung deserts, and surrounded by twelve seas. Towering mountain ranges extend through the interior of five continents. Broad, sun-baked plains cover the other three landmasses: two of these are more expansive than Earth's Sahara. This planet, whose desert ecosystem is surprisingly varied, supports a colorful array of reptilian, dinosaurian and insectian life, as well as some fascinating plant species. In her seas are large numbers of fish, vaguely reminiscent of the primitive life forms from Earth's Age of Fishes.

The three remaining outer planets in the Alpha Piscis Austrini solar system are gas giants. Like the majority of this type of planet in our galaxy, they are noted for their banded, gelated atmospheres filled with large, geometric multi-colored anomalies, which range from large 'spots' to vast, interconnected, multi-sized patterns.

Description of Home World

About 200,000 years ago, this sphere, called 'Mok'Qa'SlQ' ('Place of Life') by her dinosaurian/reptilian inhabitants, was first settled by colonists from the constellation of Orion. Measuring almost 6,000 miles (9,600 kilometers) in diameter, she contains eight oceans and five huge continents. She has a three-layer firmament that supports an ecosystem renowned for its diversity of reptilian, amphibian, dinosaurian and other unusual aquatic life forms.

Generally, this home world has a semi-tropical climate and is cooler only at the poles. Like all other planets, Mok'Qa'SlQ is a hollow sphere whose inner environment is inhabited, even for this ecosystem, by some very peculiar creatures. The 400 million Beings of this world live in special, populous cities scattered across the inner planet.

This large water world has a highly oxygenated atmosphere that is recognizable by its purple tint. Her skies swarm with billions of fantastic, dinosaurian birds and other flying creatures, such as an enormous, bat-like reptilian. Three of her continents, like those of some other worlds in this galaxy, are famous for their wide meadows of wildly colored grasses. Her other continents are noteworthy for their broad mountain ranges, dense jungles or thick forests and vast inland seas.

Pleiadean human colonists settled the third planet approximately 250,000 years ago. Called Erpa ('Home World'), she measures 9,000 miles (14,000 kilometers) in diameter – slightly larger than Earth – and has four moons. Across Erpa's largely unspoiled surface are scattered a series of temple sites, surrounded by small communities of 6,000 souls. Each settlement supports the temple site and constantly monitors the major node located at its exact center. There, ritual, which may include chant, dance and spiritually animating music, is performed each day.

The atmosphere of Erpa's semi-tropical water world is similar to that of Mother Earth. Her six diversely sized continents are surrounded by twelve boundless seas. Distinctive surface features cover them, including great mountain-walls; impenetrable jungles; sweeping, grassy plains; towering coastal mountain ranges; endless deserts and undulating meadows. Embraced within the ring of this fascinating topographical mix lie a series of enormous, inland seas. Erpa's diverse ecosystem includes flora and fauna common to most of this galaxy.

The fourth planet, Khapa ('Land of Spirit'), bears a vague resemblance to your own. Measuring 8,000 miles (12,800 kilometers) in diameter, Khapa consists of a wide ocean encompassing six immense, interconnected islands that vary in length from 2,300 miles (3,700 kilometers) to 3,000 miles (4,800 kilometers). Her surface resembles Erpa's in its physical geography. She is particularly noted for her extensive jungles, which teem with some of the most bizarre classes of insects in this sector of the galaxy. However, unlike the other water world, Khapa's aquatic life forms are extremely diverse, representing a broad spectrum of fish, dinosaurian, reptilian and mammalian species.

Erpa is home to the headquarters for the Confederation of Fomalhaut. In its inner world capital, established nearly 20,000 years ago, two very different founding races have joined together to build a unified star-nation that has endured through the ages.

Fomalhautan Society and Its Contribution to the Galactic Federation of Light

By merging the best points of galactic human society to those of the clan-like dinosaurian/reptilian one, the Fomalhautans have created a culture that works. Although they were unable, initially, to grasp how their culture could conform to that of the Galactic Federation of Light, the process of first contact changed their minds, making them enthusiastic adherents of what the Galactic Federation represents.

The Fomalhautan Confederation closely interacts with liaison groups that have been sent to the Andromeda Galaxy. They are teaching Beings in the Galactic Federation of Light to help people understand first contact, especially when it involves a neutral non-Federation state. That is to say, exactly how can a special culture, with its own unique technical skills, become comfortably a part of the Galactic Federation?

This is an important consideration because many neutral states, initially, feared both the galactic wars and their affiliation with the Galactic Federation. In actual fact, the Fomalhautans have given Galactic Federation liaisons an understanding of how first contact applies to neutral star-nations; the best way to approach neutral states eager to join the Galactic Federation; and techniques for establishing liaisons that can successfully carry out that first contact.

Physical Description

Fomalhaut humans are of two very distinct body types. One closely resembles the so-called 'Nordic' type of ET and is usually blonde with bright blue, hazel or steel-gray eyes. Men of this ilk are muscular and stand approximately six feet (1.85 meters) tall. Their women are well favored, and range from about five feet, six inches to slightly under six feet (1.63 to 1.83 meters) in height. The second type has darker, almost tanned-looking skin, and dark hair with brown, gray or black eyes. They have the same relative height and appearance as the first-mentioned Nordic group. Both classes require between 2 and 4 hours of sleep per day.

The dinosaurian/reptilian inhabitants of the Confederation of Fomalhaut are hybrids who originated from the star Bellatrix in Orion. Typically, they are very scaly and bony. The upper head is surrounded by a large, bony crest and the eyes are large and set forward just above and to either side of a very small nose. The mouth is characterized by thin lips that extend from one side of the head to the other. The non-existent ears are recognizable only by an extra-smooth, 3-inch (7.62 cm) circle on either side of the head and just behind the eyes. The large eyes, resembling those of Earth's reptiles, are either red or dull yellow. The skin is scaly, like that of a crocodile, and can be green, yellow, brown or red. A small, bony crest stretches up the middle of the back and connects to a larger crest on the crown of the head.

This Being is a biped. Its hands are thin with six long, clawed fingers, and its feet have five toes that each end in a small, knifelike claw. The tail is very short and thick like a crocodile's, and reaches only to the feet. On this planet, the male is shorter than the female. Bellatrician-like males stand between 8 and 10 feet (2.44 and 3 meters) tall, while female height ranges from 8.5 to 10.25 feet (2.6 to 3.12 meters). They require between 4 and 6 hours of sleep per day.

Beings in the Confederation of Fomalhaut are noted for their expertise in all scientific endeavors. Currently, the first major Science and Exploration Team sent to the Andromeda Galaxy, 2 million Light Years from our own, consists largely of personnel from Fomalhaut.

The human Fomalhaut language sounds both lyrical and guttural, while the dinosaurian/reptilian tongue is more guttural.

Ships of the Fomalhaut Confederation

The scout ships of human Fomalhautans are egg-shaped, like a water drop that is about to fall from a tap, and measure 60 to 85 feet (18.3 to 26 meters) in diameter.

Their motherships, shaped like huge, multi-layered cigars, range between 2 and 1,200 miles (3.2 and 1,920 kilometers) across.

Scout ships of Fomalhaut's dinosaurian/reptilian Beings are shaped like huge beetles and are approximately 100 feet (30.5 meters) in diameter.

Their motherships are notable for their amoeba-like shape, and measure between 8 and 900 miles (13 to 14,400 kilometers) across.

Afterword

The Beings described in this volume were transmitted to me in a most unusual way. Those of you who have read my book, "Your First Contact", know that I have a series of implants that act as a sort of holographic television. They are the means by which I obtain information for my updates on PAO's website. For this book, the committee involved in these 'broadcasts' consisted of at least three Beings from each of the star-nations represented in the twenty-two chapters of this work. Every one of them provided me with their unique energies. Those with whom I had rarely worked proved to be the most physically demanding. In many cases, I was subjected to painful alignments that made it extremely difficult to type out the knowledge given me. In an effort to remedy this situation, I was aided by a marvelous healer from Arcturus named Supa who balanced and maintained my alignment during each session with the twenty-two star-nations involved. Without her constant help, the volume that you have just read could not have been written. However, the difficulties that I encountered were confirmation of the severe emotional and physical discord that continues to seethe within us concerning many inhabitants of former member-worlds of the Anchara Alliance. These Beings inflicted grievous harm upon the many star-nations of the Galactic Federation of Light and its predecessors. Now, the thought forms created by these previous encounters need to be transformed and new, positive thought forms added that can aid us in our future meetings with these many, newer members of the Galactic Federation of Light.

The purpose of this book is to prepare you for a coming first contact with these Beings. In working on it, I also noticed that much of my initial apprehension had dissipated by the time I edited my first manuscript. It was as if I became a kind of sounding board for how best to alleviate the thoughts and many bodily discomforts that I had observed at the beginning of this project. It was interesting, too, to notice how surprised each former group of the Anchara Alliance was by my original deep reactions and how sincerely they wished to redress them. As a result, with the help of Supa, they made a series of adjustments that appreciably modulated the communication fields that surrounded my body. Each group also learned to 'broadcast' at a level more in keeping with the needs of my body. The outcome, by project's end, was a unique and marvelous experience. The many worlds and diverse societies of the former Anchara Alliance are undergoing immense changes. Their home worlds are very different from ours. While a few appear to be one large swamp, most others are semi-arid. Few have any similarity to our own. In all cases, one's first impression, on these physically alien worlds, is of excessive heat, near desert-like conditions or, infrequently, very high humidity. The skies on these worlds appear fantastic as well, with their varied hues of deep orange, light to dark purple and every shade of blue.

The Beings, too, differ in body shape, general appearance and size. To us, the most important point is that they are our allies. Human or not, they have cultivated a great and abiding love and a keen interest in the changes that we as Earth humans are undergoing. This unparalleled consciousness shift of ours is making it possible for an entire galaxy to come together. It is providing us, as well, with the opportunity to transform our ancient fears and realize our full potential. In this, we are becoming the instruments chosen to end a galactic war that has lasted far too long. In the course of writing this book, I became profoundly conscious of these reflections. I was delighted to discover how the ambassadorial team of each star-nation adjusted to me. Equally fascinating was how eager each one was to reveal their world to me and describe their culture. In doing so, they wove together the many distinct strands that made up the former Anchara Alliance. This experience gave me a better understanding of their adjustment to the sweeping mosaic that is the Galactic Federation of Light.

Moreover, this experience allowed me to comprehend the diversity and immensity of this galaxy. Literally hundreds of thousands of star-nations have come together in harmony to correct the immeasurable damage caused by a seemingly endless galactic war. We sit here on Earth, blissfully unaware of the events that are unfolding around us. I was made vividly aware of the extent of our ignorance by the many Beings who participated in the research for this book. I was most heartened by their willingness to share information and enable me to communicate their words to you. The great outpouring of Love was universal. They made every effort to ensure that I correctly portrayed their worlds and their culture. Nonetheless, much remained unsaid. It was decided that I would leave their final, full story to them. First contact with such a wildly diversified population as the Galactic Federation of Light needs to be made directly. It will be realized once we have achieved full consciousness and are able to overcome our most ancient fears.

A special Galactic Federation of Light first contact liaison team chose the Beings that I described to you in this work. The principles of first contact need to be carried out in layers. On the first level, appreciate that we exist and that we are your space family. In the next, understand our common origins and intertwined history. In the final tiers, perceive how that past has carried us into the present and is conveying us forward, toward a future that we will share with each other. In that future, all of us will overcome a profound, genetically determined fear of former members of the Anchara Alliance. Often, their shapes, sizes and even their scents are too much for us to bear. The special first contact liaison team intends this work to give you both an appreciation of human galactic societies and some understanding of the many societies that they are so swiftly reshaping. Like you, these former members of the Anchara Alliance wish to develop Light Bodies and return to the Light. The long night of the dark in the Milky Way Galaxy is about to end quickly.

Finally, I have written this book to give you a glimpse into the workings of twenty-two star-nations that are part of the Galactic Federation of Light. Of these, eight are human galactic societies, while five others are former members of the Anchara Alliance. Regardless of its size, each galactic society is proof that we are not alone and that a vast space family awaits us. That space family has cheerfully shown you a little bit of what makes it special. They have done so to welcome you home, and to peel away the thick layers of xenophobia in which you have encased yourselves. Once, this galaxy was an exceedingly dangerous place. Right now, because of your great shift, it is becoming much friendlier. We each have much to learn, to accept and to discover about the infinity of worlds that twirl endlessly in our galaxy. The intention of this book has been to light your way as you begin your amazing journey.

Selamat Ja! (Sirian greeting: 'Be in Joy!')

Sheldan Nidle and the Twenty-Two Ambassadorial
Teams from the Galactic Federation of Light

About the Author

Sheldan Nidle was born in New York City on November 11, 1946 and raised in Buffalo, New York. His first extraterrestrial and spacecraft experiences began shortly after his birth and were highlighted all through his childhood by various modes of contact phenomena, as well as accompanying manifestations – light-form communications, extraterrestrial visitations, and teaching/learning sessions on board spacecraft. For most of his life, he has enjoyed ongoing telepathic communications with the Galactic Federation of Light via etheric and physical implants. Sheldan has visually observed and physically experienced spacecraft throughout the years. What makes his information unique is that it is transmitted to him directly without channeling, scientific when necessary, and encoded in a spiritual language.

Around the age of fourteen, Sheldan asked the Sirians and their Galactic Federation of Light allies to discontinue communications with him because he was experiencing overwhelming conflict between their scientific and societal knowledge and that which he was learning here on Earth. The Sirians and their Galactic Federation of Light allies left, but told him that they would be back when it was time for him to complete his mission for planet Earth and her people. In high school, Sheldan was placed in advanced science programs, in subject areas such as physics, chemistry and calculus. He graduated from the University at Buffalo in 1964 and earned a Master's from Ohio University in 1970. Between 1974 and 1977, he attended the University of Southern California as a Ph.D. student, and obtained a second Master's there in 1975.

Because of Sheldan's education in science and the social sciences, and his extensive research in Nikola Tesla's alternative energy technologies, etc., he is able to bring a rational and scientific approach to this controversial subject.

Sheldan is a lecturer and the author of the best-selling You Are Becoming a Galactic Human (1994); Your First Contact (2001); Selamat Ja! A Guide for Galactic Humans (2001); and Your Galactic Neighbors (2005). In the 1970s, with Syntar Productions, he co-created a documentary on the life and accomplishments of Nikola Tesla, the genius who invented the technology of the twentieth century. From the 1970's through the mid-1980's, he did scientific research on alternative sources of electrical energy.

In the mid-1980's, his E.T. contacts resumed and subsequently led him to the spiritual and galactic information that is provided in his weekly website updates, videotapes, books, workshops and lectures.

Sheldan is the founder of Planetary Activation Organization (PAO), an organization with over 1,800 registered groups worldwide. PAO's philosophy is to empower the individual in order to transform the world. Under PAO's sponsorship, small semi-autonomous groups called Planetary Activation Groups (PAGs) prepare for full consciousness, first contact, galactic society and Earth stewardship. PAGs are inner-guided and self-organizing in the way they serve and activate their communities.

ADDENDA I

The following is taken from Chapter 4 of "Your First Contact". It is included here, in its entirety, since the principles of galactic society are the very basis for the transcendent changes occurring now across our galaxy. Throughout the course of this chapter, the fundamental Laws governing galactic society, as well as its fundamental structure, are explained by a number of specially chosen 'guides'.

Galactic Human Society

I am your tour guide, Sandara.

Previously, we have seen your physical and spiritual transformations. Let us now look at your coming societal changes. To enable us to do this, our starship cruise will be entering a new phase.

You are about to experience the wonders of our hyper-dimensional drive. We ask that you please remain seated and look at the forward video screens. Ahead of us, my friends, is a wormhole that our ship's drive is now forming. Our navigation system has calculated its exact location and a precise exit point. You will soon see a vast stream of luminescent colors hurtling toward us, and in roughly seven minutes, we will enter the Sirius star system. Sirius is a multi-star system composed of nine stars of different classifications. In order to study how your planetary society can evolve into a galactic one, we are heading for the 'B' star system. Now, please prepare for wormhole entry. We are about to begin another chapter in our journey.

Your global society's next evolutionary step is to become a galactic society. When this new reality happens, your civilization can emulate a societal model first established by fully-conscious humans in the constellation of Lyra some 6,000,000 years ago. The foundation of galactic society is Love. Complete Love is based on a profound inner compassion for your soul's growth and a sincere outer compassion for each other. To these are added sacred societal laws given by the Spiritual Hierarchy. These laws aid galactic human society by creating a divinely inspired social structure. Let us now explore the society of Sirius

'B' and learn how this galactic human society actually operates.

As we enter the Sirius system, dear Hearts, notice that we have just traveled past a very large blue star. This is Sirius 'A'. Its eight large planets are under the divine jurisdiction of a most loving species of fully-sentient Lionoids. They request simply that they be left to their divine task of holding the energy for what is this galaxy's primary spiritual stargate. Through this stargate pass all the great spiritual Beings who wish to enter and assist in the sacred development of this galaxy. Our current destination is the 'B' star. We are now passing through a beautiful light blue dust cloud. Ahead is our destination, the planetary system of a much smaller bluish-white star with six planets. Our journey's end is the fourth planet from this star. The Sirians call this solar system 'Akonowai' or 'the place of the Great Blue Lodge'. As we begin our orbit of the fourth planet, we welcome aboard Washta and his entourage of ten fellow Sirians. They have joined us to give you an overview of Sirian society and its complex culture. Let me turn you over to them.

Selamat Ja, fellow explorers! My name is Washta. Together, my colleagues and I will be your tour guides. We are happy to assist you in your tour of our beautiful and sacred realm.

We Sirians first came to this sacred land some 4.3 million of your solar years ago. We arrived here under the divine guidance of the galactic Spiritual Hierarchy and with the permission of the Lionoid people who inhabit the Sirius 'A' solar system. You are about to explore a society that is known to myriad sentient species in this galaxy as one of the prime examples of a galactic human society. Let us now teleport down and begin this trek through 'Sakara' or 'the soul of female creativity', our unique and very beautiful land.

You are presently near a small bay at the edge of our great central sea. This one large ocean makes up about eighteen per cent of our planet's surface area. The rest is a huge, interlocked continent. As you have noticed, we Sirians enjoy a semi-tropical climate. Our atmosphere's oxygen content is 36 per cent and may make you feel somewhat light-headed. The Sirian sky is naturally purplish. In it, high above us, hang two moons, each one slightly bigger than your own. Off to your right is our major mountain range, which we call the 'Shadota' or the 'many fingers of Heaven'.

Dear Hearts, most of our population lives underground in specially formed holographic chambers that are larger than most of your Earth's metropolitan areas. These enclaves are many miles high, several miles in diameter, and faithfully reproduce our Mother World's surface conditions and day and night cycles. There is no difference between them and any city we can construct upon our beloved planet's surface.

Using our advanced technology, inhabitants personally create their own houses and entire neighborhoods. The innumerable entertainment possibilities this sub-terrestrial world offers liken it to paradise. A few major temple and other ritual sites remain as surface signs of our existence. Before we teleport you down to one of our large urban complexes, let's review some significant aspects of a galactic society.

Galactic human societies are founded on the twin precepts of realized full potential (achievement of one's life purpose) and observance of divine societal laws. Based upon Love, they are the Laws of the One, Two, Three, and Four (see page 198, Figure 13). Each is part of the foundation on which any galactic society is predicated. Complete Love is seen as the ability to thoroughly understand another soul force and, from that knowledge, to better understand oneself. It is also recognized that the intimate Light of Life shines in all of us in its own special way. The service of friends and podlet (the more immediate kin circles) helps this Light enter each person in its fullest and most complete brilliance.

The Law of the One governs the prime importance to society of a well-balanced and fully centered, sovereign individual. The wholly realized individual's path is to achieve her/his possibilities (life purpose) utterly and, in the process, to fully support others.

Civilization's foundation rests on a belief that the individual's growth in consciousness can develop only by completely exploring the higher soul purpose and, concurrently, by giving service to others. It is based in personal sovereignty and founded on complete liberty and a high sense of self-worth. The individual is free to question and to investigate those things that lead to the fulfillment of her/his life purpose. In the process of this discovery, inspiration to offer one's divine service to others flows freely from within the self.

In attaining their full potential, individuals know that a unique

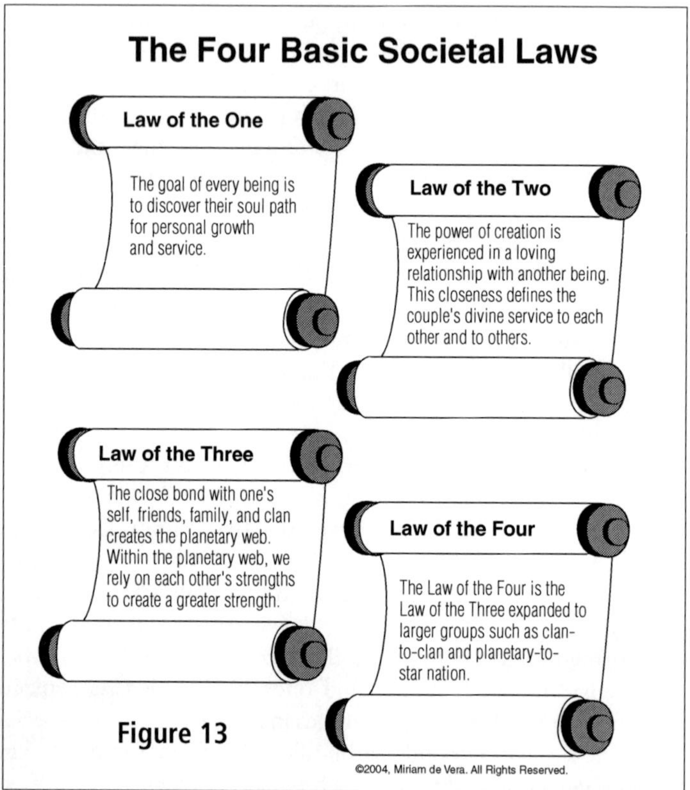

Figure 13

someone can assist them in achieving their complete union with Spirit, higher wisdom, and inner growth. This special other is their 'closeness' or a full embodiment for them of the societal Law of the Two. One's closeness has the ability to comprehensively understand one's personal soul force. Possessing that profound knowledge, individuals can then enjoy an extensive awareness of themselves and their special other. Theirs is an interconnected process, as well as a deep relationship. It is based on their mutual, integral desire to explore the divine link between two beings, by means of which they are enabled to clarify the meaning of their divine service to others.

The Law of the Three is based upon the concept of divine service and support to others. Service of, or to, friends and podlet (kin) helps bring Light (divine Love) into its fullest and most complete radiance. Galactic human society is an expression of the intense interconnection between the individual and her/his fellows. Each soul is a truly divine Light that reflects an important aspect of the entire society. Galactic society exists to support the individual in this sacred quest and to obtain her/his support in return. The complex dynamics of this particular process are embedded in the Law of the Three.

The Law of the Four embodies a union of like-hearted star-nations. As such, the Galactic Federation represents a direct outcome of the last of the four societal laws. Since galactic human society is closely entwined, the four divine societal laws symbolize the entire planetary society's gradual, interlinked development and permit it to serve other star-nations.

Long ago, the ancestors of present-day galactic humanity learned the joy of extending their service and support, in the Light, to other sentient star-nations of the Milky Way Galaxy. In this manner, they are assisted in aligning, in their own unique way, with the nature of Spirit's purpose. Out of this growing unity has emerged the Galactic Federation of Light. This magnificent organization of fully-conscious Beings has long been the symbol for Light in this galaxy. It is a shining example of the embodiment of these sacred societal laws.

Your society stands at a crossroads in consciousness, and we wish to describe to you a model for its future. Every galactic human society feels a great need to assist and support any other society that has reached the point yours has. You have the right to develop your own model. Our purpose is merely to assist you to move forward in those areas that may cause you to stumble. During this tour, watch what we do, and see how it can apply to your next evolutionary step in creating a healthy and solution focused society. Let us begin to exhibit our society's organization by allowing you to view its micro-levels.

Galactic human society is usually broken down into what can be termed very small 'clans' or 'podlets'. We call these very small clans 'Bhada' or 'the essence that reflects each other'. Podlets (see page 200, Figure 14) consist of up to 64 individuals and are customarily built around a specific life purpose: healers; spiritual warriors; engineers; scientists and/or priestess/priest classifications. Podlet elders provide education, and the podlet's many adult members supplement their teachings. Knowledge and wisdom are honored, as are those adults who have learned much during their lifetimes. Parents freely share their nurturing responsibilities with the podlet's other adults, and a child can have many so-called 'aunts' and 'uncles'. The goal of child rearing is to foster high self-esteem, personal sovereignty, and mutually shared Love and joy in all individuals.

The Characteristics of a Podlet

Figure 14

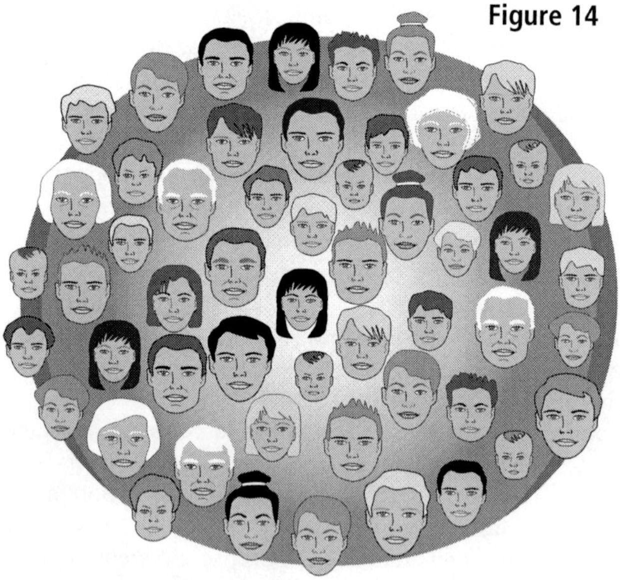

There are up to 64 people to a podlet. A podlet is a group of elders, counselors, members and children. The podlet leaders are appointed by podlet members.

Although education and knowledge are vitally important to the podlet, the child's spiritual development is even more important. The gifts and abilities that God has given for this particular lifetime come forth only as the miraculous energy of Spirit is fully acknowledged. Consequently, every child's early education is filled with reverence for the awe and wonder of Spirit. To a galactic human, Spirit is everything. This marvelous life energy directs you toward the realization of your Life's purpose during this physical life span. It is also the source of your connection to the Creator's cosmic energies that makes all realities possible. Spirit is the starting point for all inner inspirations and ideals that guide your daily experiences within physical life.

We Sirians are very proud of our spiritual heritage and the galactic Spiritual Hierarchy's acknowledgment of it. Over the past few million years, we have become spiritual teachers and guides for much of this galaxy. As a part of this process, we have become 'home' to the Great Blue Lodge that includes the divine Council of the Nine, carrying their profound messages to every part of this galaxy.

We are no more than humble wayshowers for Spirit. The way of Spirit touches each and every one in its own unique and wonderful way. There is no greater joy than to watch each new flower in this galaxy blossom, adding its beauty to the grand bouquet. The process of 'wayshowing' leads us now to a description of our counselors.

A vital aspect of galactic society is its use of a very comprehensive counseling system. It is genuinely felt that the human ancestors of this Galactic Federation's vast array of star-societies desired to create a social system that fully nourished the individual. To accomplish this goal, a system of counselors is built into each society. Counselors are divided into four major types. Each is thoroughly trained for almost twenty years at a special academy and then field-trained for an additional 75 years. Counselors are a highly skilled and universally respected part of galactic society. In many ways, they are the element that binds this society firmly together and keeps it solidly on track.

The first type is the parental-child counselor. These special individuals help during pregnancy and assist podlet elders in the raising of every child. Their major task is to guide the child in fully comprehending her/his abilities and discovering her/his life purposes. The second category is the 'closeness' or relationship counselor. They are experts in helping resolve any possible difficulties that may arise before or during the course of a primary relationship. Third is the pod counselor who assists elders and adults in carrying out, clearly and efficiently, the various stated purposes of the podlet. Last is the liaison counselor. These marvelous Beings assist each podlet in working successfully and in complete harmony with the others.

Each podlet has a governing council that functions according to the principles of Fluid Group Dynamics™. This system is based upon the fact that each sovereign individual possesses a unique set of gifts, the use of which permits the podlet to complete an assigned task smoothly and easily. The podlet appoints a certain individual to be in charge of a particular task. The rest of the podlet wholly supports her/him. When different gifts are required, another suitably talented individual steps forward to manage and complete the additional task. An organic rhythm develops in the podlet that expresses the fluidity (easy interaction) of the group. It also demonstrates each member's complete commitment to Spirit and support of all others' talents and abilities. Competition is a distinctly foreign concept in galactic society.

Figure 15

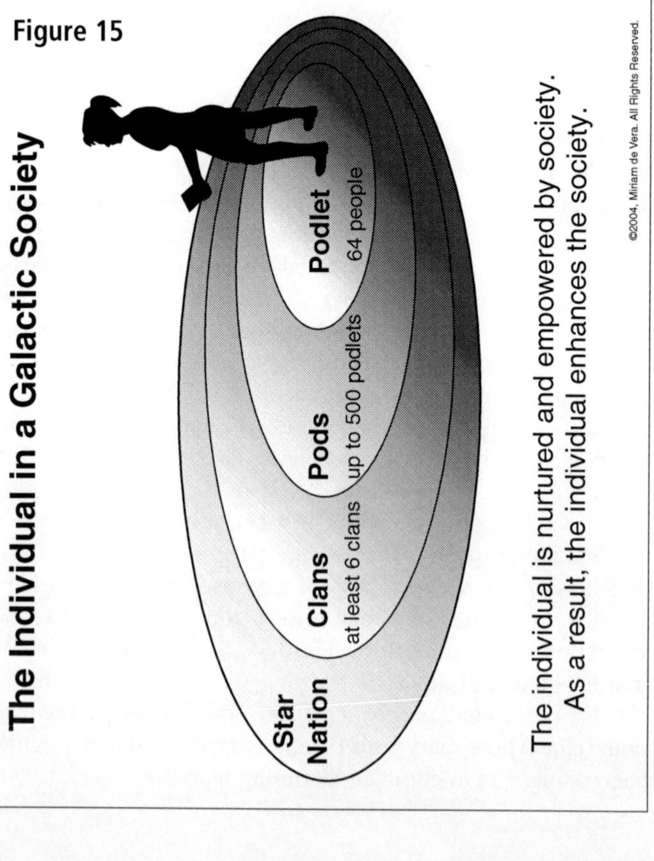

Your planetary society is now evolving toward full potentialization of the group. This accelerating process leads to the development of a new type of extended family, composed of like-minded individuals who fully understand their shared purpose and support their members' self-growth. Humans exist in a web of reality that includes necessary levels of complimentary interactions. These communications permit the continual development of inner confidence (self-esteem) and self-growth. This web of reality moves incessantly in both an inward and an outward direction. Our Sirian government is a prime example of the heights to which this development can lead.

An additional division of our galactic society is centered on the number of clan councils contained in Sirian society (see page 202, Figure 15). Here again, both the principles of Fluid Group Dynamics™ and the use of liaison counselors are widespread. Governance is perceived as the fulfillment of divine service. Since every member of the society is sovereign, government's purpose is simply to mirror the divine will of the Spiritual Hierarchy and to assist each clan in successfully completing its most sacred goals. In governing councils, divine service is perceived as a way to honor specific individuals for their many wonderful services to the community. Ultimately, governance is left up to the will of the many realms of Spirit as expressed through the divine plan of the Creator. Thus, galactic society carries out the divine plan, and the Light of God is brought to its highest intonation in the physical world. Galactic human society is based on an absolute respect for the divine WILL of the Creator. The society's purpose is to serve the divine plan as perfectly as possible. At all times, it dedicates its service to perfecting and carrying out the sacred plan of Heaven. This it accomplishes in a number of ways. First, there is constant interaction between a star system's local Spiritual Hierarchy and that star system's governing council. Collaboration is founded upon a periodic assessment of how best to implement the divine plan. The entire procedure unfolds in right divine relationship to those specific lessons and acquired wisdoms that the society may need to embody.

Moreover, there exists a continuing obligation to check on the specific life purposes of each member of the society. Members operate at a specific frequency that changes according to their inner development and the achievement of their purposes.

There is a sincere need to maintain the resonance that keeps the sacred balance between a planet and its human inhabitants. As a planet's population develops and grows spiritually, the resonant frequencies of that galactic society continually shift. Hence, endless sets of moments or eternal 'Nows', that change according to the perceived reality, constantly take place. This changing balance between society and planet is maintained by positive group ritual. Ritual is one of the many responsibilities that each podlet joyfully shares with every other. It is an important part of daily life that expresses and maintains the vital connections among planet, individual, and Spirit. Rituals also assist in communicating a sense of the profound. It is this bond that is mainly responsible for all souls' happiness and growth. Ritual is one of the essential ways in which the podlet educates its many members.

Ritual is performed according to the regional location and the specific purpose of each pod. It is also carried out simultaneously on a global basis. Galactic society is established in such a way that many pods of similar purposes are scattered throughout the planet. Intermingling of pods assures that the planet's resonance can be balanced easily. It also permits each pod to come in contact with as many different purposes as possible. The key is to teach all how to blend their energies and join most efficiently and effectively. So, you may ask, what is it that they do?

Positive ritual is lovingly performed at the many primary energetic nodes on a planet's surface. Here are located the great ritual temples of galactic society, always constructed according to the principles of sacred geometry. Temples serve as sites for properly balancing the planet's numerous resonant frequencies (see page 205, Figure 16).

Balancing ritual consists of prayer, meditation, intention, and song, accompanied by the inspired use of many great crystals, instruments and drums found at the temples. In solemn procession, members of different pods bring into being the sacred geometry and chant the sacred oaths of their people. They perform this ceremony to create new balance and give sustenance to their holy Mother – the sacred, living Being that is their home.

Dear Hearts, now that we have returned from one of our subterranean enclaves, you can see how magnificent they truly are. Living in them is not like being in a cave. It is exactly like living on the surface of our very beautiful world. We are, at present, approaching one of our larger ritual temples. This temple is noted for its huge, 250-foot (over 76 meters) high columns and its vast, 'sacred geometry-inspired' galleries. It is magnificently adorned in hues of green, brown, blue and coral pink. Its immense gold roof is engraved with the icons of our sun and this master clan. The combined thoughts of its clan created each part of this temple. One of our planet's 128 major node points is located in its center.

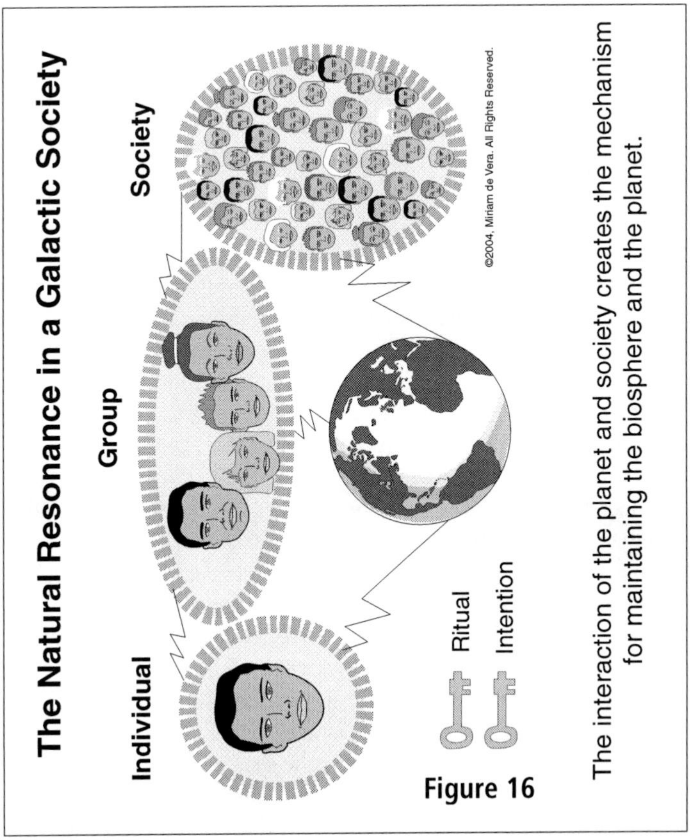

Figure 16

The interaction of the planet and society creates the mechanism for maintaining the biosphere and the planet.

As you enter, you will hear the large, specially decorated, sixteen-foot-diameter drums, which are attuned to the frequency of this planetary node. Also, you will hear what sounds like a chorus of harps and saxophones amplifying the drums. You will see many dancers at the node point, as well as those in a large circle who seem to be in meditation. The outer ones dressed in coral pink robes fine-tune this energy and send it into the planet's node. This ritual is based on various fundamental truths.

Their holy Mother planet is maintained, sacred and alive, in her pristine condition. Her biosphere is kept functioning as Mother/Father God intended. Each species of life on the planet has a distinct and divine purpose founded on the main resonance patterns of the sacred Mother. Dedicated scientists and engineers monitor every aspect of her biosphere. The purpose of society's sacred ritual is to preserve our mother world's natural balance. This vital process determines one of the main tenets of a galactic society: to celebrate the sacred nature of all planetary life and the importance of Love and Compassion.

Galactic society sees itself as an agent of the Spiritual Hierarchy and as a divine servant of God's holy WILL. Embedded in this perception is the concept that all celestial bodies are sentient life forms. Life is defined as that which contains life force and purpose. In the case of celestial bodies, that life purpose is to sustain the physical universe. Humanity exists to aid this sacred task and to learn, in the process, many necessary lessons. Humanity's existence in physicality is tempered by the need to understand the nature of physical reality and to employ it as a means to grow spiritually, as well as to serve the Creator.

The highest form of the observance of God's WILL is divine service. Consequently, galactic society is focused on service, freely offered, as part of the spiritual inner growth that all galactic humans undergo during their many lifetimes. Each lifetime is perceived to contain a divine purpose. After many lifetimes, the accumulation of divine purposes leads to a full understanding of the nature of Life and the ways of Spirit. This wisdom is applied to your podlet and to the many sub-pods existing above it. Each aspect of galactic society resolves itself into a primary clan.

These points return us to the temple sites and to the very nature of our divine service. Fully-conscious Beings exist in a realm that includes all of Creation. Our energy is then focused on a specific point in physicality in which we are completely present. Each of us communes, simultaneously, with one another. This shared act spreads our focus and increases our presence. We become one with this point and with each other. The planet is calibrated and, with it, all forms of life in her biosphere. Thus, joint ritual activates all points on the planet. We ask you to participate and to feel the energy. Such sacred energy leads us to a harmony with each other and a harmonic union of our clans.

Through the wise use of their liaisons, clans come together and form a planetary government for the entire star-nation. This government is different from that on Earth. Here, it is a great honor to serve one's clan, one's divine planet and, above all, the Spiritual Hierarchy. Galactic humans' relationship with Spirit is extremely deep, for it is Spirit that determines their lives and sets the life contracts that contain their primary purposes. To galactic humans, Life is a great, undulating flow – a river of Spirit mixed with the many powerful lessons of physicality. Yet, in its midst, the need to experience Life fully and to find the reason for and joy in physical life exists.

Galactic society is infused with a rich culture filled with many rituals, formal and casual parties, and joyous occasions! Life has been stripped of its outer struggle. Housing, clothing, food and transportation are freely provided. No monetary exchange is apparent nor is any recognizable economic system in existence. Life's focus is the pursuit of one's purpose, a quest ruled by the twin concepts of personal sovereignty and great compassion for others. The connection among all is clearly known and respected. High self-esteem is reflected by the grace, ease, and openness with which individuals relate to each other.

The concept of free and prolific innovation is the engine that drives society. Individuals have certain gifts that enable them to contribute uniquely to society. From the earliest years of childhood, the creative innovation process is encouraged, and, at the appropriate time, we begin making our life-long contributions to society. Our offerings take many forms. They include creative problem solving for our extended pod or the development of new inventions for society's benefit. Donations are rewarded through a special honoring system, either by the podlet or by the sub-clan.

This honoring system permits Spirit to recognize those persons who have brought forward an idea or device. It acknowledges the personal sovereignty and self-esteem of the individual. Galactic society encourages both the sovereignty of the individual and her/his necessary growth in Spirit. Sovereignty is a concept that many on your planet have yet to wholly comprehend. It transcends any perceived rights and refers instead to the individual's liberty to grow in Spirit according to God's wishes.

True individual sovereignty is crucial to the operation of galactic society. Within such societies, the soul's freedom to grow in the great Light of the Creator is sacrosanct. Before returning to Mother/Father God's holy side, every sentient Being has a specific soul path to complete. This sacred path is encouraged by parents, podlet, and by the many counselors encountered during one's lifetime. As one's Spirit is enriched, so, too, does it enrich the Spirit of humanity.

Each aspect of your Being is unique, yet it is also connected to every aspect of every other Being in Creation. Your inner growth assists these others and provides a means to elevate galactic society to new heights. This interconnected process is the reason that galactic society is contained within a highly intricate, organic structure.

The nature of galactic society is truly organic. It is a living organism with fluid or mutable shape, based on the dynamic of flow and tied to society's natural rhythm. This rhythm is determined by the natural resonance of the planet and its many inhabitants. It is fluid because the concept of a definite hierarchy is absent. Everyone in the society contributes effectively to its open dynamic. Yet, this organism is graceful and elegant in its inner growth and in the spread of its vast compassion. It fully nurtures all of the sentient Beings in its midst.

Let us return to one of our subterranean enclaves and examine how this society operates. Coming into view is a podlet of 32 that is participating in its temple ritual. As you can see, they have begun their procession out of the temple. They live in an urban area called 'Jaga' or 'the city of great joy'. As they emerge, you will notice that each one goes to the central meeting place, a large octagonal room more than 60 feet (over 18 meters) across. Here, individuals express their gratitude to, and their love for, each other. This ceremony of extending gratitude and nurturing is paramount to our society and brings us to an important concept.

Nurturing the individual is a pivotal aspect of galactic civilization. From the moment of birth through adulthood, parents and all other podlet members engender in each person feelings of self-esteem and social worth. The very fact of your existence, and the enduring contribution you have made to the podlet simply by entering into physicality, is always consistently recognized. Each child is constantly reminded that, at the right divine time, she/he will begin to bring forth creative innovations that can enhance the podlet and the entire galactic society.

The feeling of being cared for and heard magnifies everyone's self-esteem and assists the individual in overcoming any potential shyness. Members are taught to contribute to the podlet and to be of assistance when the gifts of others are being manifested. This dynamic encourages a natural and fluid exchange that flows endlessly according to the very essence of the podlet's many members. An immense, dynamic consciousness field continuously surrounds both the podlet and the whole of galactic society.

Intention and its manifestation are a primary result of this dynamic. Consequently, an air of creative innovation and inspiration is continuously present. Part of this vast dynamic field is the realization of each person's full potential. Galactic society exists to encourage the complete achievement of one's divine life purpose. In this realization, the individual flowers fully, as does the entire society. It is this remarkable dynamic that keeps galactic society so open to change and to reinventing itself as necessary.

Regular interchange among members of the podlet is evident in the varied types of communications that take place. A steady flow of expressed feelings and beliefs occurs at both spoken and telepathic levels.

In the community room or in separate households, this web of Love (consciousness) envelops them. Out of a genuine happiness that flows from one individual to another comes a candid openness, encouraged and rewarded by all.

Using your multi-functional scanners, step into this situation and view what is happening. Full presence and multi-dimensionality have set the stage for the scene you are witnessing. Complete empathy is the guiding principle. True emotions and feelings cannot be concealed. Yet, a structure underlies this process.

Galactic society's only structure is composed of divine societal laws and the sacred divine plan of the Creator. Each of these foundations encourages its organic field dynamic. Bear in mind that galactic society is a container that operates somewhat like a multifunctional, dynamic force field. It contains the encompassing dynamic field, and the entire society has the capability to expand it, as necessary.

This ever-dynamic consciousness field has one primary purpose: to give the society a direction. In turn, galactic society employs this dynamic consciousness field to establish and maintain the fulcrum upon which its essential works are performed.

The consciousness-oriented dynamic field that galactic society has created also serves as a basis for the individual's inspiration and development. Manifesting simultaneously in this dynamic consciousness field is a concurrent past, present, and future. This interactive energy pattern proves decisively that contributions you make to society and to yourself are both ensured and strongly encouraged by all concerned. Accordingly, you are positioned to achieve your full potential and to encourage others to do so willingly. This energy dynamic further enlarges the podlet's consciousness field and permits it to achieve its own unique full potential. During all periods of the society's ever-evolving eternal 'Now', this activity directs the field dynamics toward the completion of the divine plan.

As noted, all individuals feel completely connected to their fully conscious selves and to the fully conscious essence of their podlet. This amazing exchange of energy flows unceasingly, back and forth, at the maximum resonance frequency of this complex field dynamic. As the podlet's field grows, it encompasses the planet and the entire star-nation. Additionally, it includes numerous energies that emanate from the local Spiritual Hierarchy and from the Creator. Cosmic energies from the heart of Creation envelop this growing consciousness field and transport it into very high levels of ecstasy!

Clearly, galactic society functions on many levels that interact naturally with one another. Each one of these levels (individual, podlets, pods, clans, and planet's governing councils) is separate yet 'interpendent'. 'Interpendence' can be defined as 'a free association of sovereign Beings who have come together in a particular moment for the purpose of solving any problems. Each Being's sole purpose is to interact dynamically with all others, using their combined creative manifesting talents and their collective actions to achieve a desired outcome. That outcome can then be presented to the society and used as a model for further actions.

This multi-layered network of fully potentialized Beings is based on the above principle of 'interpendence'. As situations warrant, these groups expand and contract constantly in size. Hence, the boundary between each level is purely organic and extremely fuzzy. The number of fully-sentient Beings involved varies only with the nature of the particular problem to be solved. Those problems that directly affect the entire society involve all members, while smaller problems can involve only the members of a specific pod or podlet.

Innovative problem-solving is achieved through ongoing use of this organic field dynamic. Problems are seen as opportunities to better understand the self and society. Each problem permits those directly involved to achieve a measure of inner growth. Inner growth, in turn, allows the podlet to more profoundly comprehend its reality and to add new perceptions to its inner truths. This organic approach to reality permits the podlet and its members to grow in many directions at the same time.

The same series of principles applies to galactic society. For instance, our governing council is different from any organization you currently may conceive of. It is intrinsically embedded in our society and grows in wisdom with it. Like a hologram, each part of the whole (the many levels of our galactic society) contains the immense diversity of the whole within itself. This dynamic permits discernible, conscious interaction and the continuity of organic development.

To explain this process, let us travel to the main council chambers of the Sirian star-nation. Here, you can see that each person not only represents a clan but is also a Being who wishes to use her/his abilities to solve potential problems harmoniously. In addition, you can watch the liaison counselors in action. They bridge each group and help to maintain overall flow. The result is a consciousness field that solves potential problems and guides the societal field ever outward. If you will use your multifunctional scanners, you can more easily pick up these nuances and sense how this system creates its own 'history'.

Galactic society is energetically involved in creating a field of memories or stories that are utilized for problem-solving. All problems have an inherent solution that involves expansion of the perception of both group and/or individual soul. The solution is a wisdom that aids your inner growth. It is a divine object, provided to assist you in understanding those particular perceptions that your Full Self and the Spiritual Hierarchy create together for the purpose of your soul's growth. An old Sirian proverb on this matter states, "A problem has a purpose. To discover this purpose, one has only to understand the solution."

Full consciousness permits a society to function in the 'Light of the Angels'. It also allows galactic society to see itself as it was, is, and will be. The artificial divisions of past, present, and future converge and are replaced by consciousness modeling. This level of excellence stretches advancement to the maximum and permits every individual to interact with all others at the highest possible levels.

Accordingly, galactic society is embedded in a continuous inner communication – a natural, telepathic network. This system acts as a source for information that aids and enhances your soul's inner growth. It also creates a natural resource for any type of information you could possibly require.

The network's overall purpose is to act as a catalyst for fresh, new ideas. All individuals are born into a living sea of consciousness that helps them feel that they are not alone. All fully-sentient Beings lovingly support each other. They share a fondness for life's various inner passions and easily offer compassion to each other. Innovation flows from this highly sensitive sea in enormous waves of Light. Every member of the society seeks to fully utilize this marvelous medium for co-creation.

Podlets add to the mixture by honoring innovation and sharing these new ideas with the other podlets and pods in their clan. In all cases, the particular Being (chosen by the Spiritual Hierarchy as the vehicle for a new idea) is duly honored. According to an ancient proverb, it is believed that "Everything happens for a desired, divine purpose". Life is a series of great joys that assists you in completely understanding your reality. When you intend the best for yourself and all others, only the most positive events can possibly occur in your reality.

Fully-conscious Beings are individuals who have an understanding of their past, present, and future. They create and manifest in a time frame that encourages their success. Each person is tied to a particular life-stream or Lineage of Heaven and becomes incarnate, fully prepared to express the nature of this life-stream during the course of her/his lifetime. You create with full knowledge of the future and of the ultimate consequences of your innovation. At the same time, you are always endowed with the knowledge of your natural telepathic network to draw on whenever you evaluate potential new ideas.

Using your multi-dimensional scanners, please 'tune in' to your Full Self. Feel how it connects with you in so many varied and quite magnificent ways. Sense the absolute psychic, mental, and emotional rush that this connection suddenly gives you. Experience your deep joy and know how much you are connected to each other.

This exercise demonstrates how full consciousness feels and can be realized. A fully-conscious Being lives in a reality quite unlike yours. Yet, that Being is you – the Being who enjoys her/his fully realized potential. It is the Being you are in the process of becoming. The society you are now observing is the type of environment you shall choose for yourselves. Its reality is part of the implicate order you are creating for yourselves every day. Such a society is in a continuous state of creative flux.

Galactic society is constantly reinventing itself. The many natural networks within it act as fulcrums for communicating wisdom, knowledge, and universal, integral principles. These processes assist the evaluation of ideas and help to spread them throughout society at the speed of thought. Hence, change occurs organically. In a galactic society, tradition is merely a basis for the positive, global ritual of change.

Galactic society is always adjusting to minute changes in its various consciousness fields. Each consciousness field continuously mirrors the inner growth of its many members and any alterations in their perception. For this reason, every individual is viewed as a very important microcosm of the entire society.

Let us now look more closely at this important microcosm – the individual. You will see that each is a special Being Due to the telepathic networks and the fields of merged time (past, present, future) that surround them, each is a true representative of the whole – a hologram, if you will. Yet, at the same time, each personifies a unique and fully-conscious, sentient Being. Such multi-level ability gives these individuals an absolute sense of self.

At the same time, it gives them total comprehension of every aspect of society. This ability is also woven into daily interaction with the Spiritual Hierarchy. Further, each Being is fully conversant with the life essence of her/his planet. This marvelous Being exists in Love and has worked itself through what you call 'ego'. Inner growth is 'interpendent', and your physical existence is viewed as part of a great sacred vortex, the divine blossoming of physical Creation.

Each type of fully-sentient life form is designed both to live upon and to maintain the planet it inhabits. One of our main techniques is group ritual. As a galactic society builds its highly dynamic consciousness field, it also constructs (through ritual) a means to energize the planet. A symbiotic relationship rapidly develops between our society and the planetary biosphere. As the consciousness field grows, it enlivens and enriches every aspect of the living planet. This necessary interaction allows galactic society to fulfill its part in the revelation of the divine plan.

A fully-conscious Being acts as a responsible and compassionate physical Angel, bringing in the life (Love) energies required to maintain its world. Fully-conscious Beings assist the Spiritual Hierarchy in carrying out the divine plan in their sector of the galaxy. This interaction engages the local Spiritual Hierarchy for their star-nation and also embraces the galactic Spiritual Hierarchy. Their purpose is to aid the physical progression of the divine plan in both their star-nation and their galaxy. This procedure eventually leads them into interstellar space, to a first contact, and then to union with other like-hearted galactic societies.

Thus, a societal consciousness field is extended to the galaxy as a whole and, through it, a much larger one is established. Such galactic organizations function under sacred societal laws similar to ones previously given to all galactic societies. These laws guide the growth and development of star-nations. A subsequent set of societal laws guides this galactic union and acts as the foundation for future first contacts with other developing star-nations.

Free will, possessed by each individual and every galactic society in the development of the exquisitely complex divine plan, is this pattern of choice. The Creator has provided a special labyrinth through which the individual and her/his respective society can grow and, at the same time, can help to reveal the Creator's most marvelous design. Mother/Father God has conceived a pattern, producing special situations that continuously generate a unique overall field dynamic. These situations arise to test and prove the validity of each segment of Creation's freely chosen development. The beauty of this Creation labyrinth is that, by following it, you can eventually achieve oneness with all others.

The intent of physical Creation is to develop the maximum possible alternatives to its progression. These different processes are to be put together miraculously during the consciousness growth procedures that Creation's specially constructed labyrinth has provided. While quite complex, this process is designed to produce eventual union among all involved physical, sentient Beings. Consequently, physical Creation becomes an environment both for moving physical Beings through various stages of consciousness and for the formation of their varied dynamic fields.

The crux of this entire procedure is the Creation labyrinth itself. It has been established to produce a vast range of effects, at different moments, for all the diverse aspects of physical Creation. These varying sentient aspects can therefore 'learn' from each other about the awesome nature of Creation. Creation proceeds in a unique way that stems from this interaction. Usually, this wisdom is then passed throughout the dynamic field created by the society. Galactic society is primarily a vehicle for fully-conscious Beings to discover the innumerable ways in which the dynamic process flows. Ultimately, the Creation labyrinth is the tool used to pass this wisdom on to the next generation of individuals.

The wisdom of full consciousness lies in the fact that its design is fluid. That is, a fully-conscious Being wholeheartedly accepts the fact that she/he both acts, and is acted upon, by Creation. This dual process produces a special relationship involving a fully-sentient Being, its physical environment, and the vast realms of Spirit. It also brings forth a special, conscious dynamic that exists both for growth and to process the development of this wonderful form of sentiency. You are about to experience a most marvelous adventure in consciousness that will lead you eventually to a meeting with all of physical Creation.

Dear Hearts, we are now returning to our spaceship. As you return to your seats, please go within and feel the absolute wonder of this adventure that is consciousness. It is an amazing path that transports you to the micro-world of the physical body and its changes and, subsequently, reveals to you the macro-world of our galaxy and all of Creation.

This present aspect of our journey is a case in point. You have discovered, now, how fully-conscious societies co-create in this galaxy. After a few questions, which Washta has graciously agreed to answer, let us begin another leg of our journey into Spirit and find out how it fits into your grand adventure!

Questions and Answers

Q: Can you describe what a fully-conscious reality is like?
A: Reality such as this is truly multi-dimensional in form. You need to accept that fully-conscious individuals exist on two levels simultaneously – the personal and the group. In effect, such Beings are a true hologram of the whole, as well as a full representation of themselves. Their degree of presence is truly astounding. Moreover, they are filled with grace, compassion, and a natural understanding of others. They call upon the wisdom of their ancestors and their own past lives, are in contact with the Spiritual Hierarchy, and are true physical Angels. Their reality is one that most Earth humans may have difficulty actually grasping.

Q: What inspired the Spiritual Hierarchy to create galactic society in the first place?
A: The Spiritual Hierarchy created galactic society as a vehicle for the inner growth and development of fully-conscious humanity. It was also formed as the means for God's physical Angels to carry out their sacred tasks in aiding the full blossoming of physical Creation.

The foundation of this holy structure is the societal laws. Each law functions as a basis for one of the four aspects of galactic society. Those four aspects are: inner growth of the individual, finding of true love with another, use of this compassion to assist others in the immediate group, and, lastly, mastery of universal harmony and its application to society.

Q: What is personal sovereignty?
A: Personal sovereignty is the right of the individual to freely follow her/his purpose in life and extends to the complete respect of others in how she/he undertakes this life's work. It implies that you are able to use your God-given gifts to express

this purpose and/or search to others. It also means that your beliefs are totally respected by society. In other words, you are seen to be a person of worth with the capability to manifest those situations needed to complete your deepest desires.

Q: How does the process of innovation work in a galactic society?

A: Innovation is seen as the lubricant that turns the wheels of society. Every moment and every interaction of any individual's life is interwoven with the application of creativity. Rather than an event being viewed as a problem, it is seen simply as a matter that has yet to be creatively addressed.

The concept of failure or 'less than' is absent from such a society. At all times, you are encouraged to contribute your special talents to any detail that has yet to be addressed. This environment fosters creativity and encourages innovation. It also makes possible the great self-esteem, grace and gratitude that permeates it.

Q: In this mini-tour, there is a discussion about the creation of a consciousness field dynamic. How exactly does that work?

A: When fully-conscious Beings conduct group ritual and focus their conscious life energy, a specific consciousness field is produced. This consciousness field is influenced by the daily changes in its resonance frequency caused by the inner growth of each individual in society. Day by day, continual group ritual, and the changes being created by society as a whole, intensify this field and alter its resonance ever upward, creating a fluid dynamic. The consciousness field dynamic is also immediately attached to a merged past, present, and future.

All of these variables come together and cause the field to produce a notable side-effect – an organic Being whose every thought and intention mirrors those of the entire society. This organic whole is simultaneously reproduced in every individual in the group. Thus, it functions on two levels: the individual and the collective.

Personal and group mind are linked together, always cross-pollinating each other. They establish a dynamic field resonance with a large number of possibilities, each directed toward inner growth and creative ideas.

Acting as a guide in this process are the Angelic Realms, who ensure that this conscious dynamic field closely follows the intentions of the divine plan.

Q: How are the various branches of galactic society organized?
A: Galactic society is organized on three major levels: a plethora of podlets, numerous pods, and clans. Clans are established throughout the society and are organized according to a specific function or necessary occupation, such as engineer, scientist, or administrator. In addition, pods which can consist of up to 500 podlets are under the clan's banner. Podlets contain up to 64 related members. At each level, there is also a committee of the whole, which operates according to the principles of Fluid Group Dynamics™.

Every clan has its own set of colors, mottoes, and a cultural tradition. A clan also has an honorary council that carries out the express desires of the clan and of the Spiritual Hierarchy. In all cases, the divine plan and its sacred work, and each member's divine life purpose are blended by the Spiritual Hierarchy and the society's counselors into a cherished holy harmony. Overall, the many divisions become fuzzy, due to the dynamic of the consciousness field surrounding this society, and the amount of grace given to all by the Spiritual Hierarchy.

Q: How exactly do the different types of counselors work with the individuals of a galactic society?
A: Counselors are taught and then learn to apply two major methods of contact. The first involves the inner Angelic guardian councils or guides that all sentient Beings possess. Their purpose is to consult with the inner councils and then with the individual. From feedback, each counselor can discern how this inner growth pattern is to be created in alignment with the individual's present life-stream.

A second procedure is to take the individual all the way back to Source and collect important data along the way. When the two procedures are in alignment, key points concerning how a life purpose is intended to work out can be shown.

In addition, the point of eternal 'Now' can be employed and brought to the future, past, and back again. This technique permits the counselor to manifest how life purpose can be accomplished and to identify some of the more important people able to assist in achieving these goals. The salient point remains how the individual sets up her/his contract with the Spiritual Hierarchy and significant others.

Q: How do liaison counselors keep two or more diverse

groups in harmony with each other?

A: Because the joint actions that brought these groups together are based on Fluid Group Dynamics™, there is a creative reason for their union in the first place that lends itself to creative solutions. In addition, this association causes a group consciousness field, which also develops an environment conducive to creative solutions. All of these points can be used to produce harmony and a successful outcome in the merging of two very distinct groups.

Q: How does a podlet operate?

A: A podlet is the very core of this society. It acts as both a committee of the whole that employs Fluid Group Dynamics™, and a positive and open environment for the nurturing, upbringing, education, and life preparation of its young. It is an extended kin circle.

In addition, it engages many counselors, whose primary task is to see that every part of this process remains operational. The result is an organic group that functions according to its changing daily situations, and is fluid and nimble enough to keep itself completely operative. Out of this functional mode can emerge those creative solutions or innovations necessary for its continued existence.

Q: In what manner does the clan council come to its decisions?

A: The clan council bases its decision-making on two principles. First, their purpose is exclusively to honor and sanctify the innovation process. Each clan member swims in an ocean of consciousness, the waters of which the Spiritual Hierarchy has provided. As sovereign Beings with a full sense of self and purpose, their ideas add profoundly to the society's dynamic.

According to the second principle, their task is simply to follow the divine plan as the Angelic Realms have presented it to them. This process allows them to provide the clan with guidelines to which the local Spiritual Hierarchy has previously agreed. The clan council is solely a place where those honored for their service to the society, and to the clan, are duly appointed.

Q: During the course of this mini-tour, you have discussed the individual and the society. Just how does an individual fit into this society?

A: The individual stands at the very heart of this society. From the moment of birth through full adulthood, you are at the very center of life in your podlet. You conduct sacred ritual with your pod. Your podlet and pod educate you, and your podlet counsels you. Relatively early in your adolescent years, you begin to make yourself known as an innovator, which leads to a life-long involvement with inner growth, innovations, and divine service.

This process is based upon a need for divine service and a mutual, deep compassion. You are a fully conscious and highly purposeful Being, part of an individuated and collective mastermind that continually re-creates itself on all levels. Hence, it is easy to describe what is happening, and it becomes effortless for you to feel and sense what is really going on.

Q: How is the present Ascension or soul/body transformation process related to the creation of such a society on planet Earth?

A: On your world at present, your Spirit is descending into your physical body. When completed and fully integrated, this procedure creates a fully conscious Being. This fully-sentient Being produces a society similar to that which we have just described. Galactic society is a special spiritual vessel that such a Being prefers to inhabit. Our respectful role is to wait for the right divine moment and then to bring that blissful vessel to you. You are permitted to creatively modify it as you so choose.

Q: In this mini-tour, you have talked about one of the reasons why the Galactic Federation was formed. How does the Galactic Federation of Light fit into a galactic society?

A: The Galactic Federation is a union of like-hearted star-nations. As such, it is a direct outcome of the last of the four societal laws. The fourth law explains that, when fully-conscious Beings come together, they desire to create a harmony and to expand their consciousness field into new areas where additional innovations can be found.

Full sentiency seeks companionship through 'interpendence'. Utilizing its procedures, full sentiency finds the creative solutions to its challenges and the means to understand itself in a much clearer, brighter Light. This fundamental need to explore inner and outer space is sanctified by the Creator and Heaven's holy Lineage, and leads naturally to the formation of a federation of connected star-nations.

ADDENDA II

The Basic Principles of Fluid Management™

Fluid Management™ is a process for managing large or small organizations that Galactic Federation personnel first taught me when I was aboard their ships in the 1950's. It is a self-organizing system that depends on the rapid interchange of the tasks and personnel needed to carry out any objective.

The Three Principles of "Fluid Management"

"Fluid Management" has three major principles:

The first is that any objective is decided upon by the group or organization concerned. The task is undertaken only when the group as a whole is fully committed to its successful completion.

The second principle is that the 'project leader' chosen to manage the project is the one whom the group decides is best able to guide the plan to its completion. This 'project leader' does her/his work in full cooperation with the entire group. The 'project leader' also has the right to appoint staff to aid her/him when necessary.

The third principle is that this direction is given openly, with all the steps of the project made known to the group. There is constant feedback of information between the 'project leader', her/his staff and the group at large. In this way, they can obtain whatever available resources will ensure the task's success. The group sees itself as devoted friends or family. It is a team, interacting in full partnership, harmony and cooperation.

Finally, the group evaluates the completed project and reaches a consensus in choosing its next project. It then applies the above three principles to achieve that goal.

"Fluid Management" is based upon recognition of all members of any group as Sovereign Beings with purposive talents and abilities. Each member is fully dedicated to unleashing their creativity and focused on using their talents to solve whatever problem can occur in completing the objective.

The group encourages a free flow of information. It is dedicated to being fluid enough to reorganize itself when necessary. Each 'project leader' originates from the group and leads only because her/his talents and abilities are appropriate for the successful completion of the specific objective. At other times, these same individuals give of themselves to fully support another selected 'project leader'.

In turn, the 'project leader' is fully aware of her/his abilities and can resign from the position if she/he feels unable to complete the task. Here, the group is fully supportive of such a decision and, through its Love and caring for each member, ensures that the learning experience remains totally positive.

In Fluid Management™, there are no hierarchical structures and no firm assignment of tasks. The organization, whether large or small, sees itself as an organic entity capable of changing its form or shape whenever necessary. At its core are an inner integrity and a complete adaptability of the components that make up its whole. Everything is kept fluid and as creative and synergistic as possible.

Every member of a Fluid Management™ team is fully aware of their own inner purpose, as well as of the main purposes of the organization. The key is to find, and use, the method that most satisfactorily can solve all problems and achieve the agreed-upon objective.

For "Fluid Management™" exercises, refer to the book, "Selamat Ja! A Guide for Galactic Humans" (To order Salamat Ja!, see page 244)

GLOSSARY OF IMPORTANT TERMS

Anchara: Entity commanded eons ago by Heaven to bring forth a great darkness upon this galaxy and, at the right divine time, to shift this galaxy toward the Light.

Anchara Alliance: A former galactic organization, consisting of various dark empires, star leagues and star-nations, dedicated to the conquest of this galaxy in the name of their dark overlord, Anchara.

Anunnaki: For 13 millennia, the Anunnaki were Earth's dark, off-world masters. In 1995, they changed sides, abandoned their Earth minions (the "Illuminoids" or "Illuminati") and advised them to do likewise.

Divine Plan: Holy and divine blueprint of Mother/Father God. Through it, the many Creations are carried out.

Elohim: Chief inter-dimensional Creator Beings. Use the sacred, spiritual energies given by Angelic Realms to help Angels formulate and maintain physical Creation according to the divine plan.

Four Laws of Galactic Society: Galactic human societies are founded on the twin precepts of realized full potential (achievement of one's life purpose) and observance of divine societal laws. Based upon Love, they are the Laws of the One, Two, Three and Four. Each is part of the foundation upon which any galactic society is predicated.

Fluid Group Dynamics™: Primary organizing axiom of the Galactic Federation of Light. Non-hierarchical and goal-oriented, it relies on the talents, leadership and accord of its members. Also known as Fluid Management™.

Full Consciousness: State of unlimited reality in which physical, mental, emotional and spiritual bodies are fully integrated. Denotes full use of now-untapped mental and spiritual capabilities, including possession of Light Body and full range of psychic abilities, such as telepathy and telekinesis. Also the capacity to instantly manifest what is physically desired and enjoy full rapport with spiritual and other higher dimensions.

Galactic Human: Fully conscious human Being. Also called Physical Angel. Retains full recall of its Akashic records and true life purpose.

Galactic Federation of Light: Light union created, over four million years ago, by various stellar civilizations in this galaxy. Its divine purpose is to serve as Physical Angels called upon to carry out divine destiny prophesied for Milky Way Galaxy long ago.

Great Blue Lodge of Creation: Order of Heaven decreed by Lord Surea and entrusted to act as supreme guides of the Light in all of physical Creation. This august and holy place is presided over by the Council of Nine and led by Lord Aescapulus. Headquartered, in this galaxy, on Sirius B.

Heart Logic: The natural, intuitive logic of all fully sentient Beings. Sourced by inner, true Love and the connection of one's Soul to the wisdom of the Supreme Creative Force (God).

Hybrid: Offspring of two Beings from different sentient species and genetically manipulated to produce specific, inherited characteristics.

Illuminoids: Earth minions of the Anunnaki. They include royalty, various secret orders and powerful individuals.

Light Body: Spiritual energy vehicle of a fully conscious Being. Contains the fully integrated physical, mental, emotional and spiritual bodies, transformed into a ball of Light that can travel almost instantaneously to any part of Creation.

Ritual: Specific set of procedures celebrated on a regular basis according to defined purpose or goal. Prime example is group or individual use of meditation or vision quest to achieve divine purpose, e.g., to heal Earth or better oneself.

Treaty of Anchara: Peace agreement signed between the Galactic Federation of Light and the former Anchara Alliance. Concluded after Anchara's sudden declaration to its priests and priestesses that the time of prophecy had come. Anchara ordered its galactic minions to end their wars and join with the Galactic Federation to form one harmonious whole.

Living with Sheldan Nidle

Aloha!

People often ask me, "What is it like to live with Sheldan?"

Sheldan and I have been Life partners for the past 8 years. For over 11 years, I have known him and supported his message. Because Sheldan is in constant contact, 24/7, with his galactic friends, many assume that I, too, experience contact in the same way he does. That has not been true for me. Certainly, while I have enjoyed a few personal galactic encounters, I could count them on the fingers of one hand. When Sheldan started writing this book, it was as if a high-frequency vortex had opened in our home, giving me, at least for the duration of the book's writing, the gift to connect telepathically with our galactic neighbors.

When I first partnered with Sheldan, he was presenting two weekly updates from the Galactic Federation of Light and Spiritual Hierarchy. When he sat down at the computer to take dictation, I quickly learned not to sit behind him, as the intense energies and high frequencies immediately put me to sleep. Throughout the years, I have adjusted and no longer react that way.

I enjoy the days when Sheldan receives the update information because he is in such a euphoric state of Beingness. I call him my "Bliss Bunny". This joy permeates our entire home. However, the night before an update, Sheldan invariably falls asleep around 8 pm, during which time he is receiving inserts of data and involved in discussions "upstairs" concerning the next day's information.

For me, the energies are buzzing on the night before an update, and I am routinely wide-awake until about 2 or 3 a.m. When I enter our bedroom, I usually find a beautiful, large blue, Sirian ball of light above Sheldan, and hundreds of tiny dots of white light twinkling all around him. I've grown accustomed to this and no longer consider it unusual.

When Sheldan started to write this book, the first Galactic Federation members to work with him were of the human race.

I would come home from my errands and, as I walked up the stairs, I could feel loving, uplifting energies from the visitors he met that day. When I asked with whom he had worked today, he would give me a brief outline of the information they had given him.

My 'Bliss Bunny' would be happy, but also very drained. During these sessions, he was instructed to drink lots of water and found himself taking long naps in the middle of the day. He would also sleep his usual 8 hours at night. For weeks, all he did was eat, sleep and write.

One day, as I returned home from shopping, I felt the usual uplifting, loving energies. But instead of being wrung-out and drained, Sheldan was energized. "I began with the non-human members today, the Arcturians to be precise," he informed me. "They are so loving and gracious. They are renowned healers throughout our galaxy. They invited Supa, a female Light Body Assistant, to align my energies during our session. I feel great!"

Several days later, I came home and, as I climbed up the stairs, I felt a very dense, coarse energy. Sheldan was lying on the couch, barely able to lift his head to greet me. "Whom did you meet with today?" I exclaimed. "The Bellatricians," he muttered. "They are a dinosaurian/reptilian hybrid. Their energy is very daunting. All day I felt hot, like I had a fever with strange aches and twinges that came and went." It was obvious to me that his session with the Bellatricians had been physically challenging.

I suggested that he ask Supa to be present every day to align his energy fields with those of the various visitors. This he did, and Supa was assigned to us during the writing of this book. We grew to Love Supa, and both of us cherish our time with her.

My Time with Supa

Supa became a frequent visitor in our home. I was curious about her personal life, her culture and her Earth experience as a "Light Body Assistant". In the beginning, my communication with her was through Sheldan. We would talk with her and he would tell me what she was saying. Soon, I realized I knew what was being said before Sheldan could translate for me. With Supa's nurturing and Sheldan's patience, I learned to trust what I was receiving: pictures complete with emotions, the whisper of a voice and the intuitive impressions that can only be interpreted through the heart. Telepathy is the language of the soul. Sheldan's caring help escalated my ability to successfully communicate, first, with Supa and, later, with other galactic Beings of Light.

The time I spend with Supa is filled with Love and laughter. She looks at the bright side of life. It is with great honor that I introduce Supa to you, through sharing a combination of questions and answers, and a few short stories.

Q: Supa, what brought you to Earth?

Supa: *About two years ago when I came to observe your world, I was awed by Earth's beauty, the diversity of humans living both on and in your planet, and with the variety of animals, insects, fish, birds, minerals, flora and fauna. Earth enjoys a unique representation of all Life found throughout our Milky Way Galaxy. Your planet abounds with nature's splendor.*

After soaking in Mother Earth's beauty and paying homage to her, I went to the more populated areas. The conditions of people living in squalor absolutely shocked me. I observed whole clans literally living on garbage dumps and surviving. My heart broke, and I vowed to help Mother Earth and all her inhabitants to transform and realize their potential. I consider it an honor to participate in the awakening of Earth's humanity.

As my research continued, I found the hearts of your people aching to be liberated and to live in peace. Your oppression has been great and you have been manipulated for over 13 millennia. And yet, with all the oppression that you have lived through, your hearts have survived and yearn to discover who you really are, and to return to our Creator. The human spirit is truly amazing. Know that you are celebrated throughout the Universe.

We, the Arcturians, have been an integral part of Earth's history for eons. Our timekeepers brought the original galactic calendar to your planet. Later, the Pleiadeans modified it. The galactic calendar is a consciousness tool used to put you in sync with the time clock of our galaxy. It helps you learn to experience time instead of just measuring it in a linear fashion. Our galaxy has a natural rhythm or pulse, providing a time to rest and a time for action. As you learn to ride the wave of energy, you will find that your life unfolds with more grace.

As members of the Galactic Federation of Light, we bring our healing expertise to the medical teams and our profound understanding of Love's grace to all Beings evolving in our galaxy. Our contributions are highly revered and honored by the Galactic Federation councils.

Since the destruction of Atlantis and your 'fall' into limitation, we have taken an active role in assisting with Earth's ascension process: your return to Universal Love.

At this time, she took the opportunity to show me a picture of Earth's horses running free with their manes and tails flowing in the wind. "There is a wild horse enjoying the freedom of the open range in every human heart," she stated. I deeply resonated with this analogy. In the movies, when a horse is returned to the open range, my heart sings with joy and I become liberated with it.

Supa On Work

Supa expressed her delight in being assigned to assist Sheldan and me for the duration of this book and with the continuing integration of our Light Bodies. We enjoyed each other's company and shared information about our respective cultures.

At first, when Supa spent time with us, she found the everyday things we did fascinating. She followed me to the grocery store to buy groceries (she was aghast at the food's lack of life force) and returned home with me to prepare meals, clean dishes, sweep the floor, vacuum carpets, dust furniture, wash and iron clothes, clean toilets, etc. It took only a couple of days' observation for her to grow weary.

Proudly, Supa told me that she has never cleaned a thing in her life. They use either replicator technology or "as they think it, so it is".

Q: Often, at Sheldan's lectures, people have expressed their concern regarding the new technologies. Some say they enjoy cleaning and don't want their lives to change. What advice can you give to them?

Supa: *For those of you who wish to keep ironing your clothes, you are welcome to do so. Once you learn to live in cooperation and harmonious community, you will have more time and opportunity to explore what brings you joy. Imagine doing what makes your heart dance and sharing your joy with others! As your individual originality is allowed to blossom, you will return to being enthusiastic co-creators with God in ways you cannot imagine today.*

Currently, in your society, you are kept quite busy just trying to make enough money to pay your rent, buy your food, and meet your car loan. It is by design from those who are in power to keep you "running in place" and too tired, when you do have time, to explore your creativity.

In a galactic society, we care for each other first, while allowing ourselves to be cared for also. Our work is joyful and we consider it to be more like play.

Q: If you were back on your home world, what would you be doing?

Supa: *I would be celebrating life and Oneness with the Universe. I belong to the Temple clan, or what you might call the priestess/priest council. Like most galactic societies, we live in the interior of our beloved planet, while maintaining sacred temple sites at specific node points on our planet's surface.*

At these sacred temples, we sing, tone, and dance around a holographic fire. The fire is for purification. Through rituals, we use sacred geometric symbols to keep our biosphere and planet in balance. We lovingly commune with our forests, plants, rocks, animals and our home world. We value and respect our symbiotic relationship to all living things. If one element is out of balance, we are all affected. In fact, our entire galaxy and beyond are affected. With this knowledge, we consider it our joyous responsibility to teach others about the importance of maintaining balanced energies through the grace of Love. Ritual is exhilarating and satisfies my soul purpose.

When I travel the galaxy as a member of the Galactic Federation of Light, I am, by vocation, a specialized Light Body Assistant. Arcturians are renowned healers throughout this galaxy and beyond. We are called to assist when a society is ready to make a dimensional shift. You and your planet are unique in that you are accomplishing your ascension in an unprecedentedly short period of time. Through the grace of our Creator, divine intervention has been decreed. We are in deep gratitude for the opportunity to assist Mother Earth and her people in their ascension celebration.

Q: What do Arcturians eat?

Supa: *We eat mostly vegetables, fruits and grasses unique to our planet. My favorite food is a sweet, starchy fruit that is orange and purple in color. It grows by the oceans on trees.*

We do not need food to sustain life. We energize our bodies through Light. We eat to celebrate our planet, each other and the Oneness of everything. Sharing food with others is done in ritual, honoring the spiritual union we have with the plants and our planet. For us, food provides an opportunity to partake in the wonders of physicality: taste, color, feel, texture. We enjoy the sensation of ingesting different foods. Food is about joy and relaxation. We eat only very small quantities.

Q: Supa, you went to the dentist with me. Please tell us how you keep your teeth healthy.

Supa: *We eat a thistle type of plant to clean our teeth. The plant contains enzymes for cleaning. As we chew it, our gums are stimulated, thereby remaining healthy. Again, we have an agreement with the plant and we always give thanks for the plant's service to us. We never have to visit a dentist.*

I was horrified observing you in the dentist chair. I found your dental practices invasive and barbaric.

Q: What is the average life expectancy on your planet?

Supa: *We live to be approximately 1,000 Earth years. In your years, I am in my late 200's, which is still very young.*

Q: Please describe your living quarters on the ship.

Supa: *My living quarters aboard our ship are very simple. I guess you would describe my room as Zen-like. The décor is primarily exotic plants and crystals from my home world. Since I have a symbiotic relationship with the plants, they provide comfort and the energy of home. The crystals are used for rituals. I have one chair that molds to my body's specifications. The chair is organic. If I entertain guests, my replicator creates additional organic seating arrangements as needed. However, most entertaining is enjoyed in the many common areas provided throughout the ship.*

Our ships are large, organic, sentient computers. The walls provide soft, natural luminescent light. You will not find doors. All we need to do is communicate telepathically with the wall for it to open and it accommodates our wishes. Since the walls and floors are organic, they are self-cleaning. The floors support us in a way that is difficult to describe. We tend to glide instead of physically walking the way you do.

We clean ourselves with sonic showers. They clean by using a non-intrusive frequency that leaves us feeling relaxed, rejuvenated and ready to go. The computer lets us know when the process is complete.

When we are living on our ships, we have hydroponic gardens to supply us with our favorite plants. The "holodeck" environment emulates the frequencies of our sun and the energy fields of our planet. This symbiotic process replicates the atmosphere required for the plants to thrive.

Supa On Laughter

One Sunday morning, Sheldan and I were feeling drained of energy, our bodies were aching and we were generally out of sorts. We were planning to go to the movies but neither one of us had the energy. Then Supa joined us. She took one look at us and started laughing, or, should I say, whinnying. Her whinny is life-altering and infectious.

Supa: *I see your life force is a little low today. Perhaps a little laughter will help. Laughter raises frequencies. I believe you have a popular adage that says 'laughter is the best medicine'. Higher vibrations transmute lower vibrations. It is a Universal Law. Laughter works on all four of your bodies: physical, mental, emotional and spiritual.*

Now let me see, ahhh, yes, I've been wondering about where all of your horse proverbs come from. It will be fun to name as many as we can.

Supa, Sheldan and I had a good time coming up with the following horse proverbs:

- You can lead a horse to water, but you can't make him drink
- That's a horse of a different color
- Don't put the buggy before the horse
- Straight from the horse's mouth
- Don't beat a dead horse
- Judge not the horse by its saddle
- Don't change horses in mid-stream
- Horselaugh
- That's just plain, old, good horse sense
- Never look a gift horse in the mouth
- Horsing around
- Horseshoes are for luck

As children, both Sheldan and I loved the 1950's television show, "Mr. Ed". It was about a talking horse. We started singing the infamous theme song as I galloped around the house. We felt like kids again, laughing and forgetting all about our aching bodies.

Supa's heart was happy. Her mission to harmonize all four of our bodies was accomplished through laughter. She told us that it is important to remember to 'horse around' when feeling blue.

Supa On Posture

One afternoon, Supa came to visit. She was returning from a Light Body symposium and I asked her what she had learned. She told me that the Angelic council chairing the gathering wanted the Galactic and Angelic medical teams to find a way to get us to sit with our legs uncrossed.

Our medical teams are giving us messages and promptings, as we sleep, to make us aware of the damage we do to our body alignments by crossing our legs when we sit. It stops circulation, damages the nervous system, disrupts the flow of our energy meridians, puts unnecessary strain on muscles and tendons, and throws our hips and spines out of alignment.

Since she brought this to our attention, Sheldan and I have made a conscious effort to break this unhealthy habit, and he has been more successful than me. From childhood, I have automatically crossed my legs when I sit. I realize the importance of correcting this habit. I want my body temple to be able to receive the incoming spiritual energies with ease and grace.

While attending my weekly women's group, I noticed, after meditation, that five out of seven women crossed their legs; I shared with them the information that the Angelics want us to sit without crossing our legs, due to the damage it does to our alignments. To my surprise, they all agreed, telling me they were aware of this and are trying to correct the habit. I found their response fascinating and a tribute to our Angelic and Galactic medical teams.

Another confirming story is from my mother. She is eighty-one years old. I was talking with her on the phone when she told me that her back hurts every time she crosses her legs. She acknowledged her awareness of the damage she has done all these years by improper sitting. I had not said a word to her. I smiled and supported her realization that she needs to sit properly. Again, good work, med teams!

Meeting the Bellatricians

The Bellatricians are a dinosaurian/reptilian hybrid. They are former members of the Anchara Alliance, acting as the chief administrators for the Draconian Empire. Nine years ago, they signed the Treaty of Anchara and became members of the Galactic Federation of Light.

As I was sitting at our computer finishing up some correspondence, Sheldan came to me, stating that my time on the computer was over. It was his turn to continue writing his book on our galactic neighbors.

I told him that I was almost finished; I just needed ten more minutes. He agreed, and I continued to type.

Suddenly, I experienced a burning, electrical sensation – a bombardment of very dense energies and frequencies surrounding me. Then I felt a rod of energy blast down the center of my being. A wave of nausea permeated my entire body. Dizziness swirled inside my body like a tornado around my spine and yet I noticed, on the outside, how extremely calm I was. I doubled over our computer and shouted for Sheldan.

"I think I'm going to be sick. I don't know what happened, it's so sudden." As I said these words, the nausea lifted and the faces of two Beings appeared before my mind's eye. They were apologizing for coming in with such force and intensity.

I was grateful that the intense physical feelings vanished as quickly as they had come. At the same time, when those two reptilian faces appeared in my conscious awareness, I was extremely frightened.

Then I realized I was in Sheldan's chair and that they were expecting him. After all, they did have an appointment. I relayed to Sheldan what I was experiencing and he replied in a very matter-of-fact manner, "Oh yes, today I'm meeting with the Bellatricians. They are right on time."

Wanting to flee, I immediately signed off the computer. Then, I made a conscious choice to breathe, take a moment to center myself and engage in a conversation with these two Beings. After all, they are my neighbors.

I introduced myself and communicated that it was my heart's desire to get to know them. They agreed, and now a third Being joined them. Our communication was through telepathy. I'm not proficient at deciphering all the images and voices, complete with emotions, that come in simultaneously, but I will do my best to share my experience.

Again, they apologized. They are learning to "walk softly". They showed me a picture of our biker gang, the Hell's Angels. They are known to 'storm' a place with their energies, giving everyone the message: "Move over, we have arrived. Don't mess with us!" And yet, once you get to know some of the bikers personally, you discover they also have a gentler side. For eons, the Bellatricians had presented themselves as tyrannical overlords in our galaxy. They were the oppressive ruling class for the Draconian Empire. Now, they are transforming. It is their aspiration to be accepted as trusted members of our galaxy.

I saw a side of them that, quite frankly, surprised me. They are very curious Beings and their hearts are benevolent. They yearn to connect with Earth humans and heal the wounds of our past. They want to exchange perspectives on our shared history. They are 3D Beings going through their own ascension process. They are very proud of what they have accomplished in a short period of time. With great pride, they are creating a new society that is actively participating in the councils of the Galactic Federation.

As my fear lifted, I took time to really look at my new neighbors. I was admiring the attractive, luminescent quality of their multi-colored, scaly skin. It was many shades of green and yellow, with some orange-red. Their yellow eyes were large and protruding, and conveyed more warmth than I had ever thought possible. Since we were communicating through telepathy and their mouths never opened, I didn't see their razor-sharp teeth.

They thanked me for acknowledging their beautiful skin. This took me by surprise. Of course, they could hear my thoughts. They were very grateful that I could appreciate the magnificence of their multi-colored skin. This gave them hope that, with time and experience, Earth humans will learn to accept them. Their hearts sent out the most loving embrace. I was moved to tears. They did confess, however, that they have yet to see beauty in a human's physical appearance.

They told me they were exploring humor that they encountered throughout our galaxy. They tend to be very solemn, serious Beings and humor is something they have yet to grasp. In particular, they fail to understand Earth humor. So much of it seems to be aimed at another's misfortune. Why is this funny? I didn't have an answer for them, because I, too, do not relate to most humor found on planet Earth. This is one reason I have felt that I don't belong here and must come from another planet.

I reminded them to 'walk softly' whenever they come to visit us. I now understand, first-hand, what Sheldan experiences when various groups come to share with him. He has learned to bridge these energies; I am learning.

They expressed to me their sincere desire to make amends for the atrocities they have performed throughout the ages. They are letting go of their self-serving attitude and learning to embrace the joy received when in service to others. They wish to have a gentle introduction to those who can open their hearts, forgive who they were in the past and accept who they are today. They are open to connecting with those who wish to have an experience in dreamtime. The more open and accepting we can be, the more likely we are to attract an 'otherworldly' experience. They shared with me a popular quote among Light workers here on Earth: "Remember, we are Spiritual Beings having a dinosaurian experience." In return, I smiled and we said our good-byes until the next time we meet.

Closing

Our global society's next evolutionary step is to become a galactic society. We are approaching the divine time when, once again, we can take an active role in our galaxy. There are millions of planets, star systems and star-nations for us to visit.

While Sheldan was writing this book, our home's vibrational frequency was raised, allowing me the opportunity to communicate with some of our galactic neighbors. I had been asking for this opportunity for quite some time, and I was ecstatic. Finally, my telepathic ability was opened! However, since Sheldan has completed the book, our home has returned to its 'normal' frequency. My telepathic connection has dimmed; it is sporadic and not nearly as clear. Nonetheless, I deeply appreciate the depth of the experiences I gained as a result of this book.

These encounters changed my life. Supa's unconditional Love expanded my heart. And the Bellatricians made it possible for me to overcome my fear, by showing me that I have the capacity to Love all of God's Creation.

It is Earth's destiny to evolve; ours, to meet our galactic neighbors. One purpose of this book is to introduce to you a few of those neighbors so that you can remember who they are and who you are in relation to them, and prepare our planet for reunion. They are offering us their sincere friendship and the wisdom of their evolutionary experiences.

Thank you, Sheldan, for this grand opportunity. I am truly forever grateful.

Selamat Ja!
Colleen Marshall

Maui, Hawaii
October 2004

PAO & PAGs

You are wholeheartedly invited to participate
in a phenomenon of global proportions;
a linking of consciousness that will make a difference
to all of humanity on a gigantic scale.

Many of you believe that we are on the brink of a planetary shift in consciousness. This call is for you, as Caretakers of the Earth, to come forth and link with us in an historic effort to usher in a new galactic civilization. Now is the unprecedented time to exercise the power of group consciousness in a 'response-able' way. You can make a huge difference by linking your consciousness joyfully with many of us around the planet in a cooperative and unified vision of manifest peace, abundance, compassion, Love and joy on Earth.

A growing number of us are awakening to the call to assist in birthing a New Earth. Together, we have the power to make this world a better place for all – a society that nurtures the individual's growth to full potential as a Galactic Human; a society that is in total alignment with the prompting of Spirit.

Using heart logic and clear guidance from within, Planetary Activation Groups, also known as PAGs, create projects that are intended to raise and shift consciousness in their respective communities; to awaken the community to its full human potential; and to empower humanity to act as Earth's Caretakers, serving the greater good of the entire planet.

Furthermore, PAGs serve as a proving ground for practicing Fluid Group Dynamics™ (a new way for people to work together harmoniously in an organic structure similar to that of flowing water). These groups are non-sectarian, solution-focused, and semi-autonomous. Our only request is that each Planetary Activation worker or group maintain a communication link with the Planetary Activation Organization by reading Sheldan Nidle's updates from the Galactic Federation of Light and the Spiritual Hierarchy.

We are the Planetary Activation Organization. We invite you to link with us on a planetary level, as an individual or as a group, to create a global network of Light. You can make a difference! If you are drawn to be a part of history in the making:

Call or write us now. Your spiritual galactic family awaits you!

Planetary Activation Organization (PAO)
P. O. Box 880151, Pukalani, Maui, Hawai'i 96788-0151 U.S.A.
Voice mail: (808) 573-3110 ~ Fax: (808) 573-2867
E-mail: pao@hawaii.rr.com
Website: www.paoweb.com

Planetary Activation Group Application:

(to be detached or photocopied)

To become a part of our worldwide web of Light, please fill out the following form. Thanks!

Date ______________________________

First Name ______________________________

Last Name ______________________________

Address ______________ City ______________________

Province/State ____ Post/Zip Code______ Country____________

Telephone Number ______________FAX Number ______________

E-mail Address______________________________

Please check mark your answer:

1. Are you current with Sheldan's Updates? ☐Yes ☐No

2. Do you get them by: ☐Website ☐E-Mail ☐Fax ☐Mail

3. Are you a PAG member? ☐Yes ☐No

If in a PAG, do you meet weekly? ☐Yes ☐No

4. Have you read "Your First Contact" ☐Yes ☐No

5. Are you willing to help activate Starseeds/Lightworkers? ☐Yes ☐No

6. Are you willing to become an Earth Guardian? ☐Yes ☐No

Please write your comments and questions here________________

____

____

____

____

Want to become part of a PAG? Visit our PAO website: www.paoweb.com and use our online form in the PAG section, "How to Participate in a PAG". Fax us at: (808) 573-2867 or send your form by snail mail to:

Main PAG Coordinator
Planetary Activation Organization
P. O. Box 880151 Pukalani, Maui, Hawai'i 96788-0151 U.S.A.

Galactic Human Activation Materials

Books and Tapes by Sheldan Nidle

Books
- Your First Contact (see page 243)
- Selamat Ja! A Guide for Galactic Humans (see page 244)
- Galactic Galendar
- Your Galactic Neighbors

Buttons
- Ummac Dan buttons

Video Tapes and DVDs
- Living in a Galactic World (DVD)
- Humanity's Future: Galactic Contact & N.E.S.A.R.A. (DVD)
- N.E.S.A.R.A.: Creating a New Reality (VHS)
- Tibet-Egypt-Lemuria Connection (DVD)
- Galactic Federation Ships, Part 1 (VHS)
- Galactic Federation Ships, Part 2 (VHS)
- The Conscious Universe (VHS)
- Consciousness and Contact (VHS)
- Consciousness, Heaven, and Physicality (VHS)

Audio Tapes and CDs
- Here Among Us (December 2, 2004) CD
- NESARA & the St. Germain World Trust (December 2, 2004)
- Tibet-Egypt-Lemuria Connection (October 2002)
- Mystery of Lemuria in Hawai'i (September 2002)
- Reality of Contact and Ascension (April 29, 2002)

To order your activation materials, please go to the products section on the PAO website: **www.paoweb.com** and use our secure shopping cart. Or send a self-addressed envelope to:

Planetary Activation Organization
P.O. Box 880151
Pukalani, Hawai'i 96788-0151 USA
(808) 573-3110 (Voicemail)

Your First Contact

by Sheldan Nidle

Illustrations by Miriam de Vera

Sheldan Nidle (author of the bestselling "You Are Becoming A Galactic Human") and his Sirian guides will take you on an amazing adventure into Earth's past, present and future. "Your First Contact" will give you a comprehensive overview of your off-world origins, your true purpose and your spiritual destiny.

In these pages, you will discover:

- How your First Contact will actually occur.
- Why your RNA/DNA is changing from 2 strands to 12.
- What role Star Beings play in your evolution.
- How Earth and the solar system will evolve.
- Why your ascension into a fifth-dimensional Being is at hand.

"Your First Contact" describes where we came from, why we're here and where we are going in this vast experiment in consciousness. Join our Sirian tour guides for the ultimate E-ticket ride of your life!

360 pages with over 35 illustrations and glossary.
ISBN 0-9665791-2-7
US $ 19.75

To order this book, please go to the Home Page on the PAO website: **www.paoweb.com** and use our secure shopping cart.

Or send a self-addressed envelope to:
Planetary Activation Organization
P.O. Box 880151, Pukalani, Hawai'i 96788-0151 USA
(808) 573-3110 (Voicemail)

How You Can Support the PAO

Sheldan's free weekly Updates contain valuable current information from the Spiritual Hierarchy and the Galactic Federation of Light. Their purpose is to inform, activate, empower, uplift, inspire and provide a bridge to the future.

With your gift to PAO, you assist us in raising the consciousness of Planet Earth. This work requires commitment, time, energy, finances and encouragement from all who resonate with this mission. From our hearts, we thank you for your generosity and support. Selamat Ja! (A Sirian salutation meaning "Be in Joy!")

To help the PAO, please see our secure online contribution form at: **www.paoweb.com/fundform.htm**

Or send a self-addressed envelope to:
Planetary Activation Organization
P.O. Box 880151, Pukalani, Hawai'i 96788-0151 USA

Or call us at: (808) 573-3110 (Voicemail)